PRAISE FOR *AFGHAN POST*

"*Afghan Post* is a deeply felt and poetically resonant epistolary memoir. I love the form and the way that Bonenberger is able to inhabit the multiple and fractured selves that emerge from the experience of combat. This is a book that will bring the madness and beauty of combat right down into your shaking hands."

—Anthony Swofford, author of *Jarhead*

"This is one of the best memoirs to emerge from our recent wars. It is painfully honest as we see the author grow from being a narcissistic Yalie weenie who judges the 'aesthetics' of paratrooping to an Airborne captain who revels in commanding an infantry company in combat—and then is crushed by it. One way to thank vets for their service is to read this book."

—Thomas E. Ricks, author of *Making the Corps, Fiasco* and *The Generals*

"With *Afghan Post*, Adrian Bonenberger delivers one of the most erudite and far-reaching soldier-memoirs I have read. This book is about much more than toughing it out as a grunt in the airborne infantry. It is also the story of a sensitive, intelligent young man as he comes to terms with conflict, privilege, duty, and ultimately, himself."

—Brian Van Reet, contributor to *Fire and Forget: Short Stories from the Long War*

"All vets who served in Afghanistan will see themselves in this memoir. And the picture that it paints will captivate everyone who reads it. It's one of a kind."

—Lt. Gen. (R) Franklin L. Hagenbeck

To Doug,
Hope you enjoy the
book. I wrote it with
a civilian audience in
mind.

AFGHAN POST

POST A MEMOIR

ADRIAN
BONENBERGER

THE *Head* & THE *Hand*

—— PRESS ——

EST. 2012

Published by The Head & The Hand Press, 2014

Printed in the United States of America

Original cover design by Claire Margheim. Cover photograph by
Emily Carris and "Iraq Sandstorm" photo by Master Sgt. Cecilio Ricardo,
U.S. Air Forces Central, Baghdad Media Outreach Team, used with
permission by DVIDS.

ISBN: 978-0-9893125-2-3

Library of Congress Control Number: 2013955452

The Head & The Hand Press
Philadelphia, Pennsylvania
www.theheadandthehand.com

10 9 8 7 6 5 4 3 2 1

For Weston Bonenberger and George Dietz, and the rest of the soldiers and vets who've gone to soil over the years.

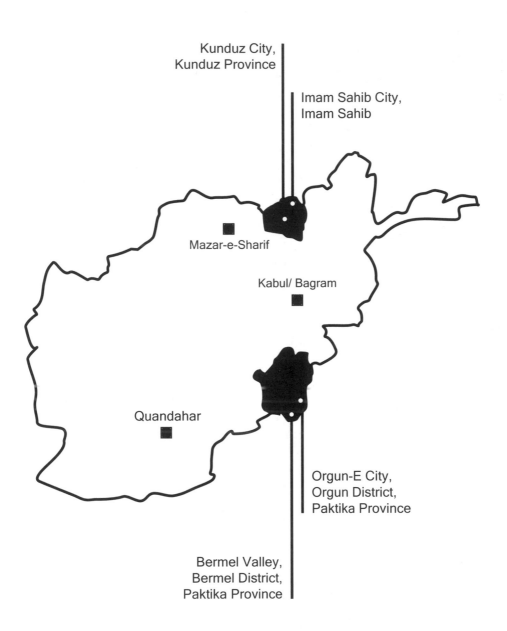

Kunduz City,
Kunduz Province

Imam Sahib City,
Imam Sahib

Mazar-e-Sharif

Kabul/ Bagram

Quandahar

Orgun-E City,
Orgun District,
Paktika Province

Bermel Valley,
Bermel District,
Paktika Province

AFGHANISTAN

INTRODUCTION

When I began this project in the winter of 2012, it looked very different from the product of today. I'd conceived of *Afghan Post* while I was leaving the army and in the middle of a bad break-up. The story that interested me then was less linear, had more characters, and focused on the failures I saw in others around me rather than deeply personal issues that I had yet to interact with in any kind of honest way. The working title at that time was *Just Another War Memoir*. Mitt Romney was the Republican party's front-runner in the primary. My memoir and I were bemired in cynicism and hopelessness.

The deep flaws and problems with this original work came to a head during a trip to Paris, when I read Louis-Ferdinand Celine's *Journey to the End of the Night* and realized that I was simply retelling others' stories, trying to fit my experiences into a narrative space that couldn't accommodate my own stories comfortably. I meditated on this for three months while living in Los Angeles, started countless drafts that went nowhere, and generally spun my wheels creatively.

As any writer can attest, reading is where good (or at least better) writing begins. I began thinking about the reading I did as a kid and the shelves in my parents' house filled with the books I loved, especially illustrated versions of *The Iliad* and *The Odyssey*. I read *The Hobbit* and *The Lord of the Rings* trilogy the same year I learned about the Revolutionary, Civil, and World Wars. When I wasn't reading, I was at my friend W.T.'s house, with Jared Brown, Ian Smith, and Scott Merrick playing "war" in the woods, or we were at my or Ian's house doing the same. We hadn't discovered sports yet, so our free time was dedicated to fighting imaginary battles: "Cowboys and Indians" or "Cops and Robbers."

It was during this age that I developed the conviction that if there was a war and I was able to serve, I would do so. I'm sure many people felt the same way when they were children, and the choices they made as they matured and grew into adulthood guided them away from that path. By the time the War on Terror arrived at our collective back door in a form that compelled service, I was in a position to join, and I did.

Seven years later, near the end of that summer in L.A., I started sketching out what would become *Afghan Post*, a nonfiction recollection delivered primarily through letters and journal entries (and based on real letters, emails, phone conversations, and journal entries). The creative inspiration for the framework came from two events: first, the revelation that I really *enjoyed* writing correspondence (and therefore would enjoy writing a book using that particular technique); second, the advice from my godfather that memoirs should be written primarily for oneself and one's family. These may sound like trivial changes in perception, but with this knowledge in the back of my head, I had sufficient direction and purpose necessary to finish the memoirs. To put it another way, it changed from a poorly-motivated and overly formulaic attempt to characterize how I thought I was supposed to have understood the war into a much more honest exploration of how the war had affected me. A story in real-time, an arc that reveals my painful, sometimes cringe-inducing evolution. For this reason alone the book has been a success; it has been the vehicle of self-reflection that I needed in order to put this experience where it belongs: in my past.

Insofar as every book is a voyage of self-discovery, the most critical thing I learned while writing this book was the extent to which my active life became compartmentalized—it bifurcated and then trifurcated under the unusual pressures of having to maintain some kind of personal identity in opposition to the army while at the same time embracing certain training and tenets that would be noxious to my civilian friends and family. At any one time I was sustaining one primary and two subordinate identities, and it was this truth that cried out to me from the correspondence that I engaged in (my journal being a sort of correspondence with myself). This is likely a fact of the modern era, of having to work in an institution or being part of a relationship, that there are multiple "yous" active at any one time: what you think of as yourself, what you consider your work or professional identity, and who you are with your romantic interest. So long as each of those compartments are fairly unified and give one spiritual and personal uplift, they are worth pursuing; my ultimate decision to leave the army was based on a recognition that while I remained with the army, those compartments would continue to be driven apart, that the unity I sought could not exist in that particular institutional framework.

A final note that should guide how you read and interact with the book—I kept as many names as I could, changing or deleting the following: names of friends who still work in sensitive positions or simply wished for their identities to remain private, names of soldiers or officers who died under circumstances that can or should not be divulged out of sensitivity to their families, names of superior officers with whom I had serious disagreements (and the source of those disagreements), and the women in my life. This may sound like a large number of identities to need changing—and it is—but as you will see, the majority of my correspondence occurs between myself and four social entities: Brent, Jim, Mike, and my parents. And while the details of what happened between me and the women in my life are emotionally true as I have written them and relevant to my development as a human being, this is not their story; it's mine. I have changed details and names to protect their reputations.

The epistolary form isn't quite as relevant today as it used to be, but it still captures a desire that drives much of contemporary media and culture: to know what's going on inside other peoples' heads. When even our own decisions and impulses can remain a vague and frustrating enigma, it can be reassuring to understand another's motivations through a narrative structure. I hope that this book provides that logic, both because I would like you, the reader, to be entertained—and because I would like to think that all the storm and fury had some broader, transcendent meaning.

GLOSSARY · SECTION ONE

Necromunda: An obscure table-top game that I and some other friends used to play at our friend Eric's house. Uses miniature figurines and dice to represent a savage sci-fi future where different gangs vie for control of limited resources on gigantic hive worlds in distant galaxies.

Manga: Japanese graphic novels read by adults. Often puerile.

Katakana: One of three Japanese alphabets—moderately difficult, versus fairly easy (*romaji*) or insanely difficult (*Kanji*). At the end of my stay I was comfortable enough with the characters where I could actually phonetically decipher place names in rural areas, which was helpful for my explorations.

Kyoto: Imperial Japanese capital. Think Boston or Philadelphia, places where political power existed early on but were quickly eclipsed by Osaka, then Tokyo. Not firebombed by Americans due to there being absolutely no military targets there—fortunate, as most of the city was built from wood, and a solid firebombing would've wiped it and centuries of artistic and literary achievement off the map.

Kobe: A Japanese port city that reminded me of San Francisco: built partly into the surrounding hillside, close to the ocean—clean and orderly like a small city (New Haven, Nashville), but accessible like its larger neighbors. An enjoyable destination, but beyond my means as a teacher.

Osaka: Vibrant industrial / commercial city in Japan, rival to

Tokyo. Gritty, real, sprawling city of millions. Sort of like Chicago versus New York (Tokyo).

Nara: Ancient Japanese capital. Think Savannah, GA, or Charleston, SC. Filled with the ghosts of centuries past, spirits darting behind every tree and trail—luckily people were smaller back then, so their ghosts aren't intimidating. Still, I wouldn't want to be messing around there after dark.

SECTION ONE

1

9 December 2001

Grandpa,

I hope this letter finds you well. It's been a memorable year—you probably heard that I'm back in school now, studying to finish my degree at Yale. This fall I took an enlightening course on A.I. with David Gelernter. There were some fascinating essays on the nature of intelligence, including one I'll never forget by George Orwell. I remember you speaking highly of Orwell—I really only know him from *1984* but was surprised to learn more about his biography—his fighting in Spain, his work during World War II. I don't suppose you ever met him or Alan Turing—why would you have? I guess it seems like the kind of crazy thing you'd do; you always seem to know weird and accomplished people with leftist leanings.

Of course, there's 9/11 too. I'd come home to do laundry and was napping on my bed when Dad ran in the room and woke me, saying "New York is under attack! New York is under attack!" At first I thought he must be kidding, but disbelief quickly gave way to anger. You and Dad prevented me from applying to West Point out of high school—probably wisely, given everything I now know about myself, I think I would've been very unhappy there—but if I had, I'd be getting ready for war now. I still don't know whether your opposition to West Point was rooted in a sense of dislike for officers or the military culture, or whether you wanted to keep me out of war (not that you ever talk about your war experiences). It felt strange, though, being on the sidelines while New York City was—it really was—under attack from terrorists. America was under attack. You were drafted, so maybe you interacted with war differently in 1943, maybe you really didn't want to be in England, France, or Germany. I hate the feeling of impotence, of being left out, of not being there with the troops who went into Afghanistan. In any case, the fighting was over before I could have made a difference.

Let's see—the girl I've been dating, I think you met her a couple times—we're on the rocks. Nothing I can put my finger on. It's awful because we've been together for a while now, but it really is failing. That's all there is to it. We don't make a good couple. So strange to be in a partnership with someone for over a year, you're in the same room with her, you're thinking the same thing, which is that the relationship is dead, and instead you talk about pesto or what's on television. And something tells me that in spite of it all I'd be happy to just keep things going—maybe happy isn't the right word!

In any case, Merry Christmas, and I hope I get a chance to see you soon; you'd better come out for graduation next spring. If you don't, I'll have to fly to Carmel and visit you myself.

Love,
Adrian

★

10 January 2002

Jacob,

Thanks for the mixtape! Never listened to The Pixies or The Cure before. What kind of a sheltered life have I led? I mean, we both went to the same academically challenging but socially awkward prep school—how did you develop a monopoly on cool, edgy music from the late '80s and early '90s? What was I doing?

Oh, right—reading, endlessly reading. If only there were some way to merge that love of reading and your passion for music, I'd be able to talk with any chick. Not that I'd have the guts to chat a girl up. I still back my way into these things. It's never a decision; it's a series of non-decisions, or allowing her to take the initiative and just following that. I guess, in my mind, the kind of courage it took to ask a girl out and have her say yes had something to do with music, rock-and-roll, and alcoholism. Sports factored in there too, somehow. I'll tell you what didn't factor in there, and that's my having a bad case of some special unnamed subgroup of acne that involves me getting these massive, ungainly pustules on my face once every month or so. Speaking of which, if there were a cure for my carbuncles involving human blood or diabolic ritual, I'd probably give up my soul. My parents and doctor tell me that the acne will recede as I get older, but I've been hearing that since I was sixteen, and I'm, like, twenty-three now...

And in spite of it all, we've made it this far, all of us, from our collective year off, and the difficulty, the ennui and heartache of sitting on the sidelines while our friends and fellow-students worked their way to degrees. Days at Brent's place, plotting and scheming, playing boardgames, telling tall tales, bullshitting, more board-games—Necromunda—beers and coffee and the rest of it. And here we are, poised to finish our degrees at long last, living in New Haven. I don't know, man, I'm impressed. I have a feeling it'll all work out for the best.

> Affectionately,
> Adrian

29 January 2002

Dear Teddy,

First things first—thank you for *The Armies of the Night*. I'm not much for non-fiction, but it ended up being one of the more challenging reads I've had this year—about as challenging (in its own way) as *A Farewell to Arms*, and appropriate given the recent prospect of a protracted war in Afghanistan, mercifully averted by our technological superiority and the great love and respect we developed with local populations through the careful diplomacy of the CIA and Special Forces. You never think those arrangements are going to work, and then sometimes they do, as they obviously have there, and you're left marveling at our administration's ability to plan and execute complicated and humane campaigns.

Vietnam casts such a long shadow over our culture; it feels like we interpret every conflict through its prism—you, Mailer, and the creative energy of your generation (and those who came through Vietnam and wrote about it) certainly dominate how people like me think about war. It's a very different narrative from the World War II books and movies. Did I ever tell you that I saw *Apocalypse Now* recently? *Full Metal Jacket* too—it's a very different experience from the black-and-white war movies where John Wayne is hip-firing machine guns and killing his way across the length and breadth of Germany or Japan with Patton's Third or the Marine Corps or the 101st Airborne. And books like *The Armies of the Night* give such an incredible background and flavor, as well as the understandable energy of a culture in flux, and the creative inspiration of a man who's discovered a formula for writing that nobody else has—it's difficult not to be carried away by the momentum while reading. As you know, you and Dad have had such a profound effect on how I view the world... reading these books is like gaining access to the stage of your generation's youth, but through plexiglass. So much has transpired since then, and the boundaries of my world are very different in ways that you guys worked to effect (civil rights, end of the draft army, etc.); having access to those days, being able to live in them through writing is a rare privilege.

I should also mention that I read Truman Capote's *In Cold Blood* on the recommendation of a friend and subsequently learned about the feud between Mailer and Capote. That was an interesting discovery, and understandable, as their styles are so similar. People who share a common passion but different viewpoints can either be fast friends or dire enemies.

Very glad to hear that you'll be able to make the graduation, I'm looking forward to seeing you. It's been a long road getting to this point, and despite the frustrations and setbacks, and the devalued nature of a Bachelor's in English, it means something to me. You've had such a tremendous impact on my intellectual development. Since I was a child, you've sent me challenging books to read, guided my internal monologue—that influence has always given me a sense of having a moral compass for "right" and "wrong."

All best,
Love,
Adrian

7 July 2002

Dear Elsa,

Thanks for the letter. I appreciate that we can still correspond, or talk, that it's not, as Phil Collins sang, "like we never knew each other before." That bittersweet bastard. Maybe that's because neither of us feels responsible for what happened. We simply drifted apart. You had your reasons. No point in rehashing the past.

I'm not trying to be manipulative here—well, a little bit—but it hurts me to see you out with other people, having such a rich social life so soon after the breakup. Going out to summer festivals, seeing guys hitting on you, knowing that everyone's going back to the same house—it's just tough. It's something I'll have to learn to live with and get over eventually. I mean—don't get me wrong, we should not be together. That's over, a dead potential. I'm with you on that. I guess I'm just saying that I'm still used to the idea of us together, and when we're not, and you're with other people—even friendship is difficult.

There's no easy answer here. I hate going out with you and your friends to an event I'm not interested in—a concert, an art show—and everyone has something to say, everyone's having a good time, and I'm dead on my feet, I've got nothing—I'm just there because you invited me. It's lame, super-lame. And spring has turned to summer. The days are so long—the solitude is intense, impossible to be awake and illuminated, for nothing—sitting at a desk in front of an empty page or a book, thinking about what's going to happen that night, followed by an art gallery and you and some tall, scruffy guy flirting with you in front of my face, and—I can't do anything about it, there's nothing to do. God, I just feel so impotent about it all. I hate myself, I hate the situation.

Look, I'm sorry—never mind. Thanks for the letter, seriously. I understand this is all a phase. I'm tired of feeling this way too. Sorry for the pitiful bout of wallowing; if I were a better man I'd just chuck this thing and write about what a beautiful day it was outside. But it was hot and humid, and disgusting. And I'm fucking depressed.

Affectionately,
Adrian

Brent,

Just sending a quick note from sunny Los Angeles. The drive out here happened in a haze of booze, hashish, some prescription meds, and, not surprisingly, she and I ended up hooking up—stupid of me to think (in retrospect) that it wouldn't happen. I'm sure once I get back to New Haven there will be a firestorm of condemnation and accusation. I'll deserve it. Not because this somehow betrays Elsa—she was the one who wanted to end our relationship—but because of Frank. That really was an unforgivable, insensitive breach of fellowship—I don't know that our friendship will ever recover. I guess if there's some hope for the future it's that there really wasn't any rancor between us before—it had nothing to do with some grudge or dispute—it was just thoughtless on my part.

She asked if I'd want to stay out here with her. I'm sure this is one of those moments where I'll look back on things in a few years and wonder how it all would have turned out if I had—but I have no money, no job, and I'd just get sucked into doing something out of necessity instead of figuring out what I really want to do. I have a strong idea that my destiny is not on the West Coast—long term, who can say, but short term, certainly not. I'd be lying if I didn't say that this girl and I—you know our history—we really do have a pretty good creative / artistic synergy. Something's off, though. Maybe it would seem too disingenuous to have driven cross country with her to escape—to never return and face the consequences of that act. Ultimately, at this point, it's more important that I set things right with Frank than taking a gamble in L.A.

You're really joining the army? That is totally wild! After all the talking we've done, the idea that you would actually take the step, go forward with it—it's inspirational. If anyone's advising you against following through, don't listen to them. Joining up is obviously the right thing to do for you—I wish I were joining too, I just can't bring myself to do it. By the time I get back to New Haven, you'll have signed up to do... what exactly? I don't understand any of that logistical or rank stuff. You'll have to explain it to me. All I know is that I'm a curious mixture of proud, jealous, and sad—mostly the first part, but a certain amount of the latter two—you'll be going on an adventure I've long dreamed of, and at a time of great national danger (at this point, largely self-imposed, but present nevertheless). Shit, man, you're probably going to war. You bastard!

It's funny, though, thinking about—I mean, tomorrow's 9/11. One year ago tomorrow, that's when all this stuff went down. Do you remember that afternoon, everyone meeting up at your place? Bringing booze, sitting around talking about it, the men in their way, the women in theirs—and then as it worked its way into our culture, the more stories came out about it, the less we all cared? We grew numb. What an impact the events of that day have had on our society, though. I was listening to NPR a couple of months later and some guy from Iowa was being interviewed—maybe you heard it—he was worried because the terrorists might attack him in Des Moines. I'm told this was a common phenomenon in the months immediately following 9/11, people talking about how "it could happen here." I don't actually feel that way, I never did, except maybe while it was happening and nobody knew how many flights were affected, and then it turned out there were more planes than just the ones that had hit the towers—there was the Pentagon plane too, and another that was maybe heading for the White House. That ended, and yet we were left with an abiding fear of terrorists infiltrating our country and affecting us. It's either symptomatic of a certain type of social hysteria, or the work of irresponsible journalism, or—I think Frank might agree with this unlikely hypothesis—in our vastly more (and better) educated culture, we just have a lot of people who've read Conrad's *The Secret Agent* and understand that the real, serious terrorist threat would be targeting places that are totally safe, like Des Moines. Because ultimately, that's where the most is at stake—our sense of safety and security. Attacking finance is something that's been done, and isn't the best way to enrage the American people—there are a lot of people I know that feel as though the towers coming down was some sort of perverted justice directed against unsympathetic exploiters, Wall Street and investment bankers. Oklahoma City was a much worse event, not in terms of death, but in terms of the questions it raises—as evidenced by the fact that nobody wanted to touch that story, or the story of Waco. An American tragedy, American citizens; Gulf War vets in the case of Oklahoma City. I mean—that's where we stand to lose, right here. When some wild-eyed religious extremists attack us, intellectually it's pretty easy to switch over to revenge mode. There isn't even much hand-wringing necessary: they've attacked the very things we dislike about our own country (Washington, the military-industrial complex, and Wall Street). They've offered us a convenient excuse to destroy them while at the same time people get to congratulate themselves on having watched a morality play unfold.

Well, I suppose you're in for it now—you can tell me all about it from the front lines. Damn man, I'm not going to lie—you've got the gears turning in my head now—I'll be watching to see how things go. If I can't stand it anymore, I may just have to follow my original inclination (you know I wanted to apply to West Point) and jump in after you. You'll probably be the only person besides my family who doesn't think I'm copying you. Meanwhile, I salute you for doing the thing I never would've had the courage to do first anyway.

Take care, man!
Your Homie, Adrian

19 January 2003

Dear Jessica,

I'm sure you've been tracking what looks increasingly like our inevitable slide toward our unjust invasion of Iraq with the same impotent anger that I have. That inevitable cliché springs to mind, the slow-motion car wreck that can't be avoided—I'd hope we could avert this disaster, but the things that Don Rumsfeld and Dick Cheney say, their intolerant and condescending comportment around reporters suggests that the truth is different. I wonder if this is what it felt like to be one of the last moderate Germans in 1939, or a Parisian restaurant owner around the same time. At least then you had the option of becoming a Communist and consoling yourself with the thought that capitalist wars of aggression set the necessary conditions for revolution and rebellion. What do we have? Communism is thoroughly discredited—there are no alternatives to capitalism. The pigs have us over a barrel and they know it.

At the same time, I can't pretend to know what I'm talking about with war. They say that the military is all in favor of going into Iraq, especially the elements that missed out on the action in Afghanistan. I've never been to war, what do I know? Do I even have a voice as a citizen? Do you worry that not having participated in war, you don't really get a vote on the matter? I wonder sometimes—but then, there are a lot of thinkers who've been to war who say it's a bad thing. In fact, most people seem to feel that peace is preferable to war if they've experienced enough of the really bad stuff.

I'm looking at spending a year in Japan teaching English. The program markets itself as a morally rewarding way to interact with another culture, which seems important (especially as an American). Get out and see a fundamentally different take on the world. Having served with the Peace Corps, you must understand this impulse better than most. Better than I do!

> Love,
> Adrian

18 February 2003

Dear Grandpa,

You would have been proud of me. Frank and I—you met him at my college graduation, I think, he was the guy with golden hair who was talking about James Joyce at that dinner—anyway, we went to the protests in New York City. It was heady feeling like I was participating in the will of the people, which was palpable. I was on 1st Ave., down by the U.N. building, and there were crowds stretching as far as the eye could see in both directions. It petered out a bit as you went toward 2nd and then 3rd didn't have much of a presence at all... something between 100,000 and 300,000 people were supposed to have turned out on a bitterly cold day.

I'd never seen anything like it.

The protests are being ignored, of course—it's frustrating, seeing the Bush administration go forward with the invasion regardless of its obvious inadvisability. Each reason they give (a case for some nascent nuclear program or "WMDs") is clearly designed to support their policy: the ends justify the means. Bush wants to take down Saddam—for what? Is it oil? Is it contracts? The father drama you read about? What's the real motivation for this? My feeling is that if Bush's administration wants to declare a crusade against militant and extremist dictatorships, there are better places to start... North Korea springs to mind... but

I'd be on board with *that*, if it's what we want to do as a nation. At least we could have a meaningful dialogue about it. The war on dictatorship and oppression. Instead of the "Global War on Terror." How are we possibly going to win that one?

I'm sure you know that the etymological root of the word "terror" comes not from *fear* (as is commonly assumed in current usage) but from a sense of being overwhelmed in the presence of the divine, or in the presence of kings—much closer to *awe* than *dread*. In other words, our "War on Terror" as understood by the administration officials who named it (out of convenience—the word terror is close to terrorist) is a war on the thing that causes us to feel dread. At the same time, the real meaning of our "War on Terror" is a war on the thing that causes us to shake in the presence of a thing or idea that causes us to feel inadequate or inferior. I think there's some truth to that—the Bush administration probably does feel a loathsome *terror* when it considers alien religions or cultures. This reaction plays directly into the hands of those cultures and religions.

It seems a bit like it must have felt for Dad's generation in 1968–69—the sense that our country's soul is being deliberately misused and misled. I don't think our reasons are unscrupulous, at least not in the way that this guy from South Africa Frank and I met during the protests meant. He was one of those guys who said that it was all about oil. I suspect this is a popular opinion around the world, and one that is, in short, idiotic. That's not the point, though, the point is that whatever reason we have for going in there isn't the reason that's being stated to us, which is that Iraq poses an immediate and direct threat to our country, and our way of life. The only way Iraq could destabilize us, that Saddam could *terrorize* us would be if we contrived a scenario in which he did pose such a threat—most of the intelligence reports seem to be testifying to the opposite. In other words, the rationale for our Global War on Terror: Iraq Edition seems at the end of it all to resemble nothing so much as the rationale I use to rent scary movies from Blockbuster. It is a War designed to frighten *ourselves*, perhaps because we're bored, or there's nothing better going on.

And lest this get overlooked in the mix: if there isn't an easily explained, easily comprehended, overwhelming and deeply compelling reason to go to war rather than staying out of war, a country shouldn't go to war. Period.

And I'm powerless to stop the march toward war. The people of the United States as well as many old and traditionally reliable allies (minus our "friends" the indefatigably colonialist Brits, always happy to push or pull us into a war that benefits their interests) stand firmly against war with Iraq—especially if you remove the fraudulent claim that Saddam is on the verge of gaining nuclear weapons and has many WMDs he's preparing to use against us—but the preparations for war continue unchecked. One hopes that we don't do the unthinkable, but there's nobody in Bush's administration putting the brakes on the thing. I would've thought Powell would be the guy, but he's been helping them sell it to the U.N. Worse than useless.

Having placed ourselves at the precipice of war, and having protested our involvement and talked with everyone I can about the issue (almost everyone up here in CT agrees with me, not that it makes a difference), I feel that I've done my part as a citizen. My conscience is clear, there's not a lot more that I can do to affect things one way or another. The professional army makes all of these decisions easy, of course, there aren't any consequences to opposing intervention.

Hope everything's well with you—looking forward to the next time I get to see you!

> Love,
> Your Grandson

1 April 2003

Jacob,

On a day like today, a letter is not just appropriate, it's necessary. We're at war again. We've invaded Iraq. It's April 1st. You can't make things like this up. Last spring we were graduating from college. Now we're witnessing the dawn of a new millennium. Tank treads and fighters and bombers. Infantrymen. Little plastic toys on a board, or pixilated avatars on a television screen. Somewhere in the desert, people like us are fighting and dying.

I had this idea about Nazi Germany recently—I was reading another book about the easy blurring of certain lines, and how the German people were complicit in the greatest crimes of the 20th century. Anyway, what if Nazism was like a social taint or disease, and it infected us somehow when we were over there in the '40s? What if the mutation, as expressed in our own society, was such that there were effective control mechanisms in place—institutions, means of propaganda—that essentially stifled dissent? I don't walk around living in a bizarre conspiracy bubble, but sometimes it's worth considering the possibility—especially on a day when your nation has done something that at *best* feels forced and unjustified and at worst might actually be destructive. Can you imagine if we get sucked into another Vietnam? We're told that it simply isn't going to happen—in the same way that we're told that we simply must intervene—everything is simple with this administration, simple choices, rendered in black and white, that are designed not to be choices at all. All or nothing thinking. I wonder how war with Poland was framed to the German people. Or war with the Allies. Or the U.S.S.R.

Well—wondering how Brent's doing—no word from the TV stations I've applied to for internships, forging on with the idea nevertheless—signing up for a mediation course this summer and looking at maybe teaching English in Japan. Nova Corp looks a little less awful than the rest. My cousin does the JET program and says the corporations are six of one, half a dozen of another—I don't think I qualify for the JET program, and in any case don't have the time to jump through all of their hoops. A good fallback, always good to have a fallback plan.

Hope the breakup hasn't hit too hard. I know the circumstances were different with you, but having moved through a pretty trying period myself, I can promise you that it gets better. Just don't go nuts with trying to move on too quickly, it erodes your capacity to be sympathetic and understanding of yourself. When you turn around on a relationship too quickly, when you go from one to another like the serial monogamist you appear to be, the person you really turn on is yourself. We should hang out soon—I know that's what the girls are doing, moving on without their unnecessary, millstone ex-boyfriends—it would be a shame to get mired in depression and stasis just as we could be exploring new places and meeting new people. Trust me.

Regards,
Adrian

5 July 2003

Dear Elsa,

Just writing to thank you for inviting me to the 4th of July party, it was a great time. I had a lot of fun. I don't find myself getting out as much anymore—been in a pretty serious and long-lasting funk, honestly—probably dating back to leaving college. I really appreciate our friendship, and that we've been able to maintain some kind of connection in spite of everything that happened last summer. Means a lot to me. Hope everything's well—maybe we can catch up one-on-one someday?

> Affectionately,
> Adrian

17 August 2003

Brent,

I hope this letter makes its way to you all right—you must be in officer training by now. The address said Fort Benning—it's impossible for me to visualize a thing like that, a fort or a barracks, apart from what I know from video games like *Civilization*. I know that a barracks is where people march and drill (?) and makes units tougher. I know that a fort must mean walls, and probably trenches and other things that could be defended by soldiers. Benning, I know from my history books, is the name of a Confederate leader of some renown—which seems like a weird source for the name of an army fort—why not Washington, or Patton, or Grant?

But maybe that's just the South. What's it like down there? Are all of the rumors we hear true? Is it like *Easy Rider*—an insular and backwards place filled with rednecks and racists? What's the food like? How's the climate? What are the girls like? Are you close to any cities? Is it really just country and Cash Money Records / Playahs, or do they listen to other music too? Are people as polite as they say?

I could go on and on with the superficial questions… feel like you're in another world or something, an astronaut, a space-walker… what's the military like, how's *training*, what's the infantry like, do you get hazed by drill sergeants like in *All Quiet on the Western Front* or *Full Metal Jacket*, are there women in your units, what does a platoon feel like, the difference between ten men and forty men, is it tough, how is it tough, are you getting stronger, do you regret your choice?

Iraq looks like it's pretty much over, they have things under control, so it doesn't seem like they'll be needing my services. I'm going to Japan at the end of August / beginning of September for a year to teach English with a corporation called Nova. The idea so far as I can tell is English for businessmen and for stay-at-home wives. I'll be doing this thing where there's a video camera on a computer, and I teach between one and four people English—over the camera—I don't know, it sounds pretty weird, but I guess I'll get used to it. Seems like the type of thing they'd do in Japan though, right? I'll have to be careful, if the computer refuses to shut off, there's probably a "kill switch" that forces shutdown lest the computer achieve self-awareness and infect the network. That, of course, would be the end of us.

I'll leave my address with your dad as soon as I get it sorted out—I understand from him that you won't be at this address by the time I'm in Japan, and mail's probably pretty slow, so no point in me barraging you with more mail if it's just going to get bounced. I'm not coming home for Christmas this year, so let me know if there's another time when you've got break and we'll see if we can get the schedules to line up. If not, no big deal, I don't plan on spending more than a year over there.

All right man, keep in touch and good luck with the training. I am constantly impressed and over-awed by your decision and discipline in doing this... I guess I should be thanking you for your service to country now too—everyone's doing this, so I feel like maybe I missed the memo, but I think it's required now of citizens.

Regards,
Adrian

2

14 September 2003

Dear Mom and Dad,

Well, I'm settled in here in Japan, land of the rising sun, in my new apartment—my roommates are great fun, an Englishman who moved to New Zealand when he was fifteen years old and is obsessed with alternative and rock bands and a six-foot-five Australian who plays competitive Ultimate Frisbee—I'm the odd man out in terms of cultural relevance. We've bonded over a shared affinity for karaoke and video games, so the evenings are pleasant. I am quite pleased with the situation—I've had bad roommates before, and it's so much nicer when everyone gets along.

Here are some initial impressions while they're still relatively fresh. I buy different ramen noodle meals on the cheap to save money (the Australian showed me a good place to shop) and eat out once a week or so. We have decent restaurants in the area, including a taco bar that's not expensive and a nice nod to home. Plenty of these lowest-common-denominator restaurants similar to diners they call *itzekia*—of course it's done Japanese style, so it's unlike any diner you've ever been to in the states—and plenty of other restaurants of varying quality. The landscape is very urban—I live in a section of Osaka called *Juso Hommachi*, and it's a rough place; lots of pimps, thugs, and prostitutes (male and female) crowd around the ubiquitous *Pachinko* parlors, their version of a casino. Pachinko is a form of gambling that's legal because you use beads instead of money (though of course you have to buy the metal beads) and therefore you aren't gambling with money.

There isn't much greenery the cityscape is largely concrete and high-rises and massive canals that direct the flow of rivers. The largest river is one that I have to cross every day to get to work. I take the train, the company reimburses me for travel (the train is packed with Japanese businessmen), then I transfer to the subway. In all it's a forty-five-minute commute, including about ten minutes of walking—if I do end up moving closer to work, it will be to cut down on the commute, as it eats up a good portion of my free time.

On the subway I either listen to music (thanks for the CD player) or read, which makes the trip fly by. My access to English literature is going to be a problem, I foresee this… meanwhile many Japanese businessmen read *manga* comic strips on the train, including some that are essentially cartoon porn—it must be weird to be a woman in a place like this, where men basically run the show.

I'm studying *katakana* and some basic Japanese so that I can do things like order food, and count, and (eventually, I hope) actually talk with the people who live here, a bit—maybe not to express thoughts, but at least on the first level. More people speak English here than I would've thought or expected, but they're also very shy about it—it's the opposite problem from a place like France where people can speak English but won't. Here they can speak English but are very, very hesitant to look foolish. In their culture, it's shameful to do a thing poorly. In ours, it's shameful not to do a thing out of fear or hesitation.

The company gives me two days off. For me it's Monday and Tuesday, the least popular days off to have (as I've just gotten here). As I get more time and seniority I'll be able to lobby for different days and different, more lucrative schedules. The teaching itself was a little tricky at first, but it's sink or swim, and I'm swimming now (albeit tentatively). I thought it was going to be more businessmen, but it seems mostly to be older people or bored housewives—some teens, whose parents want to give them more practice with the language. I listen to a lot of the other teachers and most of them seem to take on a very condescending and, in my opinion, insulting tone with the students, but these are the teachers who are rewarded, so they must know what they're doing. I will certainly *not* be staying here longer than a year unless something truly unexpected happens, as the work is less engaging than I'd imagined. I will, however, continue to seek out opportunities to explore and see new places; so far I've been to Kobe and the Osaka Castle—there are tons of things to see and do in Kyoto and Nara, as well as further north. My cousin has offered me a place to stay up where she is, so I'll visit her on a four-day, maybe next month some time.

All in all, I have no regrets with my choice. Life pushed me toward travel and adventure, and I don't have any regrets about the choice I made. It can get lonely here, but there's enough going on, enough good people, that I should be able to make it work. Miss you guys, and please send my love to Christina.

Love,
Adrian

★

Journal Entry: 21 October 2003

Today, on my twenty-sixth birthday, I crawled out of bed early enough not to need to rush into work, to allow myself the luxury of exploration. The morning was gray and heavy, the neighborhood sidewalks slick with unseen rain and the hawked spit of a thousand hurrying mouths. Uniformed schoolchildren ran on short legs into brick office buildings; electronic signs before the front doorway flashed obscure motivational messages in *kanji*, exhorting timeliness and good order. The people I passed seemed full of purpose, direction, and concentration; nobody made eye contact with me save by accident. At Mister Donut the counter girl delivered her welcome address in full.

I could smell the train stop before I got there—an acrid mix of garbage and toxic fumes from machines unseen. Teenage truants drank and roughhoused on the concrete stairs. On the asphalt platform, I was temporarily mesmerized by a beautiful, willowy, tall Japanese girl in a dress standing with her back to me—easily my height, taller in heels—why was she there, on that stop, in a filthy slum on the outskirts of Osaka? She turned and I saw her carefully made-up face—it was a man. I felt embarrassed that he had such good legs.

On the ride in, I watched as the industrial scene slid by, Japan's endless cityscape, a natural and fertile ground for the birth and growth of punk anime art. The train glided across bridges of iron and steel, crossing the great canal that separates Juso Hommachi from Osaka proper, and the smaller canals within the city. Japanese businessmen read manga, and women looked out the windows or at the floor. I listened to my favorite Orbital mix on my new CD player and it seemed like the train, the subway, the people pedaling by on the road—everyone was moving to the machinelike beat in my headphones.

13 November 2003

Dear Grandpa,

Hello from Japan! I've been meaning to write you for a while and recently had the opportunity and motivation to do so when I finally visited Kyoto. I know you're a big fan of Frank Lloyd Wright architecture—I think he's supposed to have been influenced to a certain degree by Eastern architecture and the principle of building in harmony with the landscape. I can't pretend to have much in the way of architectural training or background, but seeing some of the shrines and monasteries in the hills of Kyoto, it's hard to disagree with the idea that imagining a building as part of and expressive of its surrounding landscape makes good aesthetic sense. Kyoto's very different from Osaka and Tokyo, which hold more aggressively modern, urban attitudes toward high-rises and certain types of standard suburban or urban buildings. The buildings in this sort of city (Chicago or New York or London) become the landscape, replace hill and field with metal and concrete, which makes for a sad and dispiriting landscape. I don't like it.

There's a street in Kyoto where it's still the old-fashioned wooden buildings and basically the kind of ambiance that I was instructed by comics and movies to expect, very picturesque. I ate at one of the restaurants there where the inside was all wood, smelled amazing, and the food was incredible, fresh. It was memorable, positive—very different from my first month here when all I did was drink cheap beer and hard alcohol and go to clubs at night. That's no way to spend one's time in a place like Japan; one can experience nightlife anywhere and it will be largely the same.

Kobe's a bit different from Osaka in the sense that the architecture there is actually pretty good too—I understand (and remember, from high school) that portions of the city were destroyed in the early '90s when a huge earthquake hit and had to be rebuilt with better specifications—the architects charged with redesigning and rebuilding the city succeeded in harmonizing the new with the surrounding landscape. Behind the city, a series of mountains stretches back into the country and naturally I had to try climbing one—got a little lost back there on a series of winding trails—my payoff was a peerless view of Kobe's port. I watched the massive shipping vessels gliding into and out from the docks; together with the shimmering new urban portion a little ways to the south, I felt that the planners had done a good job. The city retains its grandeur without obliterating the landscape, unlike Osaka, which squats atop everything and dominates the nature around it. The only time Osaka is beautiful is at night, when the lights illuminate the mountains in the distance. Kobe is lovely in its own way from the street and from above.

An interesting sidenote—there's a big dispute in Japan now regarding proper deployment of their military. Apparently, Japan supported the Iraq mission with logistical elements of their "Self-Defense Forces," and this represents the first time that Japanese soldiers have been off the mainland and participating in any military deployment since the Second World War. Although Japanese schoolchildren aren't taught much about the war or their role in starting it—almost nothing, in fact—everyone has a sense that war is bad, and that even something as benign as support soldiers and a naval refueling vessel can lead to morally objectionable situations. Most of the country wants to keep the SDF on Japanese soil and not change their constitution (which, like the Bible, is pretty unambiguous about what one can and cannot do with the military). We'll see how it all plays out.

Sidenote to their sidenote—I was walking down the main shopping street in Osaka, and happened upon a military shop that sold, among other things, all sorts of World War II curios, including authentic SS uniforms, Nazi paraphernalia, U.S. WWII uniforms, Japanese WWII uniforms, and even things related to concentration camps; this section was upstairs, in a roped-off section that I and a friend were allowed into because we expressed interest (and maybe because we were white). There were pictures of Japanese people dressed in German military uniforms—it was like a club or something—this is a different place, for sure. My friend and I left in a hurry and haven't been back. I thought that kind of thing was illegal; obviously it's not, it's treated (like everything else) as a hobby. I know a few friends from back home that would take very strong exception to the existence of such a place.

I wish you could travel out here for a week or so, I think you'd enjoy the place (the aforementioned shop excepted). The food's pretty good—I've overcome my aversion to seafood out of necessity—and the mayonnaise is unique—ketchup and mustard leave much to be desired, but sake tolerable—it'd be a grand old time. Of course the flight is something like eighteen hours. But I'd be happy to host you and show you around. I won't be home for Christmas, but Christina's set to graduate next spring so shall return for that. If I don't see you beforehand—I'll see you then.

Love,
Adrian

★

1 January 2004

Jacob,

Had to shoot you a quick letter from Japan, wouldn't have been right not to. Felt like today was the best day to do it, as I'm still glowing from the best night I've had here so far. Went to Kyoto with a mixed group of French and American teachers to a famous monastery called *Kiyomisu* to watch them ring in the New Year, then had champagne afterwards at a nice restaurant. It was cold, and raining lightly, and there was a decent crowd gathered around the famous bright orange pagoda from whence hung a great, stylized bell. Well—my Japanese New Year looked like this: groups of ten Kyoto residents (whom I'm told were selected by lottery) gathered together to swing a specially blessed and anointed log into a giant bell—a total of 108 different groups rang the bell 108 times—this has some significance in Buddhism of which I'm not aware. The ringing was muted a bit by the rain, but nevertheless it was an impressive sound, and I imagined, looking out into the twinkling night, over the city, that people could hear the bell, and that it ministered to whatever need they had to hear it.

The culture itself—you and I had great fun together watching anime movies and dissecting the fungible pieces of popular Japanese culture before I moved here—it's different in certain ways, and shockingly similar in others. Like—there really is a bizarre fetishization of the high school-aged girl. When there are events where young girls—thirteen to sixteen—gather, one can generally find dirty old men in abundance—this according to women, I've never seen one of these episodes. I have heard from fellow Westerners that gropers and men who expose themselves are a common event on the subways. So—you hear about these things—they're true—and when you see noxious ideas play out on a human level, you no longer recoil in quite the same way—you have to think: *what is provoking this unacceptable behavior? What on* earth *could you be thinking to treat another person this way?* It also points to a cultural acceptance of the practice, or at least some cultural component, because I know of no country outside of Japan where this practice is common. My two cents is that it has something to do with the way women are perceived and how they feel they have to respond in certain situations—it provokes a real hatred on the part of many Japanese men, for some reason, serious misogyny.

The long and the short of it is that I think this is a pretty fun place to visit, but the more time you spend here, the more you realize that there's some serious, messed up stuff lying under the surface. That doesn't describe everyone. I've met some splendid, creative people out here, but I suspect that many of them, men and women alike, would agree that female submission and docility is sexy. As always, I spend most of my time with guys here anyway, rather than make doomed attempts to cultivate friendships with women that invariably mature into something greater down the line. A lonesome sort of life.

I'll be back in New Haven around spring sometime—my sister's graduating college so I must attend (and am happy to do so)—in the meantime, there'll be days on each end where I can be free. I understand Brent will be back in town as well following some kind of lieutenant training. It'll be just like old times. Let me know how things are if you can in the meantime, how your love life is going, what you've been up to, the usual. Hope all's well.

Regards,
Adrian

Journal Entry: 7 January 2004

Spent today in Kyoto with no agenda. Disembarked at Kyoto train station—its futurist elements almost quaint and archaic when compared to the architectural innovations in Tokyo—and explored the building. So full of space, so expansive—Japanese in suits walking quickly with their heads down, Japanese tourists with their children on holiday ambling slowly around, looking up at the ceiling, pointing. None of Osaka's subterranean claustrophobia.

The mountains are closer in Kyoto; there's a feeling that you could walk and reach them in a matter of hours. No obvious industrial areas. Wood buildings in the traditional style along certain thoroughfares and on the side streets leading into the hills. Trees and gardens poke their heads above the hedges, walls, and gates that keep them bounded. Each household a family, each family a group of individuals, related by custom or by blood.

I wandered across the river and then north, away from Kiyomizu. The river broke off into a series of smaller rivulets (channels or canals, more properly), and I followed one eastward until I came across an unusual temple. The construction and design were ornate without being pretentious—no hordes of tourists thronging at the gate. Inside, the temple—"Konchi-in"—had well-landscaped gardens and a strange sort of lonely peacefulness. The only people I saw, apart from the ticket lady, were a couple who strolled through the garden slowly, holding each other close.

12 February 2004

Dear Elsa,

Happy New Year from the island of the rising sun. And a long-over-due thank-you for the beginner's guide to Japanese—it was very useful for getting me settled in over here. As much as someone like me can be settled in Japan; there are definite limits on the assimilative capabilities of this culture. At the same time, I'm finally starting to meet a fairly wide group of people, mostly Westerners, with whom I feel comfort-able and accepted. I'm still searching for a group of adventurous Japa-nese people who can expand my access to more authentically Japanese experiences—such as *onsen*, or Japanese hot springs. The *cento* is just a hot bath, the difference being where the water comes from—geother-mally heated reservoirs or a metal tank over a fire somewhere.

You'd love the sense of that particular phenomenon—one is en-couraged to encounter the onsen or cento nude. I think it *may* be dif-ferent for women, that it's acceptable to go into the springs with some sort of covering, but as the best onsen are strictly segregated, I don't know—and there's so much chauvinism embedded in the culture that I wouldn't be surprised if there were enforced differences between the women and men. So you'd hate that part. But for the men, it's a bunch of nude guys walking around in the shower, a *ton* of sausage, with the Japanese men staring at the white guys, and, usually, me and a couple round-eyes doing things stupidly and trying not to make eye contact with anyone, least of all each other.

But then once you get into the thing, it becomes very normal. You shower, really scrub down, then rinse and walk over to the springs, which have various mineral properties. I have serious doubts that the minerals really provide the healing properties that are advertised, such as better dreams, better digestion, good for studying *math* (seriously) and nearly any other human ill you could imagine. But the heat— they're often very hot, incredibly hot by Jacuzzi standards—and the weirder springs left my skin tingling, no doubt from the mixture of minerals and the scrub and the heat. Besides this, there's also a very liberating quality to being able to feel comfortable nude in a social situation. You know I never did the nude party scene at Yale, and it might be odd around women—having a conversation with a nude woman always seemed like a recipe for embarrassment—but in a place like an onsen where sex isn't a possibility, it's just nice to live in your own skin for a little while. I always felt like this is a knowledge you had early— and it's taken me quite a while to come around to it.

There are supposed to be a few great onsen areas in Japan, and I finally have an organizing logic to my time here—I'm going to take a week in April and travel north to the Izu peninsula (which also happens to be the place that Admiral Perry landed with his Black Ships), a wind-swept and desolate place that seems to have a fairly extensive spiritual history. It's where I'll try (probably unsuccessfully) to watch Noh theater, and it's supposed to have some of the best onsen in the country. After that, who knows. Won't have more vacation until September, and that's when I'm looking at leaving. Should have one last chance for travel before I leave.

Thank you for the books and your letter. I look forward to catching up this spring when I'm back in town temporarily for my sister's graduation. Party time! Best regards to your family…

Affectionately,
Adrian

21 March 2004

Dear Teddy,

After all the talks we've had or I've overheard between you and Dad, it seems *impossible* that we could actually be playing this drama out again in my generation after everything that happened in Vietnam. The dogs of war have been loosed, and the madness of violence has fully infected our souls. We've turned a Hussein prison facility into our own chamber of horrors—a decision or non-decision that (I'm sure we'll find) was sanctioned by people in positions of real authority. What must it have been like to go from petty thievery—or fighting against the perceived invaders—to being held in a charnel house, surrounded by maniacs who tortured, raped, and even occasionally killed inmates? And not for any particular *reason* except that they could, that they were powerful and the inmates were weak? Whether anyone feels like admitting it or not, this is the beginning of the end of America. When you stop focusing on making yourself strong, and instead begin concentrating on keeping others weak, you're tiptoeing toward the fall.

The vitriol against Bush—I mean, he never seemed particularly inspired or engaged with the Iraq endeavor, but I don't feel that he would condone this type of behavior. I'm pretty sure that things like Abu Ghraib don't just "happen," but I can't point to any direct evidence of malfeasance. It seems like the type of cowardly move that Rove or Cheney would pull—people who, due to their own essential weakness and cowardice seek only to make others weaker, to impose a tyranny of relativism on those incapable of fending for themselves.

At the same time that this incident has been causing a great amount of frustration and discontent with our current administration, it's also inspiring a sort of reactionary patriotism. Seeing clearly on a public stage what my country *doesn't* stand for, it's easier for me to grasp better that there are certain things about being an American of which I'm proud. Living in Japan has also helped bring that patriotism to the foreground.

Japan has always harbored a subtle anti-American strain, most notably among the expats here, but still present among Japanese of all stripes. German, Italian, French, Spanish, British (English, Australian, New Zealand, South African), and Chinese teachers are fairly united in their dislike for U.S. policy and oppose our presence in Iraq. Up until now, I'd always stood up to them, regardless of my feelings—I just got sick of people saying "You *Americans…*" with this awful sneer—it's not like *I* invaded Iraq or did those horrible things to the prisoners—but it doesn't matter to them. The rest of the world accepts our claims at face value, that we call ourselves a democracy and so our failures become Bush's failures, and vice versa. Now—I'm dreading going in to work tomorrow. I know what's coming. I'm *almost* ashamed to be an American. But being an American is still standing up for what's right, no matter the consequences. Even if it seems right now like we bow to the law of the bully, the rule of the strong, that's not us. I don't know where to go next with that thought, what our alternatives are, but I'm pretty sure I'm right on this one and the torturers are wrong.

I'll be back home in May for my sister's graduation, so maybe I'll have a better feel for how things are, what it's like to live in America then. I've been away from home for so long, surrounded by implacable critics, that while I've developed a much better idea of how others see us, I've lost touch with what it means to me, living here. America has been reduced to a series of conveniences that live in my memory— food that I know and like, transparent institutions and mechanisms for doing everything from buying goods and services to paying bills— manners and habits—subtle things. Green, forests, nature; expanses of open space. I miss my home, but now with this Abu Ghraib thing, I also fear it—what if this stain lives in me too? What if the rest of the world is right?

Thank you for fostering a forum where I can explore these issues. If our fate as Americans is to be impotent and useless, at least we can do so knowingly—not in ignorance!

Love,
Adrian

Journal Entry: 7 April 2004

Hanami was beautiful and worth all the trouble. It must be one of the most beautiful human ceremonies on earth. Sat amidst gorgeous blossoming cherry trees—ate delicious food, drank strong sake, and enjoyed life while I had the opportunity. A stiff, chill breeze blew the trees, sending showers of petals falling to the ground like snow. Groups of Japanese on blankets laughed and smiled, experiencing the moment along meticulously established guidelines. Nothing is left to chance here, but then nothing is permanent. Somehow those two ideas are connected in Japanese culture.

I'd visit Japan simply to have an opportunity to experience this again, the petal showers in the wind, the camaraderie, the deliberate sacrifice of a day's work to the idea of aesthetic contemplation of the eternal. I have already accepted that this year's festival is likely the only Hanami allotted to me, which is one more Hanami than I thought I'd see. I feel very lucky to have made the time.

Visited my dry cleaner after the ceremony to pick up a couple suits. Had to cross a short bridge to get there, over a canal, part of the Osaka River. Looking into the water, I saw a fish swimming near the surface—looked like a carp, some kind of bottom-feeder. Even in such a hostile environment, life found a way to survive. I watched it make its way further down the canal, then lost sight of it. Threw on my suit, sank a glass of bourbon, walked down to the subway and rendezvoused with a couple friends before meeting up with our dates for the evening.

10 September 2004

Brent,

This is the final letter I'm sending from Japan—posting it from a small onsen village on the Sea of Japan—by the time you get this I'll be back in Connecticut. Your last letter was, as always, compelling and deeply engaging. I had no idea the army had a fort in Italy still—that's awesome—or that there was an Airborne unit over there. I mean, I can't even really begin to visualize what that means, is it like *Band of Brothers*? Paratroopers? The 173rd—that's your unit? I've never heard of them…

So, your news, it's breathtaking. Ranger School, an elite unit, impending deployment to Iraq (which is looking worse and worse every day) or Afghanistan (somehow against all logic we're still there—every once in a while there's a story about how a small unit got into a massive firefight at the end of the world in some forgotten valley with hundreds of tribesmen)… I don't know, man. I respect the hell out of what you're doing. Right now I only have one choice, really, that I feel I'm being presented—law school—the thought is nauseating while you're out doing your thing. When I consider that, in the morning, shaving, looking at myself in the mirror, I have to look away. I'm filled with a sense of failure and self-loathing—how could I be living this life of privilege during a time of war? What possible justification could there be for my not joining? Then I'll talk with a satisfied acquaintance, or my parents, or someone else, and they'll remind me that my thoughts are silly and inconsequential, and that joining the army is a stupid idea. I don't know. Abu Ghraib was the closest I came to chucking it all and flying back—returning to America should make the choice clearer. I'm on an alien moon right now, and everything looks odd. I can say that if something were to happen to you while I was screwing around, squandering my precious patrimony and honor on debauchery and fruitless sexual escapades, it would be a difficult thing to bear. So—if that's the score, why do I keep *not* joining?

This isn't to suggest that because you have done the thing, that I can too—I have no illusions about that. On top of which, if I haven't said so already, there's no way that I'd even be considering this right now if you hadn't blazed the trail. Sort of like how I always said Washington has to be one of the top three presidents of all time for the very simple reason that he was the first one to be a president. He could've been a king, but he went with a much less certain hunch... every other fact that his presidency produced pales in comparison to that one ultimately significant act—the most difficult of all, the decision to relinquish offered power. Sorry—bit of a tangent there—my point is that as the first to do this, you own it. I guess I'm saying that there's a feeling building in me about joining that I may be able to resist, and then again I may not; your being in the army is part of it.

Well, in any case, if you're back for Christmas / New Year let me know. I'll be in town. We'll catch up and chew the fat. See where I am in my application process to *contemptible* law school, and I'll get to live out my fantasies through your stories.

Take care,
Adrian

Journal Entry: 12 September 2004

Leaving Japan. I made one last bike trip, and nearly reached Nara from downtown Osaka. Got to the base of the pass just before sunset. After the relentless summer heat, I appreciated the first chilly evening I'd felt in months. From my vantage I could see the place where the mountains drew down into a series of navigable hills and trails, but the fading light and the dark, tangled forest gave me pause. I would very much liked to have climbed to the summit of that low pass, to have looked down into Osaka behind me and Nara to my front, but that moment will have to remain an unrealized ambition—that moment is still before me, hovering between the present and the future, somewhere just out of reach.

I must have imagined when I arrived here that Japan would be a place like any other—filled with people. If I had really understood how terrified I should be to climb onto a bus and ride five hours into Tokyo, then take three different trains and catch another bus to the end of the line, never once speaking a word of English, I never would have mustered the guts to do it. Committing yourself to a journey is opening yourself up to understanding why a thing should be done or *why it should not be done.*

23 October 2004

Frank,

Your birthday call came as a surprise to me the other day; I really didn't expect to hear from you after the way things left off. It was great to hear that you're doing so well at Stanford, it sounds like you've found a great niche for yourself and are preparing to do work you can enjoy. That's the dream, right there. And—in spite of all the crazy drama—we were all just so *close* in New Haven, packed into a pressure-cooker at first, then slow-roasted after—it is and will always be good to hear that you're prospering.

I felt that it was appropriate to set the record straight, though—I told you about prepping for law school, and my realistic ambitions in that department—I really do have to force myself to feel enthusiastic about it. I'm only motivated by the *idea* of thrilling debates and flexing rhetorical muscles, not the acts themselves. The reputation of law school combined with what you've told me about your experiences makes me feel that it's not a particularly collaborative place. Nevertheless, I get out of bed in the morning and more or less force myself to open the books, prepare for another day's worth of studies. It's what my great-grandfather did. It's what my father does. It's in my blood, apparently—why keep resisting?

Japan… at the end, I started making my peace with it. The last three months I'd hooked up with a baseball team and started finding a good group of friends—had a great time, got up to all the usual b.s., dated some really interesting Japanese women—but when it came time to leave, it was the only clear choice. I'm not cut out to be a teacher, at least not in that forum—the few students who cared about really learning English and were willing to put the time in outside "class" were joys. So—what, does that mean I could see myself as a *college* professor? The friends of mine who are going through that process are *years away* from teaching, and they started *years ago*. High school? Prep school? It doesn't feel like I have the life experience to be a credible instructor for teenagers.

If I remember those years correctly, the teachers who made the greatest positive impression on me had very colorful pasts, as well as a passion for some particular subject material. At my prep school, Hopkins, you could really have your pick of outstanding teachers. The stakes were high too because that was the moment in life where my parents started backing away from giving me moral instruction and started treating me more like an equal, capable of making my own responsible decisions—teachers and coaches were there as backstops, and they gave me alternate and plausible models for how to behave as a young person. My parents had their hands full putting food on the table, besides which their backgrounds did not facilitate the most engaged parenting style…

Well, thank you again for the call, and I'll probably pick your brain a little bit more when it comes time to make a decision. Law school feels like the end of everything, somehow—for me—the end of the dream. That's what everyone's saying I should do, so, well, so be it.

Best regards,
Adrian

Journal Entry: 30 October 2004

Was sitting at my favorite desk in the Elizabethan Club in the upper level yesterday, taking a break from the LSAT homework. Noted that the club hadn't changed a bit, the full run of *Punch* magazines resting haphazardly against one another on the bookshelf, possibly untouched since I last read through them back in 2000. The warm late-October afternoon, combined with the Club's heat, made it difficult to concentrate. Students played arpeggios on various instruments at the music school next door. Cars passed under the windows, the occasional Yale truck, small crescendos of sound. The wooden beams and floors of the Club absorbed all external energy. Later on the place filled up with students and professors during teatime, conversations filtering up through the cracks in the floor to my study desk.

After, I packed up and went to see Jacob. Met at his place around five thirty, sank two six-packs of lousy beer, (Ice House was on sale at the liquor store), listened to Frank Zappa and Talking Heads for a while. Bullshitted about graphic novel artists and the function of art in general, then wandered down to State Street where we ended up occupying bar stools. Drank through dinner, kept drinking until we got kicked out around two in the morning. Stumbled back to Jacob's apartment where we drank more and listened to Tool. An ill-advised drive over the Q Bridge, a stop at the highway McDonald's, found my bed around three and passed out fully clothed.

Twenty-seven years old—surely we're meant for more than this.

3

Dear Brent,

Well—this is unusual—doesn't feel like I've had anything truly meaningful to put in correspondence for a while, beyond whining about my perpetual existential dissatisfaction. I went to an army recruiter today. I'm going for OCS. I finally made the choice.

Here's how it went down—I'll tell it as close as I can to the truth—understanding that there will be minor details and background information that I have to largely take for granted that you'll understand in general—you're one of the few (maybe the only?) who could. I was driving into New Haven, on my way to the Lizzy to do my daily three hours of studying. Sometimes I stop by Willoughby's, especially if I'm feeling unmotivated or unfocused or tired. The one across from People's Bank. It was 9 or 10 a.m., and I was listening to NPR. Someone—Ira Glass? One of those reliable, omniscient narrators—was talking with a correspondent about the slow-burning catastrophe that we have in Iraq, and after a back-and-forth of some ten minutes, before breaking for commercials, he asked the correspondent what was happening in Afghanistan. Some units had mounted an offensive in the East to clear Taliban strongholds by the border of Pakistan. The narrator was surprised that we were still in Afghanistan, and didn't seem to really know why we were still there—and the correspondent didn't have answers.

As this was going on in the background, I waited at a red light—you know, the four-way, heading toward Odd Bins and Anna Liffy's—and these three businesspeople started crossing the street in front of me. There were two taller men in front, dressed in suits and wearing black trench coats, bankers or lawyers I'm sure, and a short blond woman in a skirt and a khaki trench coat bringing up the rear, taking two halting steps in her high-heels for every one stride the men made. The tallest man, on the left, was talking and looking at his colleague, who was laughing and nodding. The woman was looking at the tallest businessman. He looked at me, and on the radio, the narrator said: "It sounds like a different world over there."

Instead of going to Willoughby's and the Lizzy, I went to the recruiter's.

I remembered what you said about being careful of recruiters—they tried to get me to sign up for an enlisted slot with an engineer unit, or as a tanker, but I stuck to my guns and they said they'd help me put my OCS packet together. My presence—I went to the New Haven facility—caused a little bit of a stir—I guess they don't have many people from Yale making the walk down that way. I made my intent known, and—as you remember—I picked up a laundry list of tasks that I need to accomplish—recommendations, grades, health certificates, statements to write, I don't know what all. The recruiter projected that it would be three to four months before I was headed to Basic, assuming no hitches.

The most exciting news of my life—maybe, since getting accepted to Yale (I'm talking about at the time, how I was feeling)—is actually not news at all. As you know, there's no commitment, I'm not actually on the hook for anything, and won't be for months—nobody else seems to know that, though. I told my parents and they went into a state of shock. Dad didn't talk much at dinner, but they take it on faith that, having signed my name on some form (a statement of intent, maybe?) there's no way to back out. There's totally a way out! I could just not go back! Or tell them that I'm not interested. From what I gather, in fact, this is the case up until I leave for basic training.

I was very careful to let my parents know that it wasn't an option, as I don't want to get any foolish input from them. Dad's buddies are all professional draft dodgers, so their advice won't be worth much. Sitting down at the recruiter's was such a *good* feeling; for the first time in my life I felt like I was making a decision fully on my own, I was embracing my destiny. You know how the weight of my family and friends' opinions has pressed down on my neck these long years—we've talked about our similar experiences in high school, and our ambitions—which you fulfilled first. To finally throw off the shackles of expectation and stasis—the shackles are still on, but I've shrugged my shoulders and I can tell that it will be a glorious feeling once they're removed.

I'm looking forward to sharing in this experience, so please let me know everything I need to about the process, and if there are any good tips for getting through the training. Japan taught me that one shouldn't prepare too much for a strange experience, but I don't know anything about the military. Nothing at all. I'd appreciate the advice.

> Stay well,
> Adrian

1 December 2004

Dear Teddy,

Dad told me that you wanted to see me before I went to basic training, to talk through my recent decision to join the army. I look forward to it—always—but want to make sure you understand that I cannot be dissuaded from the process. I have never been more fully and *wholly committed* to following through with a project. With the war continuing in Iraq and Afghanistan—that's what it is, war, not peacekeeping or nation-building—I cannot sit back and watch as my countrymen fight and die on foreign soil. Furthermore, the excesses and crimes of poor leadership are so distasteful to me as a citizen—a healthy male, capable of carrying a rifle—that I would feel like I was contributing to the problem by doing nothing. All of these reasons and more have been building in me for a while—since before Japan, since Abu Ghraib. I can't stand it any more.

Your generation, Dad's generation, you had your fight, which was the struggle to end a deeply unjust war and challenge a corrupt administration. You won that battle, but it seems that the forces of evil have triumphed, refined the technologies and made the necessary institutional adjustments (doing away with the draft, mastering the soundbite)—as here we are again, in largely the same situation, but without the benefit of an energized population. On the contrary, the population is incentivized and energized to do nothing more than make money, preferably by discovering some clever new way to defraud others of their hard-earned dollars. When the world is unjust, and everyone participates in the crimes that unfold around and in front of them, and protest is no longer a meaningful way to effect social change, what are our options? To serve or not to serve—to engage and attempt to reconcile with the experience, not let it spin out of our understanding and control—or to cede the moral high ground to those who participate, while opting out ourselves. Senator Kerry proved that it is better to be charismatic than a valorously decorated war vet, that being a vet's no guarantee against incompetence. Even so, I'd rather be able to stand up as a citizen among my peers and have my say as a man who's risked things, who's been there, than just sitting back and making money, letting other people get their hands dirty while mine remain clean. Thanks to the professional army, conscientious objectors no longer exist. It feels like the only choices are service or silent acquiescence.

Emmanuel Kant has a quote that translates to something like this: "Experience without theory is blind, but theory without experience is mere intellectual play." The smartest, most charismatic person, a gifted orator, who has not struggled alongside his fellow men, is ultimately unreliable to me, as his ideas have not been tested against experience. Obviously it's not that this hypothetical leader is ineffective—just that rather than dedicate myself entirely to study, and the esoteric contemplation of things like The Good, I'd rather learn something of it, I'd rather be able to say *to myself* (if nobody else) that I'd grappled with life and death, and that therefore my words mean something. Again, this is for me, not for everyone, and I don't expect anyone else (or everyone else) to believe the things I do—it's just what works for me. My idea of citizenship, of patriotism, of nationalism, of being an intellectual and a good, responsible American—requires that, during a time of war, I serve in the armed forces, in the place where it's most dangerous (and I can therefore do the most good).

I chose the army because it seemed like the most democratic arm of the military. The marines feel like a proto-Praetorian Guard, and the idea that in joining them I would have to become one of them fills me with an abiding skepticism—you hear about people who self-identify as marines decades after they leave the service—I take as my example the citizen-soldiers of the American Revolution, who picked up their rifles in times of need, then put them down afterward and spoke little (if at all) about their experiences. If, in 1795, you were to have asked one of the aging former colonial Minutemen of 1775 what his occupation was, he'd say (likely) "farmer" or "cobbler" or "smith"—not "I was and am a Minuteman." The Air Force and Navy are not, from what I can tell, doing much of the actual fighting on the ground—why would I join a service where I wasn't going to actually be able to participate meaningfully in the war? Armor plays into this—from what I understand (from media and books), tanks are a meaningful part of the fighting, but are also pretty safe—I don't think the insurgents or rebels or whatever we're calling them have access to substantial anti-tank weapons. I like that idea—being immune to the fighting, but still being able to participate. Besides which, the power of an Abrams main gun is serious business... in the wrong hands, capable of leveling a building full of innocents... it would therefore be a good place for what I imagine will be my just leadership.

You had your fight in the '60s and '70s—I have mine today. This is the best place to participate in the war of my generation, and the best way for me to do it is as a combat leader, an officer.

If you're still interested in sitting down and talking through it, I'm happy to repeat the above for you in person—and either way I hope to see you before I leave for training (my application is complete, so after a few tests and a board I should be ready to ship out by late February or early March). The books and guidance you gave me are a big part of the reason I'm doing this—without that grounding in intellectualism and personal responsibility, I don't believe it would occur to me to help, to want to join and be a part of this thing. Instead, I'd be like those people who enjoy the security and safety of America but opt out of political participation, who feel that doing anything is *boring* or *tiresome* or *lame* and consequently beneath their attention—people who, in short, feel entitled without having earned that entitlement—human rights gone amok. I don't want that to be me.

Love,
Adrian

Dear Grandpa,

Happy birthday old man, and thank you for the generous Christmas gift and your thoughtful letter. I have to admit, after you threatened to disown / disinherit me if I were to apply to West Point after high school, I was really worried that you'd take my joining in the worst possible light, that it would be troublesome for you. Your reaction was essentially the opposite of what I expected. I appreciate it too, I think I understand—or I will once I've gone through the process (I'm set to ship out for basic training on the Ides of March of this year—passed all my tests and boards). You did exactly the right thing: if it was important enough to me that I felt I must join the military, then I'd risk being disowned or disinherited. It wasn't at the time, so I didn't... Of course things are different now, I have my B.A., we're at war, and you understand that I want to do my part to bring this thing to an honorable conclusion. In other words, no threats are enough to sway me.

Thank you for your stories about England and France. I'd never heard them before, or guessed at the things you did or saw, and your mention of more hidden stories for me when I finish certain training, and come back from war—when I have the knowledge to appreciate them in their proper context—I look forward to communing with you and better understanding what you went through. Keeping those and other experiences inside you for all that time, unspoken, is beyond imagining. I understand better why you were such good friends with Tom, and why his death from alcoholism was such a bitter blow. I mean—I don't get it, really, but I feel like I'm at the beginning of a process, probably the *only* process that could really let me understand or *know* what you went through on a fundamental level. That's important. Between you and me, there are times when I wish Dad had gone to Vietnam, and that I could share this with him as well—I console myself on this topic with the knowledge that he made a moral stand, and that counted for something then.

Anyway, I understand that your grandfather was in the Civil War on the Union side—a private, according to rumor—so maybe this is just something that skips generations on our side. Mom's dad (you know this) was in WWII like yourself, and her grandfather was in WWI, an artillery officer (we have photos of him with his unit after actions in 1917 and 1918; I don't know how much "action" an artilleryman sees, but that's what he was up to)—and then we have records of military service going back to the Revolutionary War—it just seems like the right thing to do; participation in war is a family tradition, and I want to take part in that tradition as well. I'll do my best to uphold the tradition of just and responsible participation.

So thank you again for being a brake pad on my hopes and dreams—it wasn't the right time to join until now; if it had been then, I would've joined regardless.

> Love,
> Your Grandson

14 March 2005

Dear Jessica,

I was in New York City recently and ran into Ralph at the Yale Club. He told me about how his career is really taking off—you must be so proud!—and how you're waiting to hear back from school—going to take your Master's in Public Policy. Cool! Meanwhile, you were at a conference in London, so I missed you—more's the pity. By now you've probably heard that I signed up for the military. I'm going to basic training tomorrow, in fact, so by the time I see you again I'll be—I don't know, an officer, I hope. Six months of training in Fort Benning followed by whatever comes next (assuming I pass the training, which seems likely but I don't want to jinx myself, I could always get sick or hurt). I'm not sure we've ever talked about this ambition of mine—as a student I was very conscious of the anti-military bias at Yale and in our community, and going into the army with the goal of seeing combat in Iraq or Afghanistan, well, I guess I didn't know how you'd react to that. It was a bunch of bureaucratic b.s. putting the packet together but I understand that the institution needs to separate the wheat from the chaff, and getting paperwork together really was the first eminently jumpable hurdle. So—I'm going to Fort Benning, the "home of the infantry" in sunny Georgia (the first time I've been to the South) to begin the next chapter of my life.

It's a strange thing—I mean, while we haven't talked explicitly about the army, about that side of my soul, in another way the conversations we've held about Homer's *Odyssey* have been some of the most enlightening and important conversations of my life, and were, in retrospect, my way of working through some of the questions that I had to answer in order to feel comfortable setting out on this journey. You were surprised—most are—when I said that I identify most strongly with the character of Menelaus, and I feel that the most accessible character for any male reader would have to be either Achilles or Odysseus (given that person's aesthetic sense). Nevertheless—Menelaus has always vibed with me—he's a good warrior (good enough to beat Paris, anyway), but just lacks something vital in his soul, some essential heroic quality beyond brute strength, beyond his status as King of Sparta. At least in the translations I've read.

I thought that I'd have more to say on the subject. I suppose there's a great deal more to be said, but probably best done in person... I can't get to sleep tonight, my last night home in a long time—I look forward to seeing the changes wrought in me: stronger, more disciplined, a better appreciation for my fellow men and for the opportunities I've had my whole life—and I look forward to having more to say about those changes with you. I'm not going to have a permanent address for a long time, months at least, but when I do I'll let you know, and I'll tell you the next time I'm in your neck of the woods. If you're not too overwhelmed with work, we can sit down for tea or coffee and talk about how we're leaving our childish notions about life behind us.

Affectionately,
Adrian

14 March 2005

Dear Elsa,

Before I hit the sack tonight—not that I'm going to sleep much, I'm sure, but I have to be at the recruiting station at 0500 tomorrow (military time!)—I wanted to thank you for putting on that going-away party for me. That was a nice thing, and it was so fun to be able to see everyone one last time before my adventure begins.

Joining the army has been like surfacing for air after being held underwater. It's the first time in years that life has seemed meaningful and important; I feel full of purpose, my life is well ordered and comprehensible in a way that's both emotional and personal—growing up it was fashionable to sneer at people who joined the army "for a sense of purpose," but what if one's sense of purpose *is* the army? You know I've been talking about this for years—you're probably the only one besides Brent and my family who truly understands the depths of my need to take part in our war. The siren's call has been blaring away for years now, and having finally unstopped my ears and answered the call, my soul vibrates with purity and harmony—there is no more discord or confusion.

People often remind me that it's a peculiarly *dangerous* thing, to want to go to battle, to see combat in war, and I suppose it will sound ridiculous or naive to assert that I do not care in the slightest bit about the danger; I can't imagine anything bad happening to me. I'm totally convinced that I will finish my training successfully, gain my officer's status, and go on to do great things. At the same time, there's an open wall in the rotunda at Yale for graduates who died in foreign wars—no alums have perished yet in Iraq or Afghanistan—if I was the first, at least I'd have some kind of footnote in history.

But enough maudlin thoughts. I'm glad that we've been able to remain friends in spite of the bad way things ended, and the really bad way they turned out afterwards. I never would have thought that a party like the one you threw would be something that meant so much to me, but I nearly teared up several times—there you have it—I felt appreciated and loved, and that's a sentiment everyone should be able to rely on. Thank you again for the support and friendship. I look forward to touching base and catching up when I return from training this fall / winter.

Affectionately,
Adrian

★

Journal Entry: 15 March 2005

Barely got three hours of rest last night. Normally during a snowstorm I'd sleep like a log—instead, the heavy, thick quiet drove me batshit. I could hear the electric clock buzzing and the switches in the lights changing as time dragged on, until around one in the morning I decided that there wasn't much point to lying in bed any more pretending that sleep was viable. Just as I was preparing to stand up and do something, anything to distract myself from the passage of time, I must have dozed off. What seemed like an instant later, the alarm was ringing, and my parents were bustling around in the kitchen.

I took the dog outside one last time. The snow was deep outside, deeper than expected—it was just supposed to be flurries, but somehow that turned into quite a bit more. Smokey loved it—pranced around like a puppy. Watching her tear through the snow, stop, sprint after imagined prey, I realized that although part of me didn't want to leave, none of me wanted to stay here. Smokey finished her playing, shook herself off, and ran up to the door to come back inside. I unclasped her collar, closed and locked the door, and joined my parents in the car. Looked at the house as our car pulled out of the driveway and saw Smokey's face at the window, watching us drive around the bend.

GLOSSARY · SECTION TWO

Army Rank Structure: In the army, your rank is your identity. The strict differences between officer and enlisted have diminished over the years, but there are still vestiges of a much less meritorious or egalitarian time in our human history.

Army Unit Structure: In previous wars, due to the necessity of massing firepower, and technologically primitive means of communication, companies (Vietnam), battalions (WWII), and even brigades / regiments (WWI / Civil War) were of primary importance. These days, it's squads, platoons, and to a limited extent (in the most difficult areas), companies.

Military Time: It's actually a really useful organizational tool. The day starts at 0000:00 and concludes at 2359:59. This is so people can't get confused. You might think in your life that there's no way you could confuse 8 a.m. with 8 p.m., but when you're on a twenty-four-hour work schedule, and everyone's tired, there's no limit to the potential for miscommunication.

Basic Training: "Boot camp." In the army, this is nine weeks of indoctrination into the "army" way of doing things. Prelude to much more challenging trials.

AIT: Advanced Individual Training. The next step for enlisted soldiers after basic training, where you learn the advanced field craft of your specialty. My "AIT" equivalent was probably IOBC, or Infantry Officer Basic Course.

OCS: Officer Candidate School. Three and a half months of the most exquisite psychosocial torture designed by man. Took me right back to junior high school.

Drill Sergeant: The sergeants in charge of training soldiers in basic training. They wear a distinctive WWI-era hat. Not always the smartest or most athletic sergeants that you will meet in the army, but generally speaking among the most disciplined. The best sergeants I worked with in the army spent time as drill sergeants.

Uniform: There are uniforms for everything in the army, and in training. You have work-out uniforms for all weather conditions, combat uniforms for intense training or just routine daily activities, and dress uniforms for official functions. One tends to act in keeping with the different uniforms—more relaxed in "PTs" (Physical Training aka uniforms), well used to the typical work and training uniform, and fairly uptight in the dress / official uniform. This probably contributes to episodes and incidents of undisciplined behavior when one is first allowed to wear civilian clothes again after months of training (or a deployment).

Tactical: Related to fighting.

Ruck March: This is how "light" or "dismounted" infantry have always approached or avoided battle: on foot, carrying their weapons and a heavy backpack full of ammo, equipment, and food.

Blue Falcon: Aka "BF" or "Bravo-Foxtrot" or "Buddy Fucker." Someone who screws other people over for personal advantage. A doucheheel.

M16: Standard army rifle from Vietnam through GWOT's opening phases. Has been almost entirely replaced by the M4. Different from the popular Soviet rifles because it's more accurate at a longer range and the bullets aren't as heavy, meaning each soldier can carry more ammo and get a couple of free shots off at their AK-47-carrying enemies. People who argue that the AK-47 is better because it's more durable and has a fully automatic setting can have that primitive and inaccurate weapon—I'll take my two free shots and extra hundred rounds of ammo and carry an M16 or M4 any day of the week.

SOP: Standard Operating Procedures. A book of rules for a unit that governs what to do in various situations, from folding clothes to how to pack one's rucksack. A TACSOP, for example, is a platoon or company's "tactical standard operating procedures," and says things like: "tapping your helmet with your open hand three times and then pointing means that you need three demolition charges on the object that is being pointed at, presumably a door," and "Green chemlights in a 'T' formation in a doorway means that the room has been cleared." When you train with these rules, consistently, it improves the efficiency with which a unit can communicate and operate.

Land Navigation: The process by which you use terrain, a compass, and a map to figure out where you are, and how to get to someplace else that you want to be (or are told you need to be). Crucial for infantry, armor, and field artillery officers. Also, fun!

Field Craft: Boy scout stuff—knots, starting fires without a match, improvising things you typically buy at a store, etc.

LTO: Lieutenant Transition Office. An awful place to get stuck waiting for a school, at which point you're basically at the mercy of sergeants who need to get details done across Fort Benning—but an *incredible* place to hang out after being done with training. Me, Mike, Bob, and a few other guys finished training and got about two weeks of free time during which our paperwork was being processed—just took off, traveled around in the South. Had other friends who hadn't made it through training yet report us present for duty. *Totally* got over, for which I'm eternally grateful.

Building Four: A hulking monstrosity of a building, built sometime around World War II by the looks of it. Headquarters for all administrative functions on Fort Benning, and also site of all of the lecture halls and therefore classrooms for OCS, IOBC, MCCC and every other classroom-oriented training course.

Malvesti: A diabolical and legendary obstacle course in Ranger School designed to encourage people to quit.

TAC NCO: An NCO or Non Commissioned Officer is an enlisted soldier who's in a position of leadership—corporal, or one of the many shades of sergeant. I don't know what TAC stands for, but a "TAC NCO" is a corporal or sergeant who has responsibility for assisting or advising officers in training soldiers at some school. I had TAC NCOs in OCS and IOBC.

Claymore: A directed-blast mine made up of C-4 and bb pellets that can be set up as quickly as fifteen or twenty seconds, or as long as ten minutes (depending on whether it's concealed, and how much). Can be initiated with a tripwire or by using a trigger or "clacker." Generally speaking, when you're at a base that is using Claymores for its defensive system, there's a sense that you're living in a dangerous area.

Splinter Village: A series of WWII-era wood shacks that hold all of the admin paperwork in the army. For some reason, the workers in Splinter Village (at least when I was there) were some of the most surly, unfriendly, condescending people with whom I've ever had to interact. Worse than the worst academic or medical administrators. So very, very bad. And of course everyone knew this, so our wise trainers advised us all to keep our mouths shut about it, that they could ruin our careers by sending us to a bad post if they felt like it. An existential nightmare where the guard to your prison cell is a psychopath.

BC / LTC: Battalion Commander / Lieutenant Colonel (or Brigade Commander, which is a colonel). A very strange and pregnant moment in an officer's career, especially an infantry officer, when that officer realizes that if he plays his cards right he could make general. I think this explains why so few battalion commanders seemed to have a goddamn clue what they were doing—many of these people were smart, capable people, but very few of them acted that way.

CSM / SGM: Command Sergeant Major or Sergeant Major. The CSM is the BC's enlisted equivalent, a sergeant with over twenty years' experience who's been everywhere and seen everything. This position attracts two types of soldiers: those who are proud of the army and really, truly love it, and want to continue serving the best they can, and those who are careerists and just want more money and power.

As with many situations, I've had the privilege to work with some of the former, and the misfortune of working with some of the latter. *You know who you are.*

Squared away: Capable, neat, disciplined.

AWOL: Absent Without Leave. Not being where you're supposed to be, or where anyone could reasonably expect you to be on a work day. A punishable offense, though not always a *punished* offense. The punishment often varied with the offender, from UCMJ to a stern talking-to. I, for the record, was never AWOL during my time in the army. Just didn't seem like it was worth it, and when your soldiers are held to a standard for which they *will* be punished, it doesn't feel right exploiting your greater relative position of power for advantage.

OPCON: Operational Control. There's a whole list of ways in which a soldier or unit can be detached from one unit and attached to another—OPCON, TACON (tactical control), ADCON (administrative control), and probably some others I'm forgetting. OPCON means you used to be attached to one unit, but have now been fully detached from that unit and reattached to another unit for a specific duration of time (or circumstances). Administrative bullshit. You know what—I'm sorry I've even subjected you to this, it's boring army stuff, and not fully necessary. Ah, hell, it's nice to have people with whom I can suffer—I'm leaving it in.

Cavalry: Still *technically* its own branch in the army, although it's technologically no longer a critical component of the Armed Forces. The insignia is crossed sabers. They wear hats and spurs and have their own traditions descended from when we used horses. Now they use Bradleys, recon vehicles, or helicopters.

CID: Central Investigative Division. The military police who go undercover and investigate other military members. They have an understandably poor reputation, but as with most such organizations are totally necessary.

Special Forces: Green Berets. The Special Forces have their official army roots in World War II, but there have always been irregular soldiers affiliated with armies. Saboteurs, trainers, heavy weapons specialists, demolitions guys, medical experts, linguists, etc. A group of up to twelve highly trained sergeants and officers.

COIN: Counter Insurgency. Contentious army doctrine that had many supporters while I was in the military, but has since been largely discarded in favor of "Counter Terror" or CT doctrine. COIN is a much more resource and personnel intensive doctrine that revolves around "winning hearts and minds," and convincing (rather than coercing) the population to agree with your presence and mission purpose. CT uses vastly fewer resources and just revolves around killing low- and mid-level enemy leadership.

Rangers: Infantry units comprised of soldiers who go through the most rigorous selection and training process in the regular army. Anyone can try out if they meet the requirements, but selection is very low, maybe in the area of 5-10%. In a traditional fight they'll get a traditional infantry target, such as a defended position or airfield critical to mission success, which happens to be where the enemy has the most defenses. The best "infantry" unit in the military.

SECTION TWO

4

Dear Mom and Dad,

I'm not in Connecticut anymore. I'm not even in America; maybe I've left civilization. This is the first opportunity I've had to think or write since I got here—what, forty-eight hours ago? Seems like a lifetime. Here, by the way, is the "30th AG" in-processing center on Fort Benning, Georgia, where recruits like me pick up their equipment, and go through "in-processing" (this means enrolling in army programs and institutions, getting pay switched on, basic admin). So—don't bother writing back to this address. There's no point, I'm supposed to ship out with my class to basic training tomorrow. *I'm not even in training yet.*

Where to begin—the kid on the bus from the Atlanta airport who was caught with a joint when he arrived… Our welcome speech from the head sergeant (which amounted to: "If you're dissatisfied with the choice you made and feel that what I'm doing is unreasonable, I was a champion welter-weight and I'm always looking for a sparring partner.")… The numerous recruits with criminal records of all shapes and sizes, including felons… The importance of having every personal possession locked, lest one of the aforementioned criminals steal your belongings … Waiting around in lines for hours, not sleeping, the anticipation of being subjected to arbitrary workouts inflicted for imagined infractions… The dread of mass punishment for real infractions, like when our entire barracks of five hundred was turned out to stand for two hours in the cold because one of the aforementioned criminals had been robbed of contraband marijuana by another criminal, and then threatened the robber's life… This isn't to say I feel unsafe here, it's just a world with different rules, and I'm adjusting to it.

The OCS guys took a corner in the barracks and holed up there. During down time—from what? We're not doing anything!—we socialize, get to know each other, the rest of it. They're from all over America, places I've never heard of, mostly the South and Midwest. Some West Coasters, and a few guys from the Northeast like myself. The handlers give us no more privilege or authority than the other trainees, and it's not like we're intentionally separating ourselves from the others because of rank (there is none now) or a sense of superiority—it's just that we know we'll probably be spending significant portions of the next six months with one another. There's not much point in making friends with someone you're not going to know in twenty-four hours.

We're full of pretentious stupidities too. I don't want to forget the embarrassing things we do and I feel just because it's inconvenient, or shameful. Everyone yells their heads off when they're told to "sound off" or any of the procedural or routine events that seem to require a constant supply of false enthusiasm such as roll call or waiting in line for lunch or receiving uniforms—anything. In the world of the "replacement facility," a person's status is reflected in the clothes they wear, with people in civilian clothes at the bottom, people wearing army sweatpants / workout clothes in the middle, people with uniforms near the top, and people with uniforms and rank (and any patches or badges on their uniform) unquestionably at the top. Nobody (except people who are out-processing or are detailed to work here) spends more than seventy-two hours here. And one can already detect the makings of tribal society.

I have my uniform, as I'm supposed to leave for training tomorrow morning. Which means my journey will have arrived at its actual beginning point, for whatever that's worth. I look at the trainees in their workout clothes, the ones who have yet to receive their uniforms and therefore the right to wear them—people who've only been here twenty-four hours, forty-eight more to go, short-timers—and think about how little they know, how much wiser I am—I want to talk with them, reassure them, let them know that everything's going to be all right—I could be a font of wisdom, answer the questions I had two days ago—then I remember that this is the most idiotic line of thinking anyone could have under the situation (though natural) and keep my mouth shut.

After all that, you must know that I'm still enjoying myself. I'm not worried about the future in the least, and still very pleased with my decision. No regrets, just an eager enthusiasm for the future challenges to come. I'll write again as soon as I have the chance—from my basic training unit, next time. Until then!

Love,
Adrian

23 March 2005

Dear Mom and Dad,

Sorry it's taken me a little bit longer than I thought to write—adapting to this place has taken a lot of energy. At night I have enough time and willpower left over to chat with the guys around me, and then it's time for bed—there's barely enough free time to recognize it as such. I'm always tired, we turn in between 2230 and 2300 (I'm going to be using this time-keeping method from now on, I stopped struggling to keep my civilian sense of time passing days ago, it's pointless), do a thirty-minute or hour-long guard shift at some point during the night depending on who's in charge, and wake up between 0430 and 0500. There are more chores and responsibilities than one can possibly accomplish during a single day, and our basic training platoon of forty has its hands full figuring out how to work as a team lest we fail the endless list of seemingly inconsequential tasks that, when neglected, result in our collectively being "smoked" or subjected to long work-out sessions that sap our strength and energy further. In other words, our lives have become attuned to the necessary task of learning how to work with one another, and not to thinking of ourselves and what we'd like to do or accomplish, such as, for example, writing letters home…

My introduction—our introduction to 4th Platoon, "Outlaws," Charlie Company, 2nd Battalion 47th Infantry Training Brigade—occurred like this: the day after I wrote you last, a bunch of us—150 or so—were herded into cattle cars and driven down the road to our barracks, each soldier with his two over-packed army-green duffel bags bulging with clothes and uniforms. Upon exiting the cars we were subjected to a phenomenon we'd been told to expect, called the "shark attack," wherein our drill sergeants, standing in a reception line, guided us to the expected collection area in the middle of the barracks. This was accomplished by screaming invectives and imprecations at us while presenting a convincing stance of physical menace. I didn't see anyone struck, but there was pushing and shoving, and trainees running and falling. Part of me wanted to laugh at the absurdity of it all, but I suppressed the instinct lest I be caught and subjected to some inevitably horrific public spectacle. Instead I kept my head down and focused on getting to the assigned meeting area. Once we were gathered in neat rows, the drill sergeants called off our roster numbers in four groups that conformed to the four platoons—which is how I found myself assigned to 4th Platoon. The roll call complete, each platoon was directed upstairs to their barracks areas. We filed up the antiseptic concrete and metal staircase and into the barracks-room, filling up the bunks as we arrived—ours was on the second floor of the southwesternmost wing—and were told how to wait at attention, which we did with nervous anticipation.

The barracks themselves—I didn't know what to expect in a barracks—on Fort Benning they're hulking, red-brick buildings that must have been built in the '60s or '70s called "starships." Each barracks holds a different battalion of 600 some-odd trainees. The battalion has a dining facility in the middle, and four-leaf clover building complexes branching off from the dining facility; each of the four clover-leaf complexes are assigned to the four training companies, A, B, C, and (you guessed it) D. The company areas hold 200 trainees (but could hold more) and are further broken into four corners that correspond to the four platoons—mine being 4th—with a few other buildings for laundry, and a place for weapons and equipment that is called the Arms Room (which is currently empty). Between the platoon buildings is a single large gathering space where we all muster in the mornings and stand before physical training, or before training events, or for roll call or anything else.

Back upstairs in my new home, I and the rest of the platoon were standing at attention in our uniforms with our duffel bags arranged according to instructions waiting for whatever was going to happen next, looking at each other and at the impressive wax floor in front of us—about twenty feet by sixty feet—with the bunks arranged in a horse-shoe oriented toward the front of the room, which was the drill sergeants' office. Our head drill sergeant, a short and impressive Filipino (we'll call him Drill Sergeant Y), walked out of the office and silently, slowly made the circuit, evaluating us as individuals and collectively, and not liking what he saw. He delivered a short speech—we are quickly learning that he is not a man of many words—the gist of which was that training was going to be difficult, not all of us would make it through, and that the only pet peeve he had was when trainees asked the question "why." Our platoon had twelve trainees like myself who were headed for OCS, some of whom I knew from the 30th AG. Drill Sergeant Y then introduced his second, we'll call him Drill Sergeant Moss, an intimidating, taller southern man who stood by with his arms crossed. Finally, Drill Sergeant Y asked which one of us owned the green sock in the middle of the room that we suddenly became aware of. When none of us confessed, we were (I am convinced, in retrospect, that this was some sort of game but at the time was murderously angry at the sock's cowardly and silent owner) put through a really devious "smoke session" for the better part of a half hour.

This was my first indication that things might actually be a great deal more difficult than I imagined. The first minute reminded me of an intense sports workout, but the novelty wore thin fast. I remember at one point, fifteen or twenty minutes into the workout, looking down and seeing a massive puddle of sweat beneath me. I looked left and right and everyone else was struggling with the exertion as well. People who could not do push-ups or sit-ups or the dreaded "front-back-go-tripwire" exercise or any of the other physical routines earned special attention from the drill sergeants which arrived in the form of yelling and insulting exhortations. In that half-hour I learned two important tenets of army training that have been critical to maintaining my sanity. Firstly, don't be weaker than the people next to you. If you're weaker, you're slowing everyone down. If, on the other hand, a quorum of weakness has developed, maybe a third of the group, it's okay to be weak—that means it's time for the drill sergeant to slow down or ease the training. Secondly, don't be special. If you're special, that means people know your name, and unlike in the civilian world where that seems to be a good thing, in the army, it's the worst thing imaginable. There's no such thing as celebrity in the army, you don't want people to know your name. On one level, basic training is about learning the basics of how to be a soldier. On another important level, basic training is about learning the "basics" of how to navigate the army's social structure. Ultimately that seems to involve not standing out or seeming to attract or wanting to attract attention.

More to follow as the platoon learns to work as a team and I set-
tle into my rhythm. Polishing my boots no longer takes an hour, nor
does folding my laundry appropriately, nor does making my bed…
I'm learning to create time, to make more room for myself—and then
there's always the hour-long shifts of fireguard at night.

Let me know how things are back at the homestead—miss you
both, my love to Smokey—give her a good chase around the lawn and
hassle her for me! I'm sure she's being especially naughty and misbe-
having now that I'm not there to keep her in line anymore…

Love,
Adrian

Journal Entry: 26 March 2005

Polished boots in record time. Laundry day for my squad. Body a
miasma of pain and soreness. Can feel the cigarette gunk of a decade
beginning to leave my lungs. No booze, no sex, no nothin', not even the
prospect of it.

More classroom tomorrow. The dreaded teach. Marching and
jumping jacks and "fall-in" from 0430 until bed. My body does not
belong to me, my agency is superfluous at best and dangerous at worst.
I am the property of the government…

28 March 2005

Dear Grandpa,

Do you remember basic training when you got drafted into World
War II? Was it as miserable and soul-sucking then as it is now? I'm
on "fireguard" now, which probably fulfills the same function as it did
when you were in, or when your grandfather was in the Civil War—
as a way to deal with predicable non-combat-related emergencies that
crop up at night. It's me and another trainee, an OCS candidate who I
get along with pretty well—this is a mercy, you know what it's like having to get stuck on guard with a jerk—conversation always makes the

time go by faster. I have an hour all to myself on a good (but not great) shift—it's after everyone else has gone to sleep, but not so late that I'll get totally shafted by the schedule. I'll have five hours of uninterrupted sleep when the shift's over. It's a cool spring night, with little breeze. Perfect for letter writing. I'm learning to take comfort in the smaller things—there are so many tedious or troubling events that when you make your way to any reprieve or sanctuary, it counts for much more than I remember when I was a civilian.

Okay, I'm still basically a civilian. It's only been two weeks since I left home, and I haven't changed *that* much. I'm easing into the discipline, to the life where every bit of thought or action is highly regimented and ordered by someone else. I haven't figured out how to own that regimentation, make it a part of my life rather than resenting the hell out of it, hating it in secret; no, I'm still a civilian, not a soldier. I'm not sure I'll ever be a great soldier, in the sense that "they" mean ("they" being the sergeants major, the generals, the people who control and contrive what a word like "soldier" means outside its context in war)—but I have no doubt that this thing is doable. It's challenging, it defeats my ego, it pushes me far, far outside my comfort zone, but smaller and less healthy men made it through before me with less, and millions have made it through in its current incarnation.

I failed the first "Physical Evaluation" or "Physical Training" test by not doing enough push-ups or sit-ups. I think half of the platoon failed, so it's not like I'm the only one… I've been training hard since, trying to get better—I'm going to need not just to pass but actually to excel, because the OCS test is harder, more rigorous, and right now me and a couple other OCS guys are in a similar boat: big brains, little biceps. Apparently it's just a matter of conditioning one's body to do a certain exercise by practicing over and over again. I'll get there, like I said, I can't imagine failing something like a push-ups test, where so many other people have succeeded—just a matter of a little bit of discipline. I had no idea that I was in such poor shape when I entered the military, and can only imagine what my ceiling for fitness is. No troubles with running, of course—it's been a joy to watch (and experience) my body's return to high school form; there's a glee, an exhilaration that comes with running at top speed, and especially when that top speed is decently fast!

Meanwhile the platoon has already shrunk from forty to thirty-seven. The first casualty was my bunk-mate and *de facto* battle buddy, a trainee I'll call Smith. He was a short, thin guy from Maine, pretty bright, with the proper motivations for wanting to serve (a mixture of patriotism and practicality, getting an education that he could otherwise not afford). Well, he started limping the second day, and although doctors couldn't find anything wrong with him, he continued to limp and was placed in the "washout" unit, where he could spend his time receiving treatment / additional testing. I was not furnished with a new bunk-mate, so the top bunk is empty, I have a bed to myself. This is nice from the one perspective (who wants a damned bunkmate), but inconvenient from the other (your battle buddy helps make your bed in the morning, it goes much faster with two people). The trainees to my left and right help me instead; I am the adoptive battle buddy of two other pairs. Yeah, it's awkward. The other two trainees who washed out had physical ailments that mysteriously cropped up as soon as we started training, prompting our drill sergeant, an impressive sergeant first class I'm calling "Y," to encourage us not to malinger. Everyone's terrified of getting sick—for one thing, nobody wants the reputation for being sick or weak, and then there's always the dreaded prospect of being "recycled," or forced to go through another bout of training.

Brighter news... so you may remember discussing my choice of branch with me. I requested armor, and I think that's probably what I'll get. One of the guys from the bunk to the left of mine is a potential OCS candidate like myself, name of John—he requested infantry. Well, we went on a three-mile ruck march, our first, and happened to be walking by one another. When we stopped, he said, "Fuck this, I don't want to be infantry," and I said, "This isn't so bad!" Our trainer, Drill Sergeant Y, has been talking up infantry every chance he gets, and long story short, John and I decided that if we get the branches we requested we're going to swap. More to follow on that front.

I don't plan on coming home between basic training and OCS, and I won't have time between OCS and whatever school I'm branched to next, either—which means that if I'm not home for Thanksgiving, I may not be home before Christmas. I look forward very much to sitting down and talking with you, pumping you for stories about your experiences, what you remember from the good old days.

Love,
Adrian

1 April 2005

Esteemed Comrade,

No, this isn't a politically-motivated letter encouraging you to vote or volunteer for some Party function—it's greetings from basic training! I've arrived, Brent, and you were right about everything—the practical supremacy of branching infantry, the importance of sleep and relative discipline, how to prepare for ruck marching—more things I'm forgetting—but most of all, the precious notion that "what one man can do, another can do." I'm sure I'd be lost here without that idea—I'd have failed several times over by now. And I've only been here a couple weeks.

It's not just that the body isn't used to this sort of thing, this kind of challenge—it's that the brain isn't used to enforcing the body's compliance in matters of pain or endurance. The three-mile ruck march with thirty-five pounds on our backs—not even a rifle, just the packs—was grueling. I understand you guys train with twelve-mile marches, and in the old days, they used to do twenty-five milers. My body can do more than it knows. Running, push-ups, sit-ups, pull-ups; I'm not used to exerting myself, but I can go the distance. The obstacle course, the bayonet course—both events where I (like everyone else) was drenched in sweat and covered in mud, and as it turned out, events that I was capable of finishing—I was up to the challenge. During the events, I had to energize myself by repeating a variation on your mantra: "I can do this, others have done this and worse." That's really all it came down to. Which is pretty incredible, that the magic solution to hardship could be so simple; at the same time, it's true, I think of the people who walked before me wearing a uniform, yourself included, in every culture and every civilization, and want to be one of them. I don't want to be one of the men who, having set out to test themselves in this environment, meeting hardship decided to walk home, shamefaced and defeated.

We begin rifle training soon. I've never shot before, and of course all the people with experience in these matters are strolling around boasting about how effective they are with rifles, how they're going to be able to hit everything and qualify "expert" with perfect scores… I'm just hoping I pass first time around. We've had the classes, and it looks more difficult than I'd thought (not to shoot—that must be fairly straightforward—but to shoot *accurately* and effectively—another story entirely). Our drill sergeant (a Hulka-type, both in terms of mannerisms and I think of actual combat experience / heroic potential) assures us both that people with no prior experience shooting are likely to do better than the others, and also that nobody will go without qualifying on their rifles, no matter how many times they have to shoot in order to qualify. Even, as he claims, if we have to shoot every last bullet in the army's arsenal and stop the war in Iraq and Afghanistan, everyone will be qualified.

Strangest thing—probably the indirect motivation for writing you today: I met another Yalie in my platoon. Jim Danly, class of '99. We were in one of those condescending classes about how to tie your shoelaces or brush your teeth, and the instructor was late, so the drill sergeants decided to have some fun with the OCS trainees for everyone's amusement, and systematically had us each stand and talk about ourselves, where we were from, etcetera. There were four or five who went before me, so I had a clear idea of what I was in for when my turn came around—I said I was from Connecticut (fag), twenty-seven years old (over the hill), got my B.A. in English (fag) from Yale (… what?). The drill sergeant started (understandably) asking me personal questions and then got bored with the game and dismissed us for a fifteen-minute break. Afterwards, one of the OCS trainees from my platoon—I'd never talked with him before, but seen him suffering on the other side of our barracks during smoke sessions—walked up to me and introduced himself. This was how I met Jim. He's easily one of the most intelligent people I've ever encountered, but also has a unique charisma—everyone in the platoon flocks to him, from the OCS trainees to the enlisted trainees to the drill sergeants. During the medical portion of the training, he pulled substantial EMT knowledge out of his past—which reminded me of the type of thing you'd do in a similar situation. Anyway—a really good guy. So far people haven't been giving either of us shit about Yale—I think maybe they respect our joining, maybe they think it's cool. That would be a first.

I'll be here for another couple months, then at OCS afterwards. I'll let you know which company I get assigned to—you're training up for Afghanistan, or about to leave, I don't know your timeline—write when you have a chance. I know nothing about the area, or what you'll be facing out there, and your exploits and adventures serve as motivation for me to keep working hard and gutting out another torturous ruck march. We did our first five miler yesterday morning, so as you know it's the most difficult thing I could imagine. Probably training harder than you are.

Salutations and luck,
Adrian

Journal Entry: 7 April 2005

Lying awake after the lights are off in the middle of a barracks full of trainees snoring and coughing is the loneliest feeling. Solitude is a peculiar form of depression, and it may be linked to the spring. Something about the seasons changing, the light expanding into morning and evening. The knowledge that as the day grows longer, people are out *doing* while we're stuck in this prison, this concrete time capsule.

Recently discovered an interesting vignette in a doctrine / field manual on tactics, describing the Soviet / German action at Kursk. All of the other vignettes cast the Americans in the role of the protagonist, so what is a German / Soviet battle doing in a book on American Doctrine? Why is the German Field Marshall Erich von Manstein cast in the role of protagonist? And why, despite him being cast in the role of protagonist, does the lesson seem to pertain primarily to the defense—how not to attack an entrenched position? These "through the looking glass" moments only serve to highlight that I'm in a place now that prizes efficiency and some complicated, obscure calculus over political sensitivities. From one perspective, the Germans fought the Russians well and effectively, and probably would've beaten them if we hadn't been shipping the Russians arms, money, and bombing the hell out of Germany around the clock—why not use the Germans' strategy in the Cold War? From another perspective, anything the Germans did—this is what I learned in High School and College—was tainted by the Nazi regime, and the horrible things its citizens perpetrated against the Jewish people. For some reason this seems like a reasonable observation to make, training for a Counter-Insurgency.

Dear Teddy,

Spring has arrived at Fort Benning, Georgia—thunderstorms, cool mornings and hot days—just in time for BRM or "Basic Rifle Marksmanship." It's the first time I've felt like this training thing is serious business—it's not marching around singing or hup-hupping with fake rifles and heavy backpacks (called—you must know this already—rucksacks)—it's using live bullets to hit man-shaped targets between fifty and 300 meters away. That's why I'm here. Medical knowledge is useful and good for morale, but not decisive. Physical training makes me feel good about myself and gets me stronger, slowly but surely, but a weak person can use a rifle to hit a target as well as a strong person. Knowing how to fire and clean one's rifle really is the most essential skill for a soldier, the thing that separates the soldier from any other group or category; an assumption of competence that allows him to carry dangerous weapons in public.

It was not easy for me to learn how to fire the M16 well, and I'm not great at it—but I'm decent. It took me a while with "iron sights"—WWII or Vietnam style, looking down the sights of a rifle, with no special scope—the most basic form of firing, where you can barely even see the target at 300 meters (the furthest target they have you practice on, though the rifle is accurate at greater distances). Zeroing was embarrassing, I was one of the last to finish zeroing my rifle. A friend I've made here, Jim Danly (another Yalie, '99) helped me finish. As with many things, he had a background with small arms and was consequently able to give me the pointers I needed to finish. I would have preferred that he or anyone else do the zeroing for me, but that's not how it works; one has to zero the weapon (adjust it for accuracy) for oneself. And that's a good thing, because I'm training to be an officer.

Zeroing—I should have mentioned this—is the process of lining up the sights with your eye. Based on where you put your cheek on the rifle buttstock, your eye makes a line to the target that the sight-post intersects, and the small, seemingly insignificant variations in cheek placement and breathing techniques and everything else make for huge deviations at 300 meters. So I kept firing, with five or six other "hard-core" [read: incompetent] shooters, and eventually zeroed the damned rifle. Obviously this is one of those things you just have to practice a lot.

Once we finished zeroing our M16s, we went down to the "pop-up" range for a week of training before the actual rifle qualification, which is required to pass basic training. The pop-up range has man-sized (and shaped) silhouette targets that, as you'd expect, "pop up" from behind hillocks in a pattern that resembles an enemy unit charging at you from 300 meters away. There are a total of forty targets, and sometimes they pop up singly or in pairs, and the goal is to hit all of them. Thirty-six hits means you've qualified "expert," twenty-seven, "sharpshooter," and twenty-three, "marksman." Lucky twenty-three. Over that week of shooting, we all learned a great deal about ourselves; I struggled up from hitting 17-20 targets to routinely hitting 25-28 targets, which after my struggles with the zeroing component gave me extraordinary peace of mind. Meanwhile many of the people with backgrounds in marksmanship had real difficulty transitioning from their habit of taking a long time to sight a target and fire an accurate shot, to the fairly aggressive pace of shooting at targets that appeared for three seconds and then disappeared. Further complicating matters were the requirements to wear body armor, a helmet that invariably dropped into your eyesight at the least opportune times, and in my case the bulky glasses I have to wear, which fogged up and slipped down the nose and were on top of everything else an intolerable nuisance while shooting. As it turned out, rifle qualification was a pretty significant challenge for a lot of the trainees; I qualified my first time out with twenty-four hits on a lane where one of the targets was malfunctioning (or I may have had twenty-seven or twenty-eight hits—the malfunction affected one of the easier targets, and the lane was shut down after I fired), but half the platoon failed to qualify and had to wait another few days for another opportunity. In the meantime, they were not allowed to wear camouflage covers on their helmets—this was how the drill sergeants punished the trainees who hadn't qualified, in case they needed additional reminders of their inadequacy.

This is a common theme I'm picking up on in the army, the idea of similarity or blending in. There is such a strong inducement to be like the platoon or squad, or to do what the platoon or squad does, that it's no longer at all surprising that atrocities seem to happen as a result of consensus. Once an idea or method reaches some sort of threshold— maybe 50% or greater—there's a high likelihood that it will be appropriated by the rest of the group. It's like a disease or a sickness, and, in fact, I could imagine that if the bulk of the platoon had some kind of cough, those individuals without a cough might subconsciously hope for a cough, just to be more like everyone else. The thing—I believe I mentioned this in an earlier letter, or perhaps it was a letter to my parents—the most important thing, above everything else, is not to stand out as an individual for any reason, good or bad. Failures are taken as failing the group, and successes are group successes that somehow reflect on the efforts of all, regardless of whether or not that has anything to do with it. I should mention that this is the part of the army that I like the least; you know that I'm fundamentally a social person, and enjoy socializing, but the sort of all-consuming desire to be alike drains my energy and enthusiasm, and is both disingenuous and dangerous. I do not feel that I should have to pretend to be like or to like everyone (or anyone) else—but I understand that I must, for the group good.

I'm writing this on "fireguard," which is what it sounds like—depending on who's in charge, a shift of between thirty minutes and an hour where you're sitting at a desk, awake, with another person, while everyone else sleeps. I pulled a shitty slot tonight, 1am to 2am, but there's not much going on tomorrow so it won't kill me. "Fireguard" is different from "roaming guard" or just "guard." In the field, roaming guard means you and someone else patrolling the perimeter of your base or temporary position. For some reason it always seems to be raining or wet "in the field," which means getting all your gear wet when you wake up to patrol or pull guard—I'm much less fond of "roaming guard" (or just plain "guard") for all of those reasons and others too diverse to mention here such as finding and waking up other people in the middle of the night once shift is over— especially when they don't want to wake up. This cuts both ways— apparently I threatened to beat one of my fellow trainees to death one night when he tried to wake me up for guard, I don't remember it, but apologized to him anyway, death threats are not cool, even if you only sort of mean them (I may have meant it at the time, a lizard brain response to extreme discomfort).

I recently started my first substantial reading project since joining the army: the *Hagakure*. You'd think I'd have read this in Japan, or before going to Japan—Jim Danly certainly thought so—of course, I went to Japan in part because I knew so little about it, not because I'd developed an idea of the place beforehand. If you've read any serious Eastern Philosophy you're aware that this genre is usually organized into analects, a series of observations and vignettes that, presumably combined with reflection and meditation, make up a philosophy or way of living. I've really enjoyed it, both the reading and the reflection. Its most famous claim, an extreme renunciation of love for life itself—a warrior should think of himself as already dead, because only at that point will he be able to act without fear or bias—is well worth chewing on. Never having been in a situation where that was even a possibility, I can't speak to its utility—but it does seem that a deliberate lack of fear would make for powerful warriors. Then again, death means "change" to the unconscious—some irresistible and inscrutable change—maybe what the book is saying is simply that warriors—leaders—must accept that their plans and ideas will meet with "death" on the battlefield (or elsewhere). Adaptability, compromise, and the willingness to accept transition rather than resisting it or fearing what is new and unfamiliar makes a warrior or leader effective.

You're probably getting ready to open the island house for the summer. I remember it fondly, the waves, the distance from shore, experiencing the journey out on the motor boat, the wonderful sense of isolation and privilege—it's going to be a long time until I even have a physical opportunity to see the island again, but happy memories give me energy and motivation to struggle through each challenge and obstacle until I am back there among friends and family.

> Hope all's well,
> Love,
> Adrian

Journal Entry: 13 April 2005

Packed my rucksack in four minutes tonight. The poncho went in its pocket, the wet-weather gear in their designated pockets. Sleeping bag, poncho liner and extra uniforms at the bottom of the rucksack—packed the lighter gear at the bottom, heavier equipment higher so it rides closer to the shoulders. Two-quart canteen full and fastened in the appropriate place.

Looked up and a few of the other trainees were already finished—most of the rest of them were talking, packing more slowly, taking their time. Jim was sitting across the barracks floor, securing the straps of his rucksack with electrical tape. Drill Sergeant Y was doing work in his office, with the doors open. Stood up and looked through my locker, made sure everything was in order for the next day. Laundry bag nearly empty, boots polished, clothes folded. Not a speck of dust to be seen.

There wasn't anything else to do, so I took a shower, wrote a letter and went to bed.

★

13 April 2005

Dear Elsa,

Figured I owed you at least one letter from training; let you know what's going on with me, how I'm processing the experience. Now you've got two groups of military-themed letters, from two different personalities—mine, and Brent's. I wonder how they intersect in terms of tone and content; if we're seeing and understanding the same things. Of course, he's much further along with this than I am—he's supposed to be deploying soon. To Afghanistan.

Here in Georgia it's getting hot—we've got a bit of spring here, which is not the beautiful spring of Connecticut, but a very wet and rainy sort of affair with mosquitoes and humidity and unpleasantness—and then the summer of the South to look forward to. I finish Basic in a little over two weeks, the beginning of May. Thus far I've learned how to be in the military, the skeleton of it, anyway—the importance of rank and deference. From my beginnings as a man taught not to see people according to their value, I've turned by phases into someone who is able to place people according to stereotypes. A strange offshoot of this maturation has been to look at people who wield real responsibility with real suspicion. I also know how to pack a rucksack, can march ten miles without stopping, can fire a rifle, and endure a certain amount of sleep deprivation. These, I understand, are the skills that will help push me through the next phases of my training.

For some reason the most important part of the experience now— or at least the one that makes most sense to describe—are the hoops I have to jump through to eat. There are three meal times: breakfast, lunch, and dinner. One generally has between five and seven minutes to finish one's meal, but if one is near the end of the line, that can be shortened to one or two minutes. There's one character, an Asian American guy who's going to OCS like myself, who is obsessed with fitness; I saw him sit down once with a plate of yogurt, hard boiled eggs, and some other protein source, and he had time to take one bite from his yogurt before the drill sergeants were ordering everyone to stand up and evacuate the dining hall. He closed his eyes and actually shuddered with rage. I'd never seen anything like it. I was nearly done with my meal, so risked an "ass-chewing" (getting yelled at by someone my age wearing a funny hat), bolted my food (you remember that I can eat pretty fast), got up and left.

The whole process is so *weird*, though—you have to "sound off" or yell the words to these various creeds from memory before you can go inside, sometimes individually, sometimes as a group, then you file in through a line, obeying certain protocols such as how to stand. You're discouraged from talking in line. And the people around you—boy, what a mixed bag. You really learn about your fellow countrymen in a place like this. There's this one ex-Navy guy with a lazy eye who threatened to kill me and a friend of mine because we were forcing him to do a detail to which we'd all been assigned but which he didn't feel like doing, and when a drill sergeant happened onto our disagreement this guy claimed that we'd called him the "n-word"—just the meanest, most depraved sort of behavior. It's always lively. Oh—"the man who cried racist" left our group; he threatened to kill some other trainees, enough to make it a serious concern, so he was removed. Don't know what happened to him after.

In any case, I'm doing all right. I'll be in OCS soon, and after that comes infantry lieutenant training, then who knows. It's hard to make plans for the future when the present is so uncertain.

Stay well,
Adrian

Journal Entry: 26 May 2005

Basic down, OCS and God knows what else to go. Now I'm really obligated. In for three years come hell or high water. Didn't feel particularly concerned or stressed when I arrived at Basic, but having learned what's at stake in the next phase, I can barely sleep looking forward to the tortures promised at OCS. Dreading failure or censure.

But I'm trapped in the decision I made—there's only one way out of this commitment at this point, and that's by fulfilling it to the letter.

26 May 2005

Dear Mom & Daddio,

Just to follow up on the phone call we had a couple weeks ago— you didn't miss anything at graduation. Jim Danly's family and friends were there, and I sort of attached myself to their party; all that happened at the end of basic training was that we marched in front of a stand, 140 of us or so, did an "eyes-right," mingled at the barracks afterward, and… that was it. I had an idea that it would be an underwhelming ceremony—I mean, it wasn't bad, but this abridged basic training wasn't the truly meaningful ceremony for anyone there. The commo privates in our class are going to follow-on training at some fort I don't know the name of, the medics are going to follow-on training at Fort Sam Houston in Texas, and we OCS-ers are going to officer school right here on Fort Benning! The second bit of training is supposed to be more difficult—especially for us as we're going to get drilled in land navigation, which is supposed to be particularly challenging. Anyway, I'd love to have you down here to pin my second lieutenant bars on, assuming I pass—I must pass—but coming down for this would have been a gross misallocation of your time, money, and energy.

I'm sitting at a hotel room in civilization for the first time in two months—seems like (feels like) forever. Being alone is a glorious feeling, and all I really want to do is lie back in my bed and close my eyes, or maybe watch a movie. Wearing civilian clothes again instead of the heavy-ply Winter Weight BDUs—our camouflaged uniforms—or the lighter-ply Summer Weight BDUs (stands for battle dress uniform). I can wear whatever I like, or nothing at all. This reminds me of the stories I heard about both Grandpa Wes and Grandpa Fado growing up.

A frightening thing happened two nights ago, before graduation. We were about to be given a *single* day off to spend with friends or family or whomever had made the trip down to see us—in my case, that would be the Danlys—we had one last test to pass, and this was to clean all of our equipment for turn-in, then pass an inspection from our company commander, a fit, tall, black captain in his mid-thirties—a very approachable but nevertheless intimidating leader. We worked for days to prepare for this inspection, scouring every piece of equipment meticulously for even the echo of dirt, developing an SOP (a plan that everyone had to follow precisely) for the layout of our equipment, and numerous trial inspections. We decided that the layout would be on our bed mattresses (to prevent dust from getting on the equipment overnight), made the slight adjustments that were necessary, helped out the people who had small last-minute problems with their layouts, and then all slept on the floor. Honestly, this was the best idea that we came up with, to sleep on what amounted to concrete. Because people were afraid of the dust. I doubted the wisdom of the idea—I'm turning into a cynic and really don't believe that it would've been *that* dusty on the floor, especially considering our being required to scrub it twice daily—but one can tell when the group has made up its mind, and then it's pointless to argue against their will unless there's something more substantial at stake than a good night's sleep. Although that's pretty substantial these days.

As luck would have it, this was to be our last night of fireguard, and everyone was assigned a shift to make the process as fast and painless as possible. I got the first shift of ten- to ten-thirty, and everyone was out like a light, sleeping by their bunks. It was a strange sight, all those bunks, configured identically with the same equipment spread out on all of them, nobody visible. I periodically bent down and checked under the beds to make sure they hadn't disappeared, which reassured me that I wasn't in an episode of *The Twilight Zone*. My shift passed slowly but uneventfully, and I handed off responsibility to the next group without issue—one of them hadn't even bothered to go to sleep, he was writing a letter or reading a letter by the light of a headlamp. I returned to the floor beside my bed, where I'd laid out a blanket and a pillow earlier, probably shook my head or sighed with resignation, and lowered my battered body to the cold tile floor.

When you've been exercising a lot—I forgot to mention that I've increased my push-ups and sit-ups substantially, I passed the test and am capable of getting into OCS, now—your extremities can fall asleep more easily, especially during rest at night. I don't know what the medical or physiological explanation is for this phenomenon, but it's real. In the field, it's not uncommon after a long day of training to go to sleep, then wake up in the morning without being able to feel one's toes, or feet, or a leg, or an arm, or a hand… you get the point.

Another important element to this story is that one gains the ability to wake up very quickly, and respond in an appropriate manner to whatever's happening—so, for example, in the field during some training event, if there's a big noise that wakes you up, or yelling, you grab your rifle and pull security. In the barracks, under those conditions, you come to the position of attention as quickly as possible, and get to the red line with all possible speed. This is called "toeing the line." Not toeing the line fast enough, or properly, got us all smoked in the beginning, and it was one of the first punishments we learned to avoid. You know, like dogs.

Well, not surprisingly it was difficult to get to sleep after fireguard, on the floor, but I did it. Don't remember much about the sleep, no dreams or anything like that, but after some very careful tossing and turning, I drifted off, maybe around 11:30 p.m. or so. Very early the next morning, around 4 a.m., I heard a boom through my sleep and felt the lights turn on. The voice of Drill Sergeant Moss, filled with anger and aggression, yelled: "Oh, Hell *mother-fuck* no!" which was all I needed to hear to understand that I'd done something terrible and was about to catch a world-class smoking, one of those marathon sessions where you need a two-quart canteen to stay hydrated. I sprang to the position of attention, as quickly as I could—but the left half of my body was numb. During the night, sleeping on that side of my body, the blood had flowed out into the center and right side of my body. I toppled over, coming down hard on my left knee but managing to twist just enough to hit the lockers with my head instead of the bunk, preserving the layout I've just slept on the floor to keep clean. I stood up again, carefully, awake now, and shuffled like a cripple over to the line like everyone else, expecting to have just compounded whatever error I'd made.

At the line, standing at parade rest (a more comfortable position than "attention" where you can move your head), I saw what had happened. The last two soldiers to pull fireguard—a young Puerto Rican future Medic and a young future commo guy who was a chubby white supremacist from Alabama—had collaborated to fall asleep on the empty beds near the drill sergeants' office. This insult, I think, was the one that inspired Drill Sergeant Moss to real anger, their comfortable bed-sleep set off against the rest of us sleeping on the floor. Everyone drifts off during guard, especially when the training's difficult, but it's understood that you're making an attempt to stay awake—that's why there are two of you on guard, one man drifts off, the other one wakes you up (or you wake him up). In a million subtle and not-so-subtle ways, you learn the idea that *sleep on guard is unacceptable*: this knowledge helps motivate you to find the tricks you need to stay awake under adverse conditions, at any cost. The important thing for the purposes of training really is the *effort*. We weren't in difficult training, we'd been cleaning gear, but let's say we had been training hard—if they'd passed out under those conditions, the future Medic at the table, and the future commo guy on the floor, literally having passed out while executing their duties, they'd have been in for admonishment, but not like this. Not sleeping on empty bunks (their presence on guard indicated that everyone before them had been able to stay awake) while everyone else slept on the floor. That deliberate disobedience, the intentional subversion of training, was too much.

It feels important to write (although it must be obvious) that I felt no sympathy for them, having subjected myself to the torture of doing anything to stay awake during guard shift. All I felt in the moment was a sense of physical relief that I wouldn't be punished, relief immediately replaced by the first pangs of pain in my knee and head. As Drill Sergeant Moss continued to castigate the two trainees, threatening them with loss of privileges, even possibly graduation, I was filled by a sense of justice. There would be no mass punishment. We would graduate together in a couple of days (as we did—we walked this morning), but in a real sense I'd already graduated: I was capable of being responsible for myself and to others, and this is how the authorities treated me. One step closer to "Big Boy Rules."

I'll write from OCS. Love to all, and thanks so much for your support and letters.

Love,
Adrian

5

3 June 2005

Brent,

Got your address in your last letter. I would've replied sooner but am at OCS now. I was assigned to Alpha Company—"Alphatraz"— you've heard all the rumors, the idiosyncratic things this company does that makes it especially unpleasant—I'm actually skeptical at this point, I think I'd be equally miserable in Bravo or Charlie or Delta Company. What's miserable about the process is seeing people from Delta wearing their white ascots, eating in the chow hall where you can take a whole half hour to finish your meal, whereas we have three minutes unless we get less; the Bravo building is empty, and the Charlie group is a couple weeks ahead of us, almost onto Blue phase. To go along with the overwhelming proliferation of other minute details that instruct on us how to behave, how to dress, how to react in every situation, and doing it in a demeaning and insulting way (Ascots!? Come on!) so that you end up elevating the loss of self and conformity as an absolute good.

It all seems trivial when stacked up against what you're going through in Afghanistan. I mean… not even sure what to write here… I'd never even heard of the 173rd when I got to the army, except from you, but here, saying "I have a buddy in the 173rd" is not substantially different from saying "I have a buddy in the Rangers"—maybe even better, as the 173rd is this sort of ultimate secret in the army. An Airborne unit in Italy. What could be better? And you're there, with this elite group, hiking in the mountains with a platoon of paratroopers, hunting for the Taliban—which I thought, really thought had disappeared in 2002 when we beat them. Iraq is all over the news, I mean, that's why I joined, the idea of being a moral leader, putting the brakes on atrocities or the willingness to commit atrocities—and meanwhile there's this *other* war that we didn't even finish in Afghanistan… takes some serious cognitive dissonance to figure that one out.

It's interesting—I don't know if you find this to be true—but I expected everyone in the military to be firmly Republican, certainly anti-Clinton. The latter is true, but the former seems less certain, less solid. There's a deep hatred for Don Rumsfeld among almost all of the senior enlisted and junior officers—anyone who deployed and saw combat—and a certain resentment surrounding the wars, how the blind prosecution of one led to uncertainty in the other. But—this is all bullshit—you're over there, you know best how you feel, that's just how it seems going through training, in my comfortable, plush armchair.

Write whenever you have the time. I passed the physical test—gotten much stronger since Basic—and am just enduring all the other petty bullshit that comes along with training. Trying to keep morale up, I know this is going to be rough. Dreading land nav, although at least there we'll get MREs and time to eat them, which will be a pleasant change. Hope all's well.

      Respectfully,
      Adrian

3 June 2005

Dear Mom and Dad,

After basic training I thought I'd be more or less prepared for the next step, this OCS business. I mean, I am—what one person can do, another can do, and tens (hundreds?) of thousands of officers have commissioned through OCS—but it's going to be tougher than I'd thought. It's far more regimented than I remember it being in basic training—or maybe I've just forgotten, already, how overly managed our time was in the first week, the shock of adjusting to my time no longer being my own. Okay—wait—I've got it—*here's* the difference. In basic training, my time was suddenly the property of the government, which was a shock, but it didn't feel like the government was going to be too focused on checking up on exactly what we were doing with that time. At OCS, all of a sudden, they're adding a wrinkle: not only does my time belong to them—no shock—but I am also being judged and evaluated, constantly, by everyone around me, including my fellow "candidates" (this is what we're called here). As you can imagine this has led to a great deal of constant and ubiquitous stress. I'm not sure how I'll adapt to it, either, though it seems likely that I will—either that, or just gut my way through it.

My platoon has decent, merit-focused leadership. The platoon leader, our chief trainer, is a black guy who looks like he could be a professional football player. He's built like a tank. I don't know if this is related or not, but he doesn't seem to feel that he needs to prove himself, which makes him a bearable leader. Leaders who don't trust their own authority are always the worst, seeing conspiracies and slights where they don't exist. The platoon "NCO" trainer or "TAC" (don't know what this stands for) is a Ranger-qualified sergeant first class who looks like he has an eating disorder—thin as a rail. He burns with a fiery, fierce intensity, and he terrifies everyone in the platoon—maybe even the company.

So, the routine is—well, different. We spend most of our time marching to "Building 4," the classroom building, standing in formation, or sitting in class taking tests. We have a half hour for each of our three meals per day, which works out to nearly three minutes per person per meal unless you're unlucky, and somebody has to stand and shout at you to eat faster. The dining facility is adjacent to a much more permissive place where you don't have to stand in a massive line—I watched a group walk into the big-boy's facility the other day and silently, secretly scowled at them, at their freedom. We sound off with various creeds, stand in line, do pull-ups everywhere, walk in a certain deeply proscribed way. We run and exercise in the morning. We sing the OCS song before going to bed at night. Every moment of our time is managed; there're often five to seven minutes between exercise and breakfast. Formations punctuate everything. Formations are mandatory. If you're late for a formation, you get punished.

Punishments vary from the informal smoke sessions I became accustomed to during Basic, to walking around in the square carrying a rifle and executing all sorts of silly facing movements—in public, along with all the others who are being punished for one of the countless infractions they might have committed—to actually being recycled to another class. Nobody wants to have to do that, to spend another month wearing the black ascot. Privileges come with the various ascots, meaning black ascot wearers must salute blue, and blue white; more importantly, white ascot wearers (the final phase, the final three or so weeks) get to take weekends off, and can eat at the nice chow hall where nobody's yelling at you. That's where I want to get to, where everyone's aiming, the white ascot. Well, graduation. The ultimate reward, a ticket out of this place.

It's a challenge. More difficult than any I've faced so far, but not beyond my ability. Jim Danly's in a different platoon, but I'm getting along fine with the guys in mine—people who are going into all different types of branches—I have a roommate who's going to be an armor officer, and a roommate who's going into AG, or the administrative branch. We have engineers and infantrymen, aviators and supply, men and women. It's going to be stressful and trying, but it'll also be over pretty fast—fast enough that I'll be walking for graduation, then pinning on my rank, and seeing you, thinking how quickly it went by and reflecting that "it wasn't so bad, after all!"

> Write when you can, and I'll do the same.
> Love to all,
> Adrian

Journal Entry: 17 June 2005

This is so much worse than Basic. There are days when I'm not sure I'll pass. Every act comes with a cost: a shower means less sleep or studying. Sleep means no shower. Studying means no sleep and no shower. Yesterday I was lucky and close to the front of the food line—had a free fifteen minutes, during which time I managed a luxurious, ten-minute hot shower—and nearly missed the post-lunch formation. Meanwhile, every advantage I've received through luck or hard work was immediately and bitterly hated by those who learned of it. I loathe almost everyone around me. My roommates are decent, thank God, or I don't know what I'd do.

I hate OCS.

1 July 2005

Dear Grandpa,

Seeing as how you opposed my becoming an officer, I figured I might as well write you from OCS and give you a little bit of feedback about the process. Before anything else—this stuff is hard. I mean, it's legitimately painful, physically, emotionally, spiritually—it's tough. No joke. So, whatever bad experience you had with officers (and I've seen firsthand that not all the jerks get weeded out, unfortunately), there was at least one moment in their lives when they were held over the fire and didn't burn. Regardless of the boneheaded and selfish errors they made later.

I can't fully reconcile my idea of what your army must have looked like—drafted, coming from all sections and areas of America—representative of its country. A sense that whatever idiotic means were being employed, at least there was supposed to be a *reason* beneath it all— the memory of Nagasaki and the Battle of Britain, a sense that if we didn't make a stand in our neighbors' yard, eventually tyranny would be knocking at our front door; the same logics I hear trotted out here, as though that's the only way soldiers know how to visualize necessary conflict, through the lens of the World War II narrative.

That probably sounds like a bunch of b.s. But—you have to understand, you guys needed that explanation, a draft army needs a good reason to fight. That was WWII. That was, to varying degrees, Korea and Vietnam—at least people could point to a unifying principle (stopping the spread of communist states) in the beginning. And when the population and the army decided we'd had enough of Vietnam, we left. I'm pretty sure that's the way it's supposed to work.

I know a fair bit of history. What I see in front of me now, in the training halls, is a group of college grads, soldiers, and sergeants who all want to be leaders in the army. They are part of a professional organization, and the country does not have any real obligation to them (by design) to provide a narrative for their participation in any war, anywhere. The Bush administration made a necessary (yet half-hearted) effort to paint Saddam Hussein as an imminent danger to us and his neighbors with his vague "WMD" program, which at various times consisted of chemical weapons, nuclear weapons, and biological weapons. That was the last time anyone tried to explain what was going on, why we were in Iraq. Our reasons for going into Afghanistan were pretty solid; I never doubted that our toppling the Taliban was just. Four years later, why are we still there? According to people who've recently been over there or are there now, all the intel assets they had for tracking bin Laden were yanked for the war in Iraq; and they're not doing much in the way of building, just giving bags of money to the Afghans. I'm sorry, that makes no sense to me.

The really interesting thing is how the professional and *volunteer* nature of our army more or less compels the leadership to confront these issues, and come up with a satisfying explanation for why we're over there, why we're doing this. You know why I'm doing this, and that's sufficient for me, but when I'm an officer and people ask me why I believe in the mission, what am I supposed to say? That I don't, I'm just doing this because I want the mission to be done morally? That's a cop-out, a dodge. It doesn't answer the real underlying question, just frames how to act—the real question being what is the *mission* here, why are we doing this?

I've told you about my friend Brent, the lieutenant in the 173rd. He has an interesting way of humanizing the conflict, but his reasons draw on experiences I don't have. At the same time, I can draw strength from the notion that so long as I stick through the training, things will become clear to me. It becomes a personal quest, to discover why you're *really* doing this thing—as that reason has not been supplied for you by the government, and hasn't been supplied to me through life events or experience. Why do we fight… I'm not sure yet, but I don't think it's for the reasons I've read about in books about WWI, WWII or Vietnam (never read a story about Korea). The books that have come out so far about Iraq and Afghanistan are, I'm sorry to say, just retellings of those narratives.

Dad said that you're moving back to Connecticut soon. I'm happy to hear that, but also sad to hear that you're leaving California. Look forward to seeing you this Christmas! Write whenever you have the time or inclination.

Love,
Adrian

13 July 2005

Dear Teddy,

It's been a long time since I last wrote, and there's been pretty good reason for that—this phase of the training has severely tested my emotional and intellectual reserves. It took a couple weeks to fall into the pattern of basic training, but here at OCS I still haven't settled in. They do a great job of making the process uncomfortable and unpleasant, a psychological trial for the refined sensibilities of an entitled and pampered college grad. It's been a month and a half.

We were "in the field" this past week—we do this regularly now, whereas we did it twice the whole time we were in basic training. Very unpleasant in the heat of a Georgia summer. Everyone dreads hosting nighttime visitors like snakes or poisonous spiders, which can run from really inconvenient, the king and queen of inconvenience combined (brown recluse), to actually dangerous (water moccasins). Since getting to Basic there have been three soldiers bitten by brown recluse spiders, and they were all immediate medical recycles—I am terrified of this possibility. My field craft is improving, though, and I'm learning basic survival tasks such as how to pick a good campsite, things that seem like common sense but aren't (at least to me).

A very useful thing we learned recently was a thing called "land navigation." This was a week-long event (or more if one takes into consideration the days of classroom instruction that preceded the actual training) that began with basic walkthroughs, proceeded to buddy pre-tests, and culminated with a day-night test that weeded out nearly a quarter of the class. I passed, but the stress was enormous. Reading a map by the light of a single red-light flashlight in the dark, or navigating by terrain association during the day, off on your own with nobody to depend on and filled with horror stories from candidates who recycled due to land navigation, the build-up was intense. In the end, I actually quite liked it. The second-to-last pre-test, as well as the final test, were remarkable for the following reason: excepting sleep, it was the first time we were trusted to be *on our own* or *alone* since starting the school late May. It was intoxicating; I had a real physical sensation of freedom as I trotted out into the forest, almost like in childhood when one's parents say that it's all right to ride your bike to the candy store alone.

I'm not doing this justice. There was so much stress and anguish over land nav, and I failed nearly every test, consistently, up until the final exercise, so it's only in retrospect that my success seems like it was inevitable. The way I can maintain an even keel about all of this is by keeping in mind that there are two more great land navigation challenges ahead of me, lieutenant training and Ranger School.

This is another development. Assuming I can pass OCS, which of course I'm certain of up to a point (barring injury), I've branched infantry. This means more land navigation, and a slot in Airborne and Ranger School if I want it. Which, naturally, I do.

I'm on fireguard tonight—it's nearly done, so I need to finish this up and get back to bed—apologies if I've rambled. Look forward to seeing you this winter, once I've pinned on my lieutenant's bars!

Love,
Adrian

Journal Entry: 30 July 2005

Nearly died on this last field exercise. Forty out of the 160 students went down as heat casualties, myself included. We were supposed to dig fighting positions, but it was somewhere in the vicinity of 105 degrees Fahrenheit, with 95% humidity. I was alone for some reason, and working (never hard enough)—at some point I started to feel faint. I found a hunk of ice—barely remember this—nobody was around— and curled up in a fetal position around it. That's where they found me some time later. I was on the last lift to the hospital. Everything checked out, so I'm back to the field tomorrow. Don't want to miss training, get recycled.

Junior-high rumors about the sexual escapades between various OCS candidates. I haven't thought about sex in two months—how anyone has the *energy* in this heat, let alone the stamina after a day of training—either they're the ones who are making me work hard through shirking, or I'm doing something wrong. Can't wait 'til this is over.

10 August 2005

Dear Christina,

Hey sis! Long time no see! It was a happy surprise to receive your letter recently… I was in the field, and so it was a particularly emotional time. I talked with you a little bit about what it's like going through this between basic training and the start of my current assignment, Officer Candidate School, and it's more of the same. Just hotter, with heavier packs and greater distances. It's not so much the physical element that gets me—I mean, sure that sucks, but you discover that your endurance is always capable of meeting such challenges (especially if, like we Bonenbergers, you have strong bones). No, it's the lack of sleep and the way that affects everything. There are so many psyche-out games that people play with you, that you play with yourself; for example, I know that if I'm to be a successful infantry officer I need to go through Ranger School, which is supposed to be infinitely more difficult than this. How will I meet that challenge, if this one seems to try me to the utmost? Well—guess I'll find out when I get there.

Right now I'm sort of in the doghouse. At the end of our last "field" exercise—the one where I got your letter—we came back in and had to pass a series of inspections in order to progress from "blue" to "white" ascot. The difference between the two is huge, I mean, you really want to be a "white" ascot. This is one of the psyche-out games I was talking about. Only about fifteen people didn't pass from blue to white, and I was one of them. Why? Well, a couple reasons. First, the way we cleaned our gear and weapons was by assembly line. I spent a good portion of my time cleaning other peoples' things, under the assumption that others would be effectively cleaning my weapon. This process worked great for almost everyone else in my platoon and not awesome for me. Second, during an inspection (I've been through many now, it's when the big officers walk around and look at all of your clothes and gear) you want to be near the end or near the beginning of the inspection, but neither the first nor the last to be inspected—five or six "inspections" from the beginning or end is ideal—which gives the inspectors time to get tired and bored, so they start finger drilling the inspection. We were first, very bad luck. So, now I have a week before my secondary inspection. I'm basically destroying my weapon cleaning it to the standards demanded. And I have to jump through all these hoops while everyone else enjoys the privileges of the "white" ascot.

Eating at the nice chow hall, taking off for the weekend, etc., etc.

Even so, I'm confident I can pass this. It sucks, but then, I was never going to be the honor graduate here, I just want to get through it. It's a load of bullshit, to be perfectly frank, but I have a positive attitude about it. The motto here is "standards, no compromise," and from the very first day the leadership made it quite clear through acts and actions that there would be "double standards" for Rangers or people who'd been through the system before, and that so long as one was willing to make "compromises" when and wherever possible, it would be more or less smooth sailing. It is this essential hypocrisy at the heart of this game, this challenge, that gives me the strength to move through it; if I can't pass, it's not an absolute judgment about my worth, but a much more damning social referendum on my value as a potential contributing member of society. I will not be exiled from the group, I will carry my weight and prove my worth.

Mom and Dad have talked about your potential as a *brewer*? I cannot give you enough encouragement in this department, please, please dear sister, please God, please Fate, let this be your chosen profession. Whatever needs to be done to realize this goal. Whatever needs to be said! Keep at it, that's the most important thing.

Thanks for the letter again. I can't promise to write back soon, but I will write, and call, occasionally. It just takes a lot of the energy I have to be using for other less important but more critical things like, say, cleaning a light machine gun without which I will not be able to graduate and pin on the second lieutenant bars that are mine by right.

Love,
Adrian

Journal Entry: 28 August 2005

Walked into the big-boy dining facility today at lunch. Finally on the other side of the courtyard after three long months. Across the way, standing in their hated lines, Bravo Company wore the black ascot of shame, going through the same dog and pony routine I'd had to endure until it wasn't enduring any more, but just the normal routine. Some of the candidates stared longingly at my freedom as I passed them by, others hated me the way I'd hated Charlie Company when the roles were reversed. Inside the dining hall I joined Jim and another couple candidates from his platoon. Picked the food and drinks I wanted. Water, PowerAid, and a cup of coffee. Passed on the dessert.

Nobody raised his voice during the meal. No leaders shouting at us, nobody yelling "move faster." Some of the instructors walked in and sat nearby, ate their lunch and left. We could have gone to Subway for lunch, could have traveled to Little Caesar's or to one of the other mess halls. This was just easier.

After all the struggle, there's no excitement in eating here, no exultation. The pleasure I was certain I'd feel here is different—standing in that long line outside, what I really wanted was just an absence of pain and discomfort—the actual absence feels empty, hollow. And I can already feel it—the need for another challenge, another unpleasant situation from which to emerge, until—until what?

6

3 September 2005

Lieutenant Hobsbach,

Okay, okay, Brent—that's the last time I'll address you as such—I am puffed up with pride, having recently pinned on my own second lieutenant bars. I am now Lieutenant Bonenberger! I may have mentioned in an earlier letter (or forgotten—the last month has been a haze, but I failed my first inspection and drove myself half-mad passing the makeup) that I did branch infantry, and so will be attending IOBC here at Fort Benning. Another six months here, prepping for Ranger School and Airborne School, then... who knows? Italy? Quite apart from the reputation of the unit, and the location, being able to serve together in the same *unit*? I mean—that'd be too much. Even if the timeline doesn't quite match up. So, yeah, by all means, please look into that. It'll be my bond, my pledge to get through every bit of training I need to get out there. Sure, it's a long shot, but nothing wagered nothing gained! The two Airborne Ranger Yale Officers in the GWOT, the link from old to new, bounding forward into the future, upholding the traditions of the past...

Jesus, I need a break, I guess OCS really got to me after all. So much subtle propaganda and inducement to perform and stay motivated. It's difficult to distinguish the enthusiasm I feel naturally from the enthusiasm I've learned to display as a part of my social persona in the army. I'll tell you what, though, Jim Danly was my one real friend in Basic and OCS, and now that he's gone, I don't know. Friendship is such an important component of a thing like the army, and friendship is difficult to contrive when the basis for communication is a series of commonplaces and blandishments. Maybe I'll feel differently when I get to a unit, but you remember what things were like in training. The constant evaluation and competition for the limited favor and emotional resources of your superiors. I'm not looking forward to seeing how West Pointers play into the mix. Until now I've been surrounded by a bunch of prior service guys and college grads who have a similar background to my own; IOBC will be easier in some regards, but I'm very skeptical about the social angle.

I'm really looking forward to catching up this winter over Christmas break. I feel like you must have answers—there's nothing to be found in training—you've been over there, you've seen it. I guess I really just want to know whether it's worth all the fuss. I mean, I'm already in, I'm obligated, I'm not backing down, I just need to know how to prepare. Should I be looking at all of this as important, vital to building the type of leader I want to be, or so much delusional hogwash? How difficult is it to do "the right thing"? Are there any generalizations one can make about it? How much of this is junk, and is there anything else I should be reading? I don't know, if I'm asking the wrong questions please point me in the right direction.

All right brother—write when you have a chance. I have your new address in Kandahar, letters seem to take three weeks or so to get back and forth, a one to one-and-a-half month turnaround for conversation. I experienced no insurmountable difficulties with land nav, by the way, really ended up enjoying it…

Stay safe,
Lieutenant Bonenberger

Journal Entry: 10 September 2005

Thank God for small favors. IOBC is not at all like OCS. My platoon is terrific. These are the "big-boy" rules I've been hearing about for so long. I have my own apartment that's a fifteen-minute walk from where we hold formation in the morning—trees lining the route, quiet in the early morning—we have tons of personal time—we're encouraged to learn, and connect, and are treated like human beings, like assets—knowing the cost, still stinging from OCS, I'm going to take full advantage of the freedoms I'm offered.

17 September 2005

Hey Jacob,

I've owed you a letter for a while in response to the big letter you sent me, along with your comics. Thanks so much, that was a huge shot in the arm. I haven't told you about the goat-rope, the fandango I've been forced through in training—figured Brent had already described it as well as I could, if not better. He's in Afghanistan now, and my trials can't be anything like the trials he's going through. I hope they aren't, anyway, that'd almost be a disappointment. I guess it's fucked up to say or think that, but that's the essence of training, right? "I need to go through this because it'll be harder when it's really happening." If it's much easier, or different, what's the point? Just a thing to satisfy our need to explain, to order? A selection process wherein certain people select themselves out through injury or failure? I don't know, man. I've seen some real shitbags slide through or even excel under these circumstances. I've squeaked through myself—I'm sure there are people who look at me and think "how'd he make it"—of course these people do not know me, don't know the violence I'm capable of. I feel that it would undermine their confidence in our system, the way we do things—but I'm not a shitbag, I'm a decent human being. It's just that at heart I'm still a civilian, and that's subversive. Training was supposed to drill that personality out of me.

When I look at the people I've come through with, I realize that there are certain types, individuals who represent ways of thinking that have as their basis a judgment of others. There's the type who believes in the national-patriotic narrative, and that's why he (I've talked with a few females, we had three in our platoon, but they're all doing this for financial or educational reasons, which is straightforward) acts in certain predictable ways. We had one of those guys in basic training, a guy I'll call "Spaulding," from Texas, a big, goofy paper mache of a man who used his superior familiarity with military customs to lord it over the rest of us—he had a Ranger Tab sewed into his PC before the rest of us even knew what one was—naturally he has become less and less talkative as everyone else gains in proficiency. Most of the time I forget he's even around. He doesn't talk too much about Ranger School any more, either, since we learned he couldn't run. Mr. Patriot, Mr. "I'm going to be a Ranger some day, closed off to others' opinions, never helping without letting you know you're weak." A bully, a thug.

Then there's the social climber, the guy who comes from a place or society (usually Maryland, for some reason) where being an army officer still means something. As you know, my going into the army wasn't a good or bad thing, it was just weird. Well, there are places—and I know a couple guys here, one from Basic and another from OCS—who believe in the righteous power of marrying an Air Force general or admiral's daughter, and being a successful officer, and that's their ticket from mediocrity into social acceptability. Terrified of being judged in a position of weakness and terrible to behold when he gets into a position of leadership—the petty tyrant, the Himmler. He sees his flaws in everyone else and is afraid of losing the thing he's earned through treachery. I thank God every day for not being one of them and hope that this faith effectively shields me from the crippling deathbed realization that all has been for naught.

Finally you have the friendly leader—doesn't matter whether he's an officer or a sergeant—who has some narrative that explains why he joined, but doesn't use it as a way to justify or frame how he acts—this type is rare, and helps others out of a sense of humanity or a general desire to watch others succeed. I am not one of those people, but I'd rather aspire to their example than to any of the others. I, like the rest of the officers, have a mixture of good and bad traits that guide my decision-making.

It's not all internal, though, which is interesting. Leadership really is a thing that you can learn, that you can understand by phases. And the training we've gone through has given me ample opportunity to learn how to be a good leader. Part of this is by experiencing bad or terrible leadership, selfish leadership. Part of this is by having (less usual, but always nice) good leadership, leaders who are looking out for your best interests. The rest has been application, trying various techniques out, finding what works for me.

You have a kid now, I'm happy for you! Otherwise I'd encourage you to give this a shot, National Guard, Reserves, something low-key. You know it's always been a daydream of mine that you, Frank, me and Brent could all go through this, form the nucleus of The Resistance in the event of some cataclysmic event (which through the logic of the fantasy we'd all survive). Why are you and Frank messing around with law school and building families? You should be learning how to sneak around and shoot heavy caliber rifles from far away to kill bad folks. Ah, well. My regards to your wife, and congratulations on being a dad.

I'm sure if you can stay away from the sauce you'll be a good one. Kidding! About the sauce part.

I'll be back in New Haven in December, so I'll look forward to catching up with you then. I understand Brent is going to be in town too, so we can hear "the real deal" about what's happening in Afghanistan. The Forgotten War.

Stay well man…

> Best regards,
> Adrian

Journal Entry: 1 October 2005

Halfway done with a week in the field. Last night, the platoon's "problem" lieutenant finally jumped the shark. He was leading a late-night ambush for his evaluation, everything under green night vision. Cold, tired, whispered questions—are we in the right area? Where is the road? Who is this? Where's the PL? When the moment came to open up on our victims, he yelled "*Fire!*" like in the Civil War, which so surprised us (the machine gun was supposed to start the ambush, that's what everyone was waiting for) that the unit we were "ambushing" actually fired on us first—he won't be making it through. I know I will.

In basic training, packing my rucksack and polishing my boots became second nature. Maneuvers are starting to feel similarly—tactics, woodland movements, in day and night—it's how to walk. Using trees to mask your movement. Looking for little bumps in the ground, anything to hide. Tying knots, using the rope to construct buildings or objects.

On the hike back from the failed ambush, nobody spoke. When we reached the base, I looked at my watch and realized that nobody had spoken in over an hour. The forest is beginning to feel like home.

22 October 2005

Dear Jessica,

I apologize for the long silence, and appreciate the letters you sent over the last months. They were well taken, and very much appreciated during a time of sparse intellectual engagement. First—big congratulations on your admission to the London School of Economics! You must be really excited, and Ralph must be so proud! Is he going to leverage that into a post out in England, continue his meteoric rise in State? And thank you for the birthday wishes—nearly done with my twenties, and here I am running through the woods and camping, playing at war with my fellow officers like a ten-year-old. I would've written earlier, and sat down to start a couple letters but didn't want to tell you that I was through a certain challenge (they got pretty hard the last portion, in OCS) and then fail it—I mean, until I pinned lieutenant, it wasn't a sure thing. I didn't want to have to tell you that I'd failed.

But now, yes, I am an officer—commissioned into the army through a long, long chain that leads directly back to President Bush himself—he expressed great confidence in my leadership ability and decision-making potential, so, you can sleep easy at night. We've got this, me and Bush and the rest of the cast you know so well from the evening news. What's different, you might ask? What about me has changed since my time as an undergraduate? A certain panache, perhaps, a swagger, a *je ne sais quoi* which is actually summed up neatly in one terrifying clinical definition: narcissistic personality disorder. That's a joke of course, but the truth is that without an astonishing amount of self-regard, acquired through innate egotism or some religious framework, most people can't hack the infantry.

The training—now that I'm well into it and can recognize certain commonalities, I can draw a few conclusions—is designed to foster this confidence, this sense of destiny and the inevitable. At each step, the pool that we started with has been narrowed by some ten to fifteen percent (at least that's what it seems like) of the beginning class, and the ones that make it through do tend to have some remarkable trait, be it guts, or leadership, or fitness, or scruples, or lack of scruples, or a combination of all of the above (plus a fitness baseline). It's really a matter of standing out without trying—in fact, while trying not to stand out. The only group of people who do not succeed in this environment, as a rule, are the people with no social intelligence—the

Autistic or mild-level Asperger's Syndrome cases—which often come over from the Navy or Air Force, where they were stuck crunching code, and now they want to lead soldiers in combat for some reason.

Through basic training and OCS I had one real friend, a guy named Jim Danly, who was at Yale the same time we were. Class of '99. He branched Field Artillery and went to Fort Sill (Oklahoma) about a month and a half ago, beginning of September. I miss him, of course; he was (for a long time, and the most important piece of training thus far, the transition away from civilian life) the one shoulder I had to cry on when I had nothing left. Thankfully, I recently met another couple of guys that I've been getting along with, from my platoon in lieutenant training (can you imagine it, a platoon of lieutenants—an organizational nightmare). One of them is a guy named Mike, who's a bigger alcoholic than I am, and who gets into the most bizarre, philosophy-motivated fistfights when he's had too much to drink. The other one is named Bob, a tall, skinny guy whose right eye gets squinty when he's deep in his cups. Mike's from Maryland and I don't know why he joined, but he wants to be infantry, he doesn't care where. Bob's from Connecticut like me and wants to get to Special Forces (unlike me). It's been a dream of his for some time. As for me, my goal is—Italy! Yes, we might be in the same general area while you're spending time in London. That's additional motivation for me to pass Ranger School and Airborne School, without which I can't get to Italy, but will be stationed instead in… wait for it… *Germany*. And I know I'll never be able to convince you to visit me out on the border of the Czech Republic, in the sticks.

I'll write more as more interesting things happen. I'm falling into a routine of building up to the next challenge, whatever that might be, and the cycle is losing its novelty. When that happens—as it has—it becomes vastly more difficult to step back and see the joy or the fascination of a given trial: a week in the field becomes another exercise in willful self-denial, a torture to endure. How to describe that in a way that's meaningful? It's brought the trainees together, made us stronger; at the same time, it's made us casual with our pain, contemptuous of it. And I'm definitely turning into a full-blown alcoholic.

Well, tell me more of your life when you have a chance; if you're still around and haven't left for the family seat in Milwaukee by then, I'll be down in D.C. with a couple lieutenant buddies on December 18th and I'd love to steal you for an afternoon. We can meet at the

Smithsonian and maybe track down some adventure. It's been a long time and by God some things have happened in our lives that bear talking about. I'll keep my fingers crossed until I get a response…

Yours,
Adrian

★

Journal Entry: 10 November 2005

It's strange to have left my social circle at Yale, where it was customary to assign real weight and value to words—words have power and can do violence, went the thinking, so best not to say things that would harm others. It's neatly opposite in the infantry, where guns and fighting ability have power and can do violence, and there's almost an insouciant contempt for words, and thoughts, and just about anything that isn't an action. I wonder if people from Yale, seeing these interactions, this deep but also fundamentally conditional racism, would be appalled or understanding. The shift has been so subtle that I just started noticing it recently.

The phenomenon must be part of our conditioning, part of the lifestyle—it's necessary to see one's enemy as sub-human, so depending on the war, one gets a full read-out on how to think properly about him / her. This could produce a downside in Counter-Insurgency, that's obvious, but it's easier for the individual than dealing with the moral reality of killing other human beings. If you haven't gone through that, don't presume to judge the infantry's derogatory terms for Middle Easterners: beeb, haj, sand-nigger, camel-jockey, goat-fucker, donkey-rapist, etc., etc., etc.

On the other hand, at the same time that one encounters the worst kind of stereotypical bluster about absolute cultural and racial values, one also encounters a truly meritocratic organization wherein skin color doesn't seem to matter. The most important things are what uniform you're wearing, how hard you work, and doing your job properly. An example of this would be our Lebanese exchange officer: he works hard and is competent, and nobody calls him anything other than his name. He's part of the group.

14 November 2005

Dear Brent,

Thanks for that incredible letter. I guess we explored your issue pretty well via email—I can't believe you were, for a time, a notorious American criminal due to being mistaken for the commander during the "Body Burning" incident—the way you explained things it made perfect sense: the bodies were rotting on the one piece of defensible terrain (the reason they were there in the first place), the villagers wouldn't dispose of the bodies, and the squads burned them. Some exploitative journalist—one of the bad ones, there are certainly good ones out there—tried to make it into a sensationalist story and didn't do his research (of course). Now that you're in the clear and people know you weren't even there, it's easier to laugh about it. I was sorry to hear that you lost a friend—I don't have much context for understanding the importance of a squad leader in a platoon, but everything you said makes it seem like he had an outsized influence on the lives around him. And a Chechnyan sniper? I mean, Jesus. Hope you were able to track the guy down and bring him to justice.

It's embarrassing to talk about my own trials in this context, so I won't spend much time squawking about how I actually had trouble with land nav this time around, had to retest once, or how I'm basically just cruising through IOBC. I don't know if this joke was around when you were there, the "ten days of training packed into twelve weeks," but I like it. On the upside, I've had a lot of time to get to know the other lieutenants, and from that perspective it's been a really productive experience. That's sort of the edge the West Point and ROTC guys have on guys like us—there are more of them, and they have four years of networking behind them, whereas we've got six months at best, and usually less (unless we're really lucky). And the place that really pays dividends is Ranger School, or so I understand... people you can rely on for assistance and not to glare at you out of malice or expediency. I'm freaking out a little bit about Ranger School, but will refrain from dumping stress on you about that while you're in *motherfucking Afghanistan*. I'll pick your brain this winter break when you're in CT.

So—the ruck marching is very tiresome, I think the worst part of it is not being able to listen to music. So, so boring—it's not the pain, the difference between rucking eight or ten or twelve miles is insignificant. I can't imagine that the difference between twelve and twenty miles would be that great either—one's mind cannot distinguish between the physical pain of one and the other, or the boredom either. The guts required to go on another step or another mile are the same after—I don't know, six miles? So—if it's a matter of mental conditioning, or "training like you fight," I get it, no iPods. If it's physical conditioning, then we should be able to use our iPods, or dip, or have energy drinks. The worst part is just how fucking *boring* it is, what a time suck, with nothing but the aches of your shoulders and knees, and the pain of existence to anchor you. I would imagine that this is a difference between training and warfare—when you're rucking, it's either to go to a place where you might be fighting, or away from a place you just had a big fight in… I'm curious about this, let me know. The big takeaway here is that I hate rucking.

See you soon,
Adrian

4 December 2005

Hey Jacob,

Sorry I missed you for Thanksgiving, I was only in town for a couple days. Hell of a thing, it's just that one doesn't get much break. I wasn't sure that I was going home until really the last minute, ticket prices were outrageous (nearly $400, should've been around $200), and consequently I was forced to make some choices about my flight, hard choices. Like coming back Saturday instead of Sunday. Super lame.

Anyway, the short update is that things are progressing as they have thus far—unexceptionally. Getting from one school to the next. Lieutenant training is nearly over, and I'm going to make the best of an opportunity to attend Airborne School. This will give me some breathing space before Ranger School, and a chance to get in slightly better shape before the big test. As you know Brent said that Ranger School was the worst. That's saying something. Other than that nothing to report, no ladies in my life, just reading a lot, sleeping, and going out drinking with a couple of good guys I met here, Bob and Mike. We make an unlikely trio; Mike's one of those Maryland officers I told you about—selfish in a personal way that approaches narcissism, but not pretentious (a lot like you, actually), and Bob's a Connecticutian from the other side of the tracks.

Let me know how things are going at school, what teaching's like. Your assumption that I know anything about it based on my experience in Japan is deeply flawed: I was more of a conversationalist than a language instructor. What you're doing now, managing personalities, getting people enthusiastic about reading and writing, imparting some of your passion for the process of studying; that takes organization and discipline that was never demanded of me in Japan. If I were in your shoes, I'd be worried about caring too much about my students, getting heavily invested in their success or failure; things that I do not ultimately control.

See you soon buddy,
Adrian

Journal Entry: 11 December 2005

In the field on our last major field problem before Christmas Break. Marched twelve miles out into the training areas—down Cardiac Hill, around the airfield, into the woods. As we crossed a bridge and approached the woodline, a C-130 rumbled down the airstrip behind us and took off, flying low directly over the formation—I felt a rush of adrenaline as the wind and roar of the plane washed over me. It was a good moment for a little boost, right on the edge of the woods, five miles into the ordeal.

It seemed like the march would never end. The pace was excruciating. Because I was in charge, I was supposed to run up and down the formation checking on people, which I did, and it just killed me. Watching the two officers in front of the formation, their rucksacks bobbing up and down in the gray winter afternoon, every step an agony, unable to complain about it with anyone because I was in charge—a strange mixture of frustration and pain. The winter woods on the side of the road passing by slowly, inexorably.

When we arrived, we set up our living areas and changed. The platoon TAC NCO, a ranger-qualified SFC, took a few officers out to find wood for a fire. He came back with a great piece of "lightning wood," a shard of pine that had been riven from a trunk by lightning and soaked in sap. We put it at the base of the woodpile, one of the lieutenants ignited it with his lighter, and the lightning wood blazed white-hot. The pile was a pyre in no time.

The ground is frozen from the cold, and the temperature hovers between twenty and thirty degrees at night—no need to worry about the dreaded water moccasins, or the hated brown recluse spider. At last, a solid night's sleep with no care.

7 January 2006

Elsa,

Just writing quickly to thank you for inviting me to the party over Christmas—it was good to see you and Brent, and just about everyone in the same place again after so long. Smoking on the back porch, drinking, just puttering around—it felt like old times, and I appreciated it. I wish I'd had more of a chance to catch up in person.

Nothing much else to report. The process hasn't been easy but it's agreed with me so far (or at least not destroyed me). I feel stronger than ever, my thinking is sharper, and taking challenges one day at a time has really transformed my life. Meanwhile, my luck's held good with training—there is a feeling of "destiny" about this decision (so naturally you're quite correct to tell me to be cautious) but if one is following one's heart, and giving everything to a purpose or idea, what can go wrong? The process of giving is what makes the experience important, not the result.

Oh—it was easier to write this than to say it, so I didn't bring it up when we had the chance to talk in person—it's incredible, the extent to which David Foster Wallace's *Brief Interviews with Hideous Men* accurately describes the social milieu in the infantry. I never talked with Brent about this, but I feel it rubbing off on me as well—a strong predisposition toward overt chauvinism bordering on (and sometimes turning into) outright misogyny. Like any other off-color joke, I've found chauvinist jokes funny—nationalist, religious, racist, politically insensitive, you name it, I've laughed at it. So long as the joke is about the *process* of the thing, that is. Take a racist joke, for example—so long as it's about the absurd logic of racism (a black person is shiftless or lazy), the joke is certain to provoke laughter (in me) because it's the idiocy of the logical mechanism, and the clever way in which one is brought to appreciate the ridiculous. Some of the jokes about women and sex are appalling, indefensible—and it seems like one of the few places (the infantry is all male) that young psychopaths feel comfortable dehumanizing, really *hating* women. Because the infantry functions as a group, an unscrupulous few have an outsized impact on the rest of the group. I'm not saying everyone in the infantry is a psychopath, just that they tend to be the loudest; and everyone else tends to just go along with the flow, rather than contradicting them and causing group strife.

I'm not claiming that it's the only thing we do when we're sitting around cleaning weapons or at the campfire in the field, or that it's a complete commonplace—just that I notice it, and it is present, undeniably. Family men, Christian men, Black and White and Asian and Middle Eastern men, everyone can bond over the one thing that keeps us together and sets us apart—our sexual identity. Imagine that.

Take care,
Adrian

28 January 2006

Mike,

As promised, I'm opening up a second line of communication between us that I hope will prove fruitful and serve as a sort of record of our thoughts and experiences. I'll open the dialogue by saying that while I found the Tucker Max site as funny as you said it would be, it was also kind of disturbing. I've been thinking a lot more about certain strains of thought in the infantry since hanging out with an ex-girlfriend over the holidays who is fairly passionate about these and related matters (the stories you probably heard about my actions and activities in New York over New Year's with that Japanese exchange student notwithstanding). The strains one finds in Max's work are not substantially different from the bullshit I've heard and delivered sitting around every campfire or on guard shift from when I was in basic training to our final evaluation exercise in November-December during IOBC—it just seems pointlessly reductive. Worth a cheap laugh at first, but—that whole business with him and the former Ms. Vermont—there's a legitimately pathological dislike of her, there, a woman who just seems to want to be left alone and write stories for children. It's tough to read, and unless that was his intent, to have us feel guilty for him, in his stead, I can't imagine what the purpose of it all is. So, I don't know. I understand that by expressing this idea I'm identifying myself as an enemy to the cause of masculinity, and I'm not sure why that should be the case—wouldn't a true chauvinist believe that the cause of male superiority would be best advanced by allowing us to defeat women on equal terms, rather than keeping them in bondage? And if not—aren't we actually crypto-feminists, acknowledging that they are the superior sex?

I did finally get around to reading *Starship Troopers*, right after I finished the Robert Owens you recommended to me, and you were right, the book is vastly different from the movie. I didn't care for the book, and it's odd that it would be on the reading list for a young lieutenant. The movie has always been one of my favorites, but as with all good things is not sufficiently well developed. How do the veterans take power? The book omits the genesis of its proposed world order as well, though it offers a clue: contact with alien civilizations. Like *Ender's Game* it imagines us as the aggressors and the ultimate victors in a galactic struggle—the movie and book—and why else write literature like that?

Airborne School isn't much of a challenge. Nobody said that it would be but it's... pretty mundane. I don't mind, I appreciate the extra time to get my mind ready for Ranger School—don't know if Bob told you but there's this National Guard pre-Ranger gag one of the other lieutenants figured out and he then put my name and his name down—I love the idea that we'll be able to circumvent the massive wait-list in the LTO by doing a prep course everyone should probably do anyway—but it will be two weeks of hell. I guess the good news is that the physical and tactical component should prepare me really well for the rest of the program.

But—yeah, I don't know what your beef is with Airborne School; I think it'll be pretty fun to jump out of planes. The paratrooper tradition is one of the few pieces of the current military tradition that I was aware of when I joined, thanks to *Band of Brothers*, which I remember you dismissing as so much pro-war propaganda. Obviously I have to go through it anyway if I want to get into the 173rd—Ranger School as well—but there's something more to it than just an obligation. There's an aesthetic that I like, maybe the only one in the regular army, the place where a thinking man can be a warrior too. Paratroopers—I'm not there, but I know a couple guys at the 173rd now and they tell me the same—are allowed a certain important degree of autonomy and individuality because everything we know about airborne warfare tells us that this autonomy is critical—that once there's a drop, often at night, you're pretty much on your own, to gather what buddies you can and create as much havoc as possible. You have to be confident in your abilities as a soldier unto yourself, first—faith in the unit or even the mission is not a precondition for success. That rings true to me about war in general, though I wouldn't take things that far. It's really more a matter of taste. And doesn't the flexible doctrine of the paratrooper fit perfectly with a thing like insurgency?

The training, though, that's a totally different animal. The "Sergeants Airborne" line us up in massive formations, and put us through repetition after mindless repetition of the same easy drills, playing childish and silly pranks on us to see who isn't paying attention. When you're in the back of a 300-man formation and someone says "rehover" instead of "recover," you're going to assume they said "recover" and take the appropriate action. If you're me and the guys standing next to me in the back row, you're then going to think that getting smoked because you couldn't hear the command is a bunch of stupid horseshit. Fuck-fuck games at their most pointless. Then the slow nine-minute mile runs are just hell on the joints and don't substantially contribute to fitness or anything else save for the legion of overweight female supply clerks heading to the 82nd—quite naturally the ones who sound off the loudest and subsequently require us to "motivate" them when they fall out because of the blistering pace we're setting—it's embarrassing. Nevertheless the class has been cut from a starting size of 450 down to 370, which is pretty incredible. I guess the jumps are supposed to knock out a few more.

That's the scariest thing to me—getting injured through some stupid freak accident caused by wind gust or a bad landing or who knows what—so close to Ranger School. I've been on Fort Benning for over nine months, with (if I'm lucky) another three or so to go, and I don't want to get hung up because I break my ankle or my leg on a jump. It's possible that people talk about the danger of injury as a way of keeping people alert, but it's also possible that bad luck plays a bigger role than normal in a thing like jumping out of an airplane.

All right buddy, looking forward to policing up Bob and heading out to Auburn for the weekend! Stay well.

Adrian

Journal Entry: 4 February 2006

The fog was thick this morning—so thick that the 200-foot jump towers, massive iron and steel contraptions recognizable from miles around, were completely obscured beyond one hundred feet. Driving to training, blurry lights emerged slowly out of the gray, marking a gas station here, the Little Caesar's there—then slipped back into the haze. The lieutenants' barracks and the airborne buildings, hulking, multi-story brick structures, were reduced to shadowy probabilities. An awful stench lingered everywhere, from a sewage treatment plant miles away. The fog suffocated light and sound; the only thing I could hear was the muted chugging of my car's engine, which somehow magnified the scent of things. The sewage treatment plant smelled like a pile of leaves and flowers rotting.

By the afternoon, the sun had emerged to burn the worst of the fog away and some of the smell went with it, replacing both with an oppressive, sticky heat. It was after lunch, and we all had a growing, uncomfortable awareness that rubber rain-gear and ponchos were double-edged swords—they could kept the water and moisture out but trapped the sweat on our stifled, drowning skin. So it is with the Georgia sun—even in winter it has its way with you, delivering precisely the worst type of energy where it's least wanted.

A few of the lieutenants from infantry training turned their backs on Airborne and Ranger training. Ranger School, extra training—at this point it isn't necessary. I could be at my unit in a matter of weeks, after Airborne School. I'm making a choice—nobody's telling me what to do at this point, where to go, what the right direction is—nothing's clear.

We'll see how I feel when I'm done. I'm tired of being treated like an asshole.

11 February 2006

Dear Mom and Dad,

I'm "Airborne qualified" now—I got my "jump wings!" This is the first badge or sign of anything special that I have for my uniform, and I'm quite proud of it. I made my fifth jump on a Thursday, and the ceremony was on Friday. The weather cooperated, sunny and in the sixties—just a few clouds drifted over "Building 4," the site of so many tests over the last seven months. A column of OCS students marched slowly away, back to their barracks—I couldn't tell if they were wearing black or blue scarves. The bleachers were filled with friends and well-wishers (for the students). Behind the bleachers was a C-47 transport, the kind they used in World War II for Normandy. The origins of the Airborne.

When I was in OCS I would march in formation (literally to the beat of a drum) by this parade field every day, barely thinking about it—about halfway through my time there, it must have been July, we marched to Building 4 and saw a graduation rehearsal for some earlier Airborne School class. One of the other candidates, a prior-enlisted sergeant explained the situation to me. I remember looking over, quickly so as not to break stride or fall out of position, and *wondering* whether I'd be standing there someday, but it was so far off, so unlikely... I learned this in training, not to imagine the future; the future is the worst sort of siren. To avoid obsessing about things over which I had no control I learned to *dream* my dreams, to indulge little secret fantasies, but to keep them away from conscious thought. And I keep showing up for graduations, only to discover that graduation was the very moment I'd been thinking of all along.

Brent may have found a way to pull me into Italy, to the 173rd Airborne. He said the first thing that had to happen was for me to get assigned to Europe. My first assignment was to a "replacement battalion" in Alaska—in other words, I had no idea where I was headed, whichever unit needed a lieutenant. There was a guy in IOBC who had a slot to a training battalion in Germany—Hohenfels, out on the border of the Czech Republic—who wanted to go to Alaska at any cost. We were the perfect match, so we "swapped" assignments (just as I "swapped" branches earlier—this is a useful but also deeply disturbing aspect of the military, the inter-changeability of its human capital), and as of right now I'm headed to Germany. Going to a training battalion would be a step in the wrong direction for me; it's not what I want to accomplish during my time in the military, so it's additional incentive to get through Ranger School. I have full confidence that with a strong effort on my part it will be possible for me to get into the best regular unit in the army—hell, the military—the 173rd Airborne Brigade.

You may notice that there is a certain amount of necessary cognitive dissonance at play here—on the one hand understanding that I am completely replaceable, on the other hand fully embracing the myth that my special destiny singles me out for greatness or success in all of my endeavors. I don't yet have a way to explain this, except that it seems possible to hold more than one idea in one's head at once, so long as one doesn't spend too much time paying attention to either! Maybe this is why the future has to remain vague and out of focus...

I start pre-Ranger training in a few days, and if I pass, Ranger School almost immediately afterwards (we get a day off), so I'll be certain to write when I have a chance. I'm really nervous about it—from what everyone tells me it's the first significant challenge where a dedicated, disciplined, and talented soldier or officer can fail for reasons beyond his control. Luck is a factor in getting through, staying healthy, staying injury free. Hope I'm lucky.

Love,
Adrian

3 March 2006

Hey Brent,

If pre-Ranger is any indication, I'm about to begin the most difficult months of my life up to this point. How I passed the two-week pre-selection process is beyond me; at no point did I feel that I'd understood or mastered the material, at no point did I feel confident or capable (unlike basic training, three-quarters through OCS, and all of IOBC). I felt physically and mentally exhausted, and overwhelmed by the sheer volume of instruction that was being delivered to us. The land navigation course was a brutal and uncompromising gut-check. Their "mini-Malvesti" obstacle course was the first time I've ever reached the limits of my muscular endurance. I made it through, I passed, and tomorrow morning I've got a free, guaranteed one-way ticket to Ranger School. This is a classic army-training maneuver: I am forced to look forward to the hellish pain I must endure, to work for it, to beg for an opportunity to be cut with the serrated blade, to thank the axe-man for cutting off my foot. That's how they get you with that volunteer stuff; "hey, you asked to be here, why are you complaining?" When the draft was still active, Ranger School must've been a truly wretched place.

One of the more interesting things to me has been how watching how my fellow IOBC students interact with the idea of Ranger School, how they deal with the prospect of this unprecedented challenge: a sequence of events and leadership lessons everyone tells them will push their abilities in ways they've never encountered before. Some people are derisive, call it "just another army school," or "gay" or "stupid," and go out of their way to prepare with a spirit of nonchalance and indifference. Then there's the other side of the spectrum, the people with Ranger Tabs sewn into their hats that their dad gave them from Vietnam, or their older brother gave them, or an uncle. They know exactly what's going to happen in Ranger School, how hard it is, what the secret is for all the challenges, how to trick yourself awake, what to say when the Ranger Instructors are yelling at you. Every step in the process, for them, is interesting and vital—asking people for advice about Ranger School, telling others what they know about the challenge, giving you tips on how best to pack your bags for the first day (you want to know where everything in the bag is because they'll have you shake it out and go through, item by item, so practice), what kind of lock to use, where to stand in line for push-ups, where to start in the run. Most others fall somewhere between these two poles, myself included. I find it difficult to allow myself the certain luxury of the latter group—the sense of destiny, the notion that if I just ask one more question of someone with a Ranger Tab then I'll know the secret, the magic answer, the comfort that goes with the asking—and having been through pre-Ranger do not feel indifference at all, rather dread.

Thankfully, there's a platoon in the 173rd urging me onward at the end of the tunnel (the one bit of fantasy I allow myself). On the bulletin board at the LTO this morning, I saw a lieutenant from West Point who'd done well as an undergraduate—I'm sorry, a "cadet"—and had selected Italy with his "duty station of choice"; he'd failed Ranger School for the second time and was posting his wish list for trades (Germany wasn't on it; Korea and California were, for whatever reason). There were already three infantry officers trying to get his attention—a strange dance, the vultures circling the soon-to-be-dead asking the dying for permission to peck out his kidney—and I'm sure there will be other opportunities available when I get through. Failing Ranger School means no Italy, and that's close enough to "death before dishonor" to do the trick.

Your humble & etc.,
Adrian

★

31 March 2006

Dear Mom and Dad,

I apologize for not writing earlier. I made it through the first phase as I told you. I'm writing this while waiting for a reconnaissance patrol to return, the guy in charge is a moron and I can already tell he's lost. We're in the mountains. We did rappelling and knot tying and some other basic mountaineering events. I'm always tired and hungry. All anyone talks about is food.

So here's a list of things I need to eat—I'll have eight hours to eat what I like before going to Florida for the Swamp phase—I've put a lot of thought into this. Put some extra in the package in case someone else needs stuff.

Snickers bar (King Size). No, two. Pepperidge Farm "Geneva" cookies. Triscuits, cheese whip, Cheese Nips, Hanover Honey Mustard Pretzels. Jelly Belly jelly beans. Nilla Wafers. "Petit Ecolier" Little Schoolboy *milk* chocolate cookies. Shortbread. Cornbread. Fudge. Mustard (*Dijon*).

God, I would kill for a grill right now with four pieces of good German cheese sausage smoking up over a hot bed of coals… buns lightly toasted, stone-ground mustard, Heinz ketchup, relish, chopped pearl onion, grated Tillamook cheese on top… I'm actually crying a little bit here, can you imagine, we marched eleven miles uphill today and haven't eaten more than two meals in a day consistently in a month and a half, the idea of grill and a couple of cold Sierras—good God—send the food, send the food, send the food.

God willing I'll be at graduation. Don't buy the tickets, I'll call you if I make it through this phase. Mom, I heard from Christina that Smokey's not doing well. I do not want to know if our dog dies while I'm here in Ranger School, do not give me that information.

> Send food,
> Adrian

★

Journal Entry: 8 April 2006

Finished Mountain phase. For the first time in months I feel capable of communing with myself again. Knots and rappelling and mountaineering and ambushes all day, all night, until everyone fell asleep on their faces. Was stretched so thin that I began attending Sunday services for the first time in over a decade—cried during singing of Amazing Grace. This trial has so tired me that I can barely think straight. It's two months since Bob and I started Pre-Ranger... here / now is doing and feeling, no thinking necessary. The mountains of Georgia recede into the distance. On to Florida.

When I called Mom about my success earlier today, she told me that our dog had died. Unbelievable.

★

5 May 2006

Brent,

I passed, I got the tab. Quick thoughts on the subject:

1) The Ranger Tab is, alongside the Ranger Scroll, one of several pure expressions of a man's ability to withstand suffering and trial. It is also similar to predestination, in that a Ranger is not made, he is born, and then at some point in his life goes through the trial and puts the Tab on his shoulder. I was always a Ranger, it was always my destiny to go through this experience, but it doesn't change anything about me, I am essentially the same person that I was before.

2) Many good people, good leaders, did not make it through. Misfortune plays a role in the process. People with very bad luck cannot be

Rangers, or are not Rangers—they are something else.

3) Ranger is a word that describes a combination of good fortune and perseverance. At least—the absence of catastrophically bad luck.

4) If one had an opportunity to test oneself in this school and did not, that says something about you as a man, as a combat leader. If you tried and failed, it says something else—especially if you're trying to get back.

5) This was a more difficult trial on the obvious physical level but less obvious emotional level than Yale. Yale was harder intellectually.

6) There is no effective way to prepare for Ranger School.

I never want to be cold again if it can be avoided. I never want to be hungry again if it can be avoided. The people in my squad through Mountains and Swamp (I shifted units after the first phase—got peered during the Darby phase despite passing both of my patrols—long story) were like family to me during Ranger School but their faces are already fading from my memory.

Well—see what you can do about Italy. It'd be awesome to join you at the best "regular" unit in the military. Catching up over the winter break was great, as was meeting your buddy from the 173rd, but it'd be better to get an assignment there, against all odds, and keep the "story of destiny" alive, wouldn't it?

And welcome back from Afghanistan!

RLTW,
Adrian

★

15 May 2006

Brent,

Quick change of plans—I know you've been having trouble locking a slot down for me in Italy, which is sort of a shoot-the-moon kind of longshot. An opportunity to get additional training fell in my lap that will give you more time to maneuver as well as making me a more attractive candidate for the storied 173rd "Herd." The commander of the Lieutenant Transition Office, a beleaguered captain who is constantly fielding solicitations for school slots and special dispensations (and whom I thought up until an hour ago did not know my name from the seven hundred others) called me and my friend Bob (told you about him over winter break) and told us to pack our Ranger bags and head back to Camp Darby for RSLC, the reconnaissance school. I know nothing about it except that it's supposed to be harder than Ranger School and my body's still healing from that ordeal (as you can imagine), but I had to take advantage, so I'm headed over there now. That gives us until June 16th—assuming I pass—as a Ranger of course there is no option but to pass—see what you can do.

I've stopped going to church—not that this is a thing that bears on Italy much, but thought you'd be interested to know—I'd been going mostly, I think, as a way to avoid being controlled by my drill sergeants / TAC Officers / Ranger Instructors. It was the one place where I could be with myself, have a bit of private space, but now that I'm a person again, that my time is my own, I just don't see the point anymore. This feels like the type of revelation that would be especially shocking to some of our classmates—being in a place where God and church were an *escape* from dogmatic lectures and thought-control. Well, back to my bad-Christian habits, where I bemoan my guilt and make up for it on Christmas and Easter.

> To the Front,
> Adrian

Journal Entry: 22 May 2006

Thank God for RSLC, this might just be the thing that pushes me over the edge for the 173rd. It's pretty clear that without the school, I wouldn't be getting to Italy—going to Germany instead, which would be an unmitigated disaster. At the same time, God*DAMN* RSLC. I'm back at Camp Darby. Saw Mike the other day, getting ready to "walk," having earned his tab. And here Bob and I are, undergoing more exhausting training than I ever did during the buildup to Ranger School. Five-mile runs with rucksacks. Grueling marches. Land navigation fit to break a bear. My body is still recuperating from Ranger School, and it's enough to nearly undo me.

Thank God for Bob. Never thought I'd say it, but having a friend, an ally that I can experience this with—it makes all the difference. Good people here, it's not that, it's just that my temperament seems to be less individualistic and more team-oriented. Think I'd crack up if I had to go through OCS again—that school was the gold standard for douchey psychological torture.

30 May 2006

Dear Grandpa,

It's been a while! There's been so much news, which I'm sure Mom and Dad are telling you, that it almost seems like no news at all. The more training I go through the more I feel that for someone like you, all you need to hear or know is that I've done it—Airborne School, Ranger School. So, you know who I am, you've seen that kind of young man before in your own time, in England, in France, in Germany— you know what I'm trying to do, who I'm trying to be. What's the point of rehashing details? Describing hunger, hatred of army food, discomfort, lack of private space or personal time? You know all of this. Even a private with one combat deployment knows more about what's going on than I do; I've never seen it before.

One of the few things that I thought you might be interested to hear was my experience in Airborne School. Most people advised me to push Airborne School off until after I graduated Ranger School, arguing that being "Airborne" in Ranger School would put me at greater risk for an injury. The people who advocated for it said that jumping *into* a phase in Ranger School was a unique experience, and well worth the risk—the risk on top of getting injured, and of course, the risk of death from jumping out of a perfectly good airplane. I weighed each side's encouragement: the pros, the cons, and as is more and more commonly the case, made the final decision on an impulse. It was the last day at IOBC, my platoon of lieutenants was saying "see you later" to each other and making social plans when the TAC NCO entered the room and asked if anyone wanted to go to Airborne School. Four of us looked at each other, shrugged our shoulders, walked down to Airborne School (about a five-minute walk from the lieutenant school) and that was that, three weeks on "jump pay" and my first badge. As it turned out the decision to go "Airborne" did not affect my Ranger

School experience much; all of the jumps in my class were canceled, the only time I even boarded a plane was in Florida, and we slept (uncomfortably) while the plane buzzed lazy circles around the drop zone for two hours during a serious rain and wind-storm, finally landing and hopping on trucks when the safety officer canceled the jump. So my decision to accept the risk of jumping in Ranger School was negated by the practical fact of there being no jumps. At least I had the courage to try.

Airborne School isn't like back in your day, when sergeants would hit soldiers to punish insubordination, and trainees had to run six miles at a seven-minute pace and then come back and hurl sledgehammers at each other and the person who was struck in the head by the sledgehammer instead of catching it had to do another six miles with no water. Or so I hear. In any case, I really enjoyed it in the end. I like to jump! Which is a good thing, going to an airborne unit. My first jump was good, a soft landing. The second one was hard, I hurt my ass and was worried that I wouldn't be able to hack Ranger School as a result (gutted it out). The third jump was the one that sold me, though. It was a night jump, "Hollywood" (which means no combat rucksack between your legs, no rifle strapped to your leg, just a parachute, very light and easy). There was a very slight breeze, and when I jumped out of the plane, and the parachute snapped open, I was surrounded by a cool, all-encompassing darkness. It was so quiet and peaceful, only the drone of the airplanes buzzing off into the distance gave me any indication of my relative proximity to other people; I was alone. I drifted down, counting carefully, trying to gauge the distance left to the ground, then stuck a perfect landing, surrounded by the rustle of the collapsing chute and the crump of other paratroopers landing in the distance. On the drop zone, there were several HMMWVs with soft red chemlights attached to their radio antennae, waving slowly in the light breeze—the chemlights resembled eyes in the darkness. I felt energized by the sense of solitude, the sense of possibility. I could almost imagine that this wasn't a training exercise, there were enemy somewhere out there, and I needed to link up with my fellow soldiers for the mission. I knew that this was the right place for me, this is what I wanted to do.

One thing I don't like about the military, about the attitude they encourage in everyone, is the drumbeat of submission. It begins with people instructing you that you, the individual, are not actually allowed to resent anything. I'm sure it must've been the same in World War II, and seems to have been in Vietnam (at least from the movies and books I've digested), where the officers always have their heads up their asses, and the enlisted man (usually a sergeant) has to figure everything out for them and save the day, and nobody really wants to be there but by God it's a bad job and somebody has to do it… usually with submachine guns and hand grenades… and the Nazis or the Vietcong are using kids for soldiers, now, the *brutes*.… That army, *your* army, draws its soldiers overwhelmingly from rural and poor, urban populations in World War II, and is overwhelmingly first- through third-generation European immigrants; not much color in there. In Vietnam, the army has been desegregated and places a disproportionately high number of black service members into the infantry. You can drink in these armies. You aren't supposed to do drugs but they're available (in Vietnam). And most importantly, there is an explicit choice to be made about the nature of your citizenship, the nature of your service. You see, the truth that drives those narratives forward is the truth of the *draft*. The choice that you faced in WWII, and an average citizen faced in Vietnam (assuming they weren't the 3-5% of the population that feels so patriotically about the cause of their nation that they immediately join) is this: "What will I do when I get drafted?" This is the choice you see play out in *The Things They Carried*, when the protagonist decides not to flee to Canada (though he makes it very clear that such a decision would be morally acceptable or even superior to the one he makes), to fulfill his draft obligation. This is a serious and important part of the character's struggle, and was presumably an important part for many Americans in WWII and in Vietnam.

Vietnam, the stand-in for an immoral and unpopular war, prompted a serious change in our society. As the war wound down, Nixon's administration ended the draft (or selective service) and the army started doing the research and setting up the institutional mechanisms necessary to recruit, train, and retain a "professional army." To bring things back to the present time, here we are with our professional army, our all-volunteer force—you hear these buzz words with a fair bit of regularity in the military, the idea of military service as just another place to learn a vocation, of being worthwhile and important on its own, stripped of the value of patriotism—the post-WWII, post-Vietnam idea that we unconsciously grew up with while watching John Wayne attack Normandy or fight behind enemy lines in Vietnam—it's not that those tales of valor are irrelevant, they're just *off*. The nature of heroism is different in an army where everyone there has decided to be there, has made a choice to serve under a variety of circumstances; who has essentially volunteered for the mission. I mean, I've made some important choices, some choices in training that were difficult at the time, even something as simple as getting out of my sleeping bag and really trying to stay awake on guard shift—I've just noticed that ideas like sacrifice and courage, people still talk about them and use examples from previous wars as though our situation is the same or even similar to those other wars. I suspect that it is not, and draft versus professional is one of the ways in which the narrative is shifting, or maybe has shifted.

This was the thing that the army figured out—they realized that in a draft army, a citizen could really say: "I did not want to be here but here I am, so I reject the premise that you have an essential authority to tell me what to do; your authority is that of the prison guard." This logic is very difficult to refute on a basic human level. You try looking another human being in the eyes and telling them, "Well you didn't want to be here, you tried not to be, you have good reasons for all of that, but you still have to do what I'm telling you to do." Now you're in some really intense shit, morally, as a leader. Everything that happens now falls on your shoulders. Well, in the professional army, you don't have to worry about most of that. Everyone here signed up, and by the time I joined, everyone understood they were going to either Iraq or Afghanistan. Even those patriots who joined up in the wake of 9/11 to fight the Taliban and by the time they finished their training got sent to Iraq instead—they joined.

I have yet to see how this plays out on the battlefield. In training, every complaint, every misfortune, every bad thing that happens in any circumstance disappears when examined by the drill sergeant or the TAC NCO or the Ranger Instructor or the Sergeant Airborne. "Don't thank me, thank your recruiter." "You volunteered for this." "He was a two-time volunteer." "Some of you… the what we like to call 'three-time volunteers', you guys are the front lines…" It's like a cult, where the more you volunteer, the more training you willingly undergo, the more responsibility you accept, the higher the stakes get. But it's not on the army. It's not on the government. They learned that lesson in Vietnam. No—it's on *you*.

Another aspect of this is the way in which the very idea of "volunteering" has shifted—the representations I've seen of World War II always have the officer or sergeant asking for a few volunteers for a tough mission. In Vietnam you tried to avoid volunteering for anything; it was probably going to get you killed. We've kept the Vietnam idea—I suppose our fathers handed it down to us—so that volunteering for a task is a bad thing, even within the military, common sense says don't volunteer—but then there's the fact that volunteering is what got you here, and is wrapped up in our idea of what it means to be a motivated or good soldier.

I noticed this first during basic training and then forced myself to forget about it until Ranger School was over. I guess one of the things that helped me get through the training was the ability to push the future out of my mind and not think about the consequences of decisions or actions. I had enough energy to stay awake, to put one foot in front of the other, and that was about all. Once Ranger School, that torture, once it was complete, I started thinking again. Processing what I'd heard, what I'd seen, what I'd written in my journal. This is a big part of it, a huge part of the wars, Iraq and Afghanistan—it's *us*. I don't know if I ever told you about my experience with responsibility in Japan, but outside America—it's not like it was for you and Grandma in the '60s and '70s, when being an "American" opened doors for you—these days many foreigners think that Iraq and Afghanistan are our fault, that we elected George Bush and so everything his administration does reflects on our democratic will. They believe our hype, our propaganda—if America does a thing, that action must mean the America *wants* to do it, that the people desire the action (for good or ill). At least we're not bullies like the Germans or the Russians. So on an international level, on a national level, on an individual level, we Americans live at a time and in a place where everyone has decided to *join*, to *volunteer*, to *vote*, to *participate*—or *not*—and the consequences of this participation are unclear but somehow mean we're fighting *two* wars at the *same time*, one in the Middle East and one spanning South and Central Asia.

I'm really looking forward to catching up. I'm eager to swap stories—my lame training stories for your interesting and compelling World War II tales. That doesn't sound fair, but it's all I have…

Love,
Respectfully,
Adrian

Dear Mom and Dad,

I'm writing from another Ranger School, called RSLC, that no-body's heard of. There's no Tab or Badge or Widget you get from it, and the classes are very small and difficult, so it doesn't attract the same number of applicants or adherents as a place like Pathfinder School (which has a Badge you can wear after you pass the course). Don't let any of that fool you, it's the most difficult School I've been to so far. Harder than Ranger School. I'm here for another couple weeks—no recycling option—you pass or fail, that's that.

It's also the best course I've been to. I've learned more in the last three weeks since getting here than I have learned in my entire time in the army. This—Reconnaissance and Surveillance—missions deep behind enemy lines, evasion and subterfuge—this was what I was meant for, likely in an earlier war. The packs are heavier than in Ranger School. You get less food. You hump longer distances. We're training to fast-rope out of helicopters, tie ourselves onto lines, and get pulled out by a single helicopter operating behind enemy lines. The team size is six instead of fifteen or forty. There's no room for error, everyone on the team is critical.

Things I've learned… the land navigation course was something like twenty miles long, and took hours to complete, running beside roads and through the brush, staying concealed. I know how to use a few really complicated electronics devices that hook into a computer and can send pictures using satellites (!). I know how to field-improvise antennae. My field craft has never been stronger (tying ropes, finding areas to camp in, bandaging myself, all that nonsense, even trapping and killing animals for food). When we go on missions we don't wear helmets. There are complicated but necessary link-up procedures designed for friendly guerrilla groups or CIA / Special Forces cells so that we can link up in bad guy territory. Claymore emplacement is very important. We've spent a week memorizing vehicle and weapon recognition, so that we can tell what model of which tank or armor personnel carrier or radar emplacement the enemy is using. Foreign army uniforms. It feels like I'm in a James Bond movie when I think about it.

But it's been really tough, the classes, the cumulative effect of irregular and insufficient sleep—I found myself broken down and in tears for the first time since I got here, totally exhausted after this one class.

Crying. I rallied. This is taking me to the extreme of my ability. I need everything I have to make it through to the end—there's a twelve-day field exercise coming up in a few days, so I'm going to disappear for a little while. When I emerge, I hope that Brent will have been able to wrangle me a slot to Italy. We'll see.

Either way, when this is done I'll be leaving Fort Benning for Europe—but I'll get a couple weeks holiday beforehand. I plan on coming up to Branford for a little while to visit you guys and just relax in general. If anyone in the area wants to see me let them know, you have permission to set appointments up on my behalf. After this it's going to be a while, probably at least until Christmastime.

Thanks so much again for your support during Ranger School, the packages were amazing. I'm really doing this, guys, I'm—it's happening. The dream was never "Airborne Recon Ranger," but it's within my grasp. Who'd've thought!

> Love,
> Adrian

20 June 2006

Brent,

Got your note this morning. Incredible news. I'm out-processing now, so it's in the works—I'll be in Italy in a month. I owe you a debt of gratitude that can never be repaid. Two debts, in fact: the first for being an example, for showing me what could be done, what was possible; and the second for actually pulling off the professional sports equivalent of a last-minute, on-the-run, under pressure, back-of-the-endzone touchdown strike from fifty yards out to come from five down and seal the win, getting me to Italy. Fucking Italy, man, this is amazing. If people knew the full measure of this story, if they understood everything that went into this, they'd characterize it as literally incredible, or some other easily-manufactured cliché.

Apart from the difficulty you must've encountered pulling strings to get my orders changed, there was one last hurdle I had to pass before writing this letter. As you probably recall, the place where they store all of the administrative files for training is a WWII-era office park called

"Splinter Village": this is where they cut your final "orders" after you've done all the other paperwork you need to complete before leaving the post and moving to your new assignment. And when you've been on Fort Benning as long as I have, in as many schools, you have to do a *lot* of paperwork. Having completed that over the course of about a week and obtained everything I needed, all the signatures and stamps that granted me access to the assignments office, I walked to a place that up until that point had been merely a builder's grade door at the top of a rickety staircase. This was where they'd print my final orders, and I would be free to leave my apartment and then Fort Benning.

I arrived at 1154, walking up the stairs in my fresh, clean ACU uniform. The sign on the door read, "Out of office between 1230 and 1330 for lunch." No problem, plenty of time, how hard can it be to print a two-page document, right? I opened the door and walked in.

The room was broken up into a series of three work areas, two of which were occupied by seriously overweight women, Tammy and Regina. The waiting area, which consisted of some old wooden chairs, was empty, so I sat in a place where I could watch the women work and be conspicuous. They ignored me for a few minutes, pecking away at their keyboards and occasionally pausing to deliberately, oh-so-deliberately click on their mouses several times before resuming the typing. I alternated between watching them and looking at a cat-clock on the wall, its shifty eyes watching as each second of my life slid by, irreplaceable. A stain in the ceiling of the office provided silent testimony to the effect entropy exerted on the larger passage of time, and I mused as I waited, lost in thought. When it became clear that there was no getting rid of me, Regina sighed and looked over at me.

"Do you have an appointment?"

Apologetically, I told her that I didn't, that I'd never gone through the process and that nobody had told me that I needed an appointment. I did not mention that my lack of an appointment did not seem to be important at the moment, as their office was not exactly a beehive of activity.

Looking over at her co-worker to corroborate that she'd heard me correctly, the woman said "He never done this before," conspiratorially, but still loudly enough that I could hear her. Regina giggled and shook her head incredulously. "Did you at least sign in?"

I hadn't and said so, eliciting more sighs and giggling from the employees whose job it was to help me. I looked around the waiting area and found a clipboard holding the sign-in roster on the top of a stack of metal filing cabinets. There were several copies of the sign-in roster, though this appeared to have been unnecessary—only the top three spaces had names written in them, with today's date on the side. The last person to come through—another lieutenant, apparently—had left two hours ago. I put my information in the fourth slot and replaced the clipboard where I'd found it (and where it would remain, untouched, for the duration of the stay).

I checked the cat-clock. 1204.

Tammy, who had yet to talk, addressed me without looking up from her keyboard. "Mmm, okay, you're going to have to come back. We're closed until 1330."

Regina nodded. "It's our lunch break," she said, and swiveled away from her computer, then *without standing up, walked her rolling chair five feet over to an immense wicker handbag, from whence she withdrew two foot-long subway subs and a full liter bottle of Coca-Cola.* "You'll have to come back later."

You know this situation; you've had to deal with civilian employees. What was I supposed to do, what could I say? One of these two women held the power of fate over me, the power to cut my orders, to send me to my next post—I couldn't risk doing or saying anything to alienate them, or assert against the weight of their mockery and derision that I too was a human being and deserved at least the acknowledgment of respect. Instead of appealing to the Enlightenment or Christianity, I swallowed my pride and became the very model of a polite and solicitous (but not ostentatiously so) gentleman. I apologized for cutting into their break. I thanked them for explaining what I needed to do, I promised I'd be back "around 1330, a little after" so they understood that I was their ally in this, I was not going to be making unreasonable demands on their precious time. Then I left to take my own lunch.

When I returned at 1430, Tammy was not at her work station. She'd left early, Regina explained, because she'd been feeling tired and "stressed-out." I glanced at the clipboard quickly to see whether the office had experienced a post-lunch rush, but my name was still the last one on there. "It's going to be busy next week," Regina added by way of explanation. I expressed sympathy, then asked how her lunch was. You know. Caring about people. We're all people.

After a bit of mindless banter we finally sat down to business. I gave her my orders, which still read "Hohenfels, Germany," and explained the situation. Her face, which had been soft and gentle, now took on a hard edge.

"I can't do that, I can't change these," she said. "You have to talk with [we'll call her] Mrs. Jones, in Virginia. I can't change these."

I explained the situation, that the orders *had* already been changed, in Europe, that it should be in the computer system. She didn't understand and insisted on calling Mrs. Jones. You remember how unhelpful Mrs. Jones was when you and I talked with her about changing my orders earlier this month. Well, Mrs. Jones gave the woman an earful about me, I could hear her unmistakable voice on the phone. How I wasn't supposed to go to Italy, I was supposed to go to Germany. You can't go where you please, you have to go where you're assigned. I had to hear that all over again. Her voice was victorious over the speaker phone, and Regina's eyes glittered as if to say, "I told you so." Then she said it: "I told you so!"

It was one of those impossible human situations where miscommunication separates two people, prevents them from speaking with one another as equals. You know, maybe I walked in there ready for a fight, ready to get frustrated and blocked by surly paper-pushers. I really don't think that was it; I am capable of treating people the way I like to be treated, and it wouldn't have been in my best interest. Maybe they were used to seeing people chisel and wheedle their way out of unpleasant assignments. Who knows. At any rate, I was failing to make this woman understand that the only thing I needed her to do was print something. That was it. I made one last appeal to her humanity. "I promise I won't ask anything else, but I *need* a new set of orders… the ones I received at IOBC have 'draft' written across the top."

Finally, she understood what I needed—the only thing I'd needed all along, not that I could have understood that (as this is not my job)—for her to type my social security number into her system thereby bringing up my amended orders, and then for her to click the "print" button. As she's doing this I have to endure a nice bit of eye rolling and I-told-you-so-ing about how my orders were for Germany and how a lot of people try to pull a "slicky-boy," and Mrs. Jones knows everything and you can't slip anything by her and the rest of the demeaning and condescending bullshit I'd been forced to wade through dick-deep since walking in the door. Like a fucking supplicant. But she *did* it, at last. She input my social security number, key by key. She slowly dragged the mouse pointer onto the print button on the screen, squinted, and double-clicked it. The printer whirred and two sets of orders came out, face-down. She picked them up and read one, then did a double-take.

"These orders are for Italy," she says.

*Mother*fucker.

I thanked her for her help and said something about how Mrs. Jones the all-knowing must just not have gotten the memo from Europe, systems out of sync or something, and left. Splinter fucking village.

See you soon, man! We're going to be in the same unit!

Love and respect,
Adrian

7

12 July 2006

Dear Jessica,

So much has happened in both of our lives. I'm sure I wasn't the only person who would've laid serious money on you marrying. It didn't seem like anything was wrong when I saw you in December, but I suppose that's how these things work: we construct stories for our friends, stories about how our lives are basically okay, and the rest of the world sees what it wants. One thing about the army that I'm coming to resent is that it takes me away from my true friends, like yourself; at moments when you need friendship and support, I'm nowhere to be found.

So—forget Ralph, he's a douchebag. You're one of the healthiest, most well-adjusted people I know, which is why I've made an effort to keep you in my life all these years—I think you have a really solid moral compass. Don't let a catastrophe like this dominate you, especially while you're getting established in London. Trust me—six months from now you're going to be in a fantastic relationship with the son of some English lord, and Ralph is going to be kicking himself. Just focus on you.

On that note, as we're about to be in the same geographical neighborhood—and if I know you, you're going to be just moping around in your apartment drinking tea and reading instead of getting out—I *have to* recommend that you visit me in two weeks in Italy (alternately, I can visit you in England, either way). My friend Brent—you remember him from Yale—pulled me in to the 173rd Airborne, a group of paratroopers positioned in Vicenza, to guard the strategically critical fresh cheeses of Asagio and Valpolicella wines from thieves and ne'er-do-wells. Now the two Yale-educated, Airborne Ranger-qualified infantry officers in the U.S. Army are in the same unit (same battalion, in fact). Long story short, you gotta get out here, Jessica.

Fingers crossed that we can meet up in Europe and catch up more properly, in person—I've lost some weight through Ranger and Reconnaissance Schools, but you'll still recognize me (if you visit later in the fall I'll have had a chance to put on some serious weight eating that good Italian food and then I'll look like a different person entirely)... write whenever you can!

> Affectionately,
> Adrian

★

Journal Entry: 18 July 2006

Drove through Benning's main gate for the last time, watching the forest slip past from side- to rear-view mirror. Thought about Mike on his road to Texas, or Bob driving in that death trap of his up to New York. Passing the downward slope toward the highway, I saw the road that marks one of the boundaries for land navigation—remembered those ordeals, tripping over vines and branches in the woods, lurching through the heat and fatigue looking for metal land nav points. Running and rucking and pushing until I was passing out. Knowing that not giving my utmost was tantamount to cheating the nation, as I was just a trainee, just another piece of know-nothing meat for which the instructors were responsible. Every challenge, every school, from Basic to RSLC—over a year of my life fading into the distance and replaced with a sudden and nearly overwhelming level of responsibility.

Slowed down at the front gate one last time. Noticed cars stopping to get checked on post as I accelerated away. Families, soldiers, sergeants, officers, struggling to get *on* post, to get *in* the gate, *back* to Fort Benning. I remembered the first day of basic training, where Drill Sergeant Y called us "know-nothing-meat" and told us not to try to escape through the forest or swamp, that they'd find us and bring us back. Fifteen months later, I finally did it, broke out of that fetid, stinking prison.

19 July 2006

Dear Jim,

Well, here we are—you're headed to Fort Carson to be an FSO, and I'm headed to Italy to be a rifle platoon leader. How far we've come from our humble beginnings as "Private Danly" and "Private Bonenberger," before we even had the specialist rank to brag about—just a couple of faceless uniforms, sweating into the green grass or onto the clean barracks floor, doing jumping jacks until our arms felt like they'd fall off, the dreaded "mountain climber," the torturous and insulting "front-back-go." At long last, we're officers, we're headed to units, and those units are training to go to Iraq. Maybe we'll see each other over there too; stranger things have happened in war. Simply meeting you—one of the very few people in my life I consider a friend—would have been sufficient to justify the army as an experience, before whatever war throws our way. The rest of it is gravy so far as I'm concerned.

I don't know if you remember Jessica Benelli, an English major like myself, I think maybe a year or two behind you—my age. Shorter girl, blond, did a lot of volunteering with the Political Union—was with Ralph Greenberg. Anyway, Jessica has been a friend for ages, and she's coming out to visit me in Italy. This is the first time I've been really excited about seeing a girl since—I don't know, in years. I saw her in D.C. over Christmas break—she's about to start at LSE. Between you and me, I dreamed about her during Ranger School. Not sexually—you don't (I didn't) have sexual dreams or fantasies in Ranger School—just about her cooking for me, baking for me; it was one of the most intensely romantic and passionate dreams I've ever had in my life, I'll never forget it. I have to acknowledge that I have serious feelings for her. And she's going to be in Europe for a while, so it's sort of the perfect time to see if we'd make a good match—inasmuch as any time can be said to be perfect, with the prospect of an impending deployment hanging over our heads.

I met another couple guys in infantry officer training that I stayed in pretty close touch with afterwards, a guy named Bob who was indirectly responsible for my getting into (though not through) Ranger School, and a guy named Mike; I think you'd like both of them, hard-drinking, patriotic intellectuals that they are. Interested in what's happening, what this is all about—interested in contributing afterwards. I remember the first time you and I talked about the future of

America—that conversation helped carry me through basic training.

Combat is where all presuppositions, all races, creeds and prejudices get swept away—here we all are, standing on the cusp of real adulthood, produced by a society that no longer values maturity, that watches athletic competition and reality television instead of war coverage, that reads *Harry Potter* instead of the classics, that resents you for bringing up "several months in the future" as a guard against foolish behavior in the present—let alone the probable consequences of our actions in ten or twenty years. No long-term vision. Well, I've seen the long-term future of America—I saw it in the faces of my comrades in Ranger School, and infantry training, and in basic training as well—and the future, I'm happy to say, looks bright.

Write from Colorado when you have a chance, and let me know when you guys are headed out. Give me a call, I know you're not supposed to talk about deployment dates over written material, I totally won't wander into a bar and tell any attractive, olive-skinned women with Iraqi accents...

> Stay well,
> Adrian

28 July 2006

Dear Teddy,

I'm in Italy now, with my unit, 2nd Platoon ("The Goats"), C Company, 1st Battalion (Airborne), 503rd Infantry, 173rd Airborne Brigade Combat Team. Doesn't really roll off the tongue so I'll just say the 173rd. The best of the line units, a secret unit, virtually unknown outside the army, not even fully appreciated within the army—I couldn't be prouder and happier to be a part of it, to have the responsibility and honor of wearing the patch and the Maroon beret (sign of the Airborne). I was picked up at the airport by one of the platoon leaders, a guy named Matt, and have been settling in nicely since then.

Thank you for the lovely dinner on the island, it was great to see you and catch up. It had been so long since I saw the island, since I spent meaningful time with friends and family in civilization, that I'd almost forgotten what it felt like. Comfort and ease come with a price, though—too much makes it difficult to train, keeping those things as uncertain possible future outcomes make the challenges worthwhile.

And the challenges have just begun. Everything I've done up to this point was to prepare me for arrival at my unit, and in now that I'm here, the training counts for little to nothing—the Ranger Tab, the Airborne wings, the officer and soldier training, the people I went through training with who didn't make it all the way through or cut deals to avoid certain parts, or went to their units—all of it served to get me to this moment, to a meeting with my company commander or "CO," to a platoon where I'm the new guy, and everyone else has one or two deployments under their belts. A lot of these guys went to war together, just got back a few months ago, and are preparing to go back—they have stories and pictures and videos—pictures and videos of terrible things—I'm not initiated. So comfort and ease and entitlement—a sense of deserving or belonging, which really amounts to the idea that I'm safe and secure (what I've just done is describe *happiness*), none of it has a place in my life right now. I need to remain hungry, to keep that sense of perspective that got me here.

But I guess that's why you and Dad and the rest of the older generation have always told me that life's a journey.

At the same time, as I meet my fellow officers, the ones I will serve with on deployment to (presumably) Iraq, I am amazed at the level of professionalism and enthusiasm they display, and I'm inspired to work hard to earn their admiration and respect. It reminds me a bit of Yale, the essential camaraderie that exists between people who generally regard themselves as superior and those around them as equals—this is a special, extraordinary unit, and from what my friends tell me of their units, maybe unique in the military. Even the guys who've been to Special Forces or Ranger units don't claim that those places were better than Italy, because they tend to attract leaders at the junior officer level who have something to prove, who feel that they haven't met their potential, and see each other as rivals. I've been here three days and wouldn't consider screwing over any of my peers for an advantage—though I'm told that such an event is fairly common. It certainly sounded that way listening to the prior service guys in OCS or at IOBC.

To answer the question you asked over dinner—I'm not reading for pleasure much, now—working on T. R. Fehrenbach's *This Kind of War* about Korea, and "A Letter to Garcia" by a guy named Hubbard, writing about an incident in the Spanish-American War. The latter was pretty quick, and I didn't like it at first—too much of the "Spirit of Manifest Destiny" impulse that probably infected everything written before 1920 (and some things after). After reflecting a bit, I decided that what the hell did I know, my superiors wanted me to get something out of it so I would—and the lesson is pretty sound: you should do everything in your power to resolve a problem or situation before troubling anyone above you for help. Coming as I have from a background where others were always happy, even *eager* to solve my problems for me, to make things easier, it's been difficult transitioning into this world where self-reliance is the first and highest "good"—necessary before one can participate as a member of the "team." When you have a group of people who are self-reliant, the group is almost unstoppable.

This Kind of War has been more informative, less *instructive*—I'd never read about the Korean War, it wasn't just "the forgotten war," it *is* the forgotten war, not much part of our cultural memory, too inconvenient, probably in the same way that Europeans don't waste time on World War I, too painful and ultimately meaningless. Interesting largely because Korea seems to have come as such a shock to us—we were totally unprepared but wholly committed to defeating the North Koreans; you don't usually see that intersection in foreign policy. Reading it I've been thinking: "if this is the type of book that our battalion commander wants us to digest and consider, then we're in good hands."

I'll write more soon, unless I'm overwhelmed with my new duties (which is always a possibility). The big event here is "battalion" or "brigade" "CQ," and I don't know what CQ stands for but I know what it means: sitting in an office all night, i.e., time to write letters. This event drives the social lives of the officers affected, and every lieutenant is affected...

Love,
Adrian

18 August 2006

Hey Bob,

That's wild, you and Mike will be deploying really soon, then. I don't think we have orders yet, but someone told me we're on the big-boy chart to deploy in spring of 2007. It can't come soon enough, it's really frustrating to know that you two will be getting into things before I've even started unit training… I know that sounds like an immature thing to say, but you understand—so few people do—you train for a thing like this, like war, you train to be an infantryman and it's all you want to do, nothing else, just get to war. That's about as far forward as I've thought, anyway.

We joke about why we all joined up—Mike because of his passionate, blind belief in America, and his general outrage over 9/11. Me because it felt like sitting around doing nothing while our officer leadership failed to actually *lead* and keep soldiers out of harm's way (physical or spiritual [in the case of Abu Ghraib]). You because you wanted to be around hot dudes, and you're too fundamentally insecure to just admit that. We all had our reasons, and ultimately (with the exception of Mike—and you, I guess) the reasons a man gives for choosing to do a thing like this are always both more and less than the full story. Then you get into a thing like Ranger School and your thinking evolves, you sacrifice so much of yourself to get to where you want to go, that it becomes like doubling down on an uncertain bet—what else can we do but go to war? What other choice remains for us? To not go? To find a cush job somewhere and sit this out, safe and sound? If we had families I guess it would be different. Mike and I don't, and you *can't* (unless you magically develop "game" with women—I'm not holding my breath).

Seriously, it'll be a tough thing seeing you guys out there while I'm training. Stuck behind, wondering if it'll all still be there when it's my turn – if I'll even get a turn. When you think about it, most of the guys we went through Ranger School with are already at their units; we were the only two who did RSLC. Some guys I think are going almost straight to theater. It's a special time to be in the infantry—we find ourselves in the heart of the opening act to whatever happens next in the Middle East—things are changing. The power dynamics of post-colonialism, of post-cold war Asia are changing, balances are tipping. Iran's getting stronger. Pakistan's getting weirder. And—God help us—the three of us will all be there this May. Needless to say, if you find yourself in Europe before you deploy…

Stay well,
Adrian

Journal Entry: 25 August 2006

Snapshot of life in Italy: Brent and I hopped in his five series BMW and cruised West to Cannes for our old friend Peter's wedding. It's always a pleasure to drive—on the Autostrada, blasting Madonna and Metallica, we passed through Verona, Milan, and Genoa as afternoon changed to evening, the sun highlighting the Alps, and then nightfall. We sped down the coast of Italy at a stupid, breakneck pace, and then into France.

Peter and his bride looked fantastic at the wedding. For the ceremony, they found one of those small, intimate stone churches that probably used to house priestesses of Isis back in the B.C.E.'s—a veneer of Christianity slapped on the rough walls. Between the vows and the reception, a few of us walked down to the beach nearby and swam out to a raft fifty meters offshore, then lounged in the sun for a while. Someone had the foresight to bring a couple bottles of some sweet wine— whiskey would've been better, but it's a real chore to lay on booze out here—Brent and I could've got some for pretty cheap back at the base, but in our hurry to pile into the car and hit the road we just forgot. After the beach, everyone reconvened at a waterfront restaurant, the party set off against another multi-colored sunset that seemed to last much longer than normal, multi-mega-billionaire yachts moored offshore, and finally the twinkling of stars on the French Riviera. Some people broke away to go skinny dipping for the after-party; I and a couple other party-goers took nightcaps at a nearby café before calling it an evening. Soaked with sweat from the heat and humidity and dancing; in the summer heat, even rotgut like Cutty Sark blended Scotch on ice can feel like a tonic.

In daylight, the drive by Monaco and up between the mountains was breathtaking—the highway close and narrow, like a goat-trail with sharp turns threatening an abrupt flight into the ocean below. The drive back was uphill, much more slow and methodical owing to the slope of the highway. Elsa came with us, sat in the front seat while I napped in the back. Good to finally feel like she's purely a friend—no more of the post-breakup, vague misunderstandings. Everything is clear and clean in Italy, no disagreements or fighting, but a hell of a lot of drinking. Life here is slow and good. Almost forget that we're paratroopers and officers, members of the best "conventional" outfit in the military. Cause that doesn't just happen—that requires Ranger-School-like-training. Well—eat, drink, and be merry. Feels like New Haven—or, the way New Haven should've been—with something more substantial beneath it all.

★

10 September 2006

Dear Jessica,

I apologize for the way I acted when you came to visit. It was great seeing you, taking our relationship to the next level—I started feeling that way about you when I was in Ranger School, and I never thought I'd be waking up in bed and seeing your face beside me. Never thought that would happen, not in this lifetime. Along with the other significant changes in my life, I didn't prepare well for this addition (although I wanted it), this change, and I handled it about as poorly as a man can handle a thing. Getting drunk, going out with other officers, speaking meanly to you, being hard on myself—your being understanding, despite the situation you were coming out of in England, with Ralph—I'm really glad you're still talking with me. "I'm under a lot of stress" sounds slick and useless and stupid, but it's true—how else can I explain booting a chance to be with you?

I've been dealing with the pressure the only way I know how, by pouring myself into training. I've been with my platoon (2nd Platoon "The Goats," C Company, 1-503rd Airborne) for almost two months, and it's challenging. I couldn't ask for a better platoon sergeant (I explained some of this to you, but the dynamics are a lot plainer to me now than they were when I arrived). He's a consummate professional, knowledgeable about all things military—also, while not well educated by some standards (which is interesting—I feel like I'm seeing the hierarchical America at work here, two bright people with different educational backgrounds, one ends up a sergeant, one a lieutenant), an intelligent and deeply intellectual person whom I'm proud to call a friend. Between the two of us and a really fantastic platoon's worth of soldiers (all of the NCOs are great, most of the soldiers are great, a couple of bad apples but that's par for the course), it's been a real joy to learn my new job, what being an officer really means. Nothing I learned in training prepared me for this.

My commander's another inspirational story—I told you my first interaction with him over email was not positive, and that translated into a rough first week at work (the week before you came out to see me). He basically told me to stop being selfish, shut up, and do my job—it's been a *steep* learning curve. He's been the best possible example for me, and deploying with him and serving under his command would be a dream come true. He caught part of the last rotation to Afghanistan, so there's still a possibility he might not get switched out. Maybe I could get a few months, five or six months as a platoon leader with him—that would be enough.

I didn't do myself any favors at the battalion level, either, also in the first week (this sounds like a litany of excuses as to why I acted like such a horse's ass, and is, because I want you to keep talking with me). Our battalion commander is a very demanding leader. The impolite way to describe him would be a tyrant, but that's reductive, it doesn't do him justice. The positive attributes: he's very management-focused, and I think on a very basic level does care deeply about the unit doing well, and about succeeding in his job. Anyway, when I got here, I didn't really understand how things worked in a unit, in the military, and opened my mouth in a couple of public situations where the input of a second lieutenant was neither needed nor wanted, consequently earning a couple of unofficial talking-tos from him and his enlisted counterpart (the equivalent of my platoon sergeant) the "Battalion Command Sergeant Major." And his second in command, the "Battalion Executive Officer" or "XO." Since that time I've been walking on pins and needles. The easy fix for this has been simply to be quiet and stay as far away from them as possible, which I'm told is the proper thing to do for a second lieutenant.

The long and short of it is that, in addition to asking your forgiveness for my behavior, I also have to ask your forbearance, because there's no way I'm going to be able to visit you in London—at least not in the short term. I'm on probation, as it were, trying not to be "special," especially as Brent's reputation is on the line as the guy who vouched for me. It's as though I'd managed to alienate or anger every professor in the English Department at Yale, even the department head, and have to go out of my way not to ruffle any feathers. This actually happened, if you remember, between my Junior and Senior year. I'm stuck here for at least the next month—then the unit's in training up in Germany for a month.

I want to see you again, Jessica—I want to give "us" a try—I haven't felt like this about a woman since college. If you can hang in there for a couple months, I'll get on the first plane to see you in a city of your choosing when I get free for Christmas break. I'm not like Ralph Greenberg, I'm not on the spaceship to professional and financial overlordship—as you know, I never put work first. Here, the stakes are high, and I have to, even though you're at LSE, you're close—I have to put the platoon first, as well as a crazy, idiotic thing like my reputation. I'm going to make sure I'm healthy with work and stress so when we see each other next (if you still want to see me—and I'd understand if you didn't), we'll be able to do this thing right, build on the incredible chemistry we have as friends and, now, more. I think about your visit often, I miss you terribly, and hope like hell I didn't blow it.

> Love,
> Adrian

Journal Entry: 15 October 2006

I am settled into my unit and responsibility now. It's been almost three months, and I'm basically accepted / tolerated as part of the group. The commander makes his expectations of us known clearly, consistently, and I've never seen him angry or judgmental. My fellow officers are, collectively, the finest and most talented group of people I've worked with since I was an undergraduate at Yale. The soldiers and sergeants instruct me rather than vice versa—this flies in the face of most of the advice I received at Fort Benning, that I would be in charge and that they would be subordinates. I'm learning too much now to say unequivocally that I know best.

The battalion commander has us read books and discuss ideas in officer LPDs (Leader Professional Development), the closest thing in the army to a classroom environment. We're paratroopers, but we're also *intellectuals*—I'm not sure many people own that beyond me, but I think in a war like COIN that's the only hope you have of winning. Squat-thrusting three hundred pounds isn't going to win us the war—understanding what worked in other places, assessing our area in Iraq or Afghanistan, and being smart (and likely unorthodox) will be what helps us achieve success.

Brent leaves for Fort Benning soon. Three months at the same post—three more months than I would've ever imagined possible. In this case, you really do create your own luck... without his luck-generation skills, it never would've happened, either.

It's still not working quite right with Jessica for some reason. It should be perfect—there is no objective reason that it can't be—but something's wrong. With *me*. Obsessing about the future, about stringing her along while I'm consumed by my own insecurities and anxiety over deploying soon—I'm hoping that it passes—I'm in Italy, come what may in the future, why can't I relax in the present? I *love* this woman, she's my equal, or maybe my superior. When she writes about my sanity, and about how she'll worry when I deploy, I can't help but think—what if this isn't the perfect time for us to have a relationship? What if this is the worst time? What if I've doomed us, by pushing for a relationship now?

26 November 2006

Dear Mom and Dad,

When things are going well, I rarely take the time to write. When they're going poorly, I can't find the words or energy to write. The prolific correspondence of the past year and a half is a combination of two phenomena: the enforced solitude of late-night guard shifts and the ongoing moves, from school to school and fort to fort. People often correspond at particularly contemplative holidays (Christmas or New Years) or during big changes—getting a new house, having a kid. The normal rhythms of life break, giving us time to reflect on how things have progressed—this seems to happen regularly in the army; between three and nine months, something is always happening, changing.

My time in Italy has been like a dream. Traveling, enjoying Northern Italian culture (so very different from what we tend to think of as "Italian"—of course our cultural prejudices against Italy are informed by the poor immigrants from Southern Italy (and especially Sicily) during the latter part of the 20th century)—training with the soldiers. The 173rd is a special unit, not "Special Forces," not "Rangers," it's just another line unit in the army, a regular unit made up of special people in a very special place. I've been taking full advantage of every opportunity I have to enjoy what Vicenza has to offer and take the training with my soldiers seriously.

Brent left recently, which is the direct inspiration for my writing—a change in my habits. Having him here to show me the ropes and plug me into the social scene—it was a real boon. Hell, I wouldn't be here if it weren't for him. With his departure in late October, the social scene shifted, and I was thrown onto my own resources—fortunately, as I alluded to earlier, the 173rd is full of special people, extraordinary soldiers and officers, and I've met some really great people. Still, it's a tough thing—I guess at this point, he's one of my best friends, and being in the same place as him for a few months, it just didn't feel like enough. Also I'd hoped that we'd get a chance to go to war together.

I spend most of my time with the unit, training. We did a land navigation course in the Dolemites, practically mountain land nav—massive ups and downs—with a couple small Italian villages and a few pastures thrown in for good measure. Italian villagers sat or stood on their porches (or in front of the cafés) watching the "Americani" run around in desert uniforms, kneeling in the shade, checking points though binoculars, looking at their compasses and maps, what to the villagers must have been inscrutable, pointless military training—it was the most fun I'd had in a long time. Our CO is a ferocious warrior whose background is shrouded in mystique. He's easily the most competent leader I've ever spent time with. A day around him is worth a month in basic training or any of the other useless schools I went to before Ranger School. Even Ranger School isn't much when it comes to real, common-sense leadership; this guy is the real deal. The timing might not work out, but I have my fingers crossed that he'll deploy us to Iraq this spring.

I don't know for sure that we're going to Iraq, but that's what everyone's saying. There are some rumors that we'll go to Afghanistan instead. The "orders" don't exist yet; everything's contingent on getting "orders." Once they arrive, we'll know where we're going and how long we'll be there. It was like me with my situation coming to Italy—until I had orders, I didn't really know which unit I'd get. The process is the same at the unit level. No orders, no plans. Up until this point we've been training to go to Iraq, learning Arabic, practicing a lot of urban warfare. The unit's first deployment was to Iraq (jumped in, the only airborne jump from a "regular" unit so far), and its second deployment was to Afghanistan (that was when Brent was up in the mountains).

It doesn't matter to me, either one's fine, though when I went to the recruiting station a couple years ago (so long!) I was thinking about deserts and the Tigris River.

Back before I understood what went into a war, I had a dream about finding bin Laden. I'd found him in a cave, in Afghanistan. I was a hero. This dream really happened. It was before Ranger School. Now, with my actual unit, the 173rd Airborne, the legendary unit from Vietnam, I feel the constraints of possibility, of probability—a platoon doesn't move that way, a company doesn't find itself around the cave where bin Laden's hanging out, it doesn't work like that. All of my pre-conceived notions about warfare have changed—people bullshit you in training, they force you to get stronger, but they are very careful not to strip you of the one thing you need to get through it all, the illusion that warfare makes sense, that individual action has an effect on the outcome of a battle, that you can be a hero. They let you keep that illusion, thank God; I don't know how anyone would make it through otherwise, if they knew the truth.

At this point, I don't even know "the truth," I shouldn't have written it like that. I know that I don't know the truth, that's the only thing I know. That the things I learned during training (they also call it "in the schoolhouse") were true of training, nothing more… all the real knowledge comes from a combination of *unit* training and experience—the rest of it is all pain and theory. It almost goes without saying that there's a very healthy bed of mistrust for the junior officers (lieutenants like myself and captains) among the sergeants—the soldiers don't know any better, so they trust the sergeants. There's a tension between people who come into the unit straight out of the schoolhouse and begin telling others that *they* know the best way to train, *they* know what's important, especially when some of those others have significant combat experience. I had the good fortune to work with a great platoon sergeant; we have a positive relationship of mutual trust, and one of the reasons it's so balanced and healthy is, again, because my commander (a captain) is such a fantastic leader. He's a terrific mentor, and the first day I arrived he "squared me away" by telling me what I should be doing as a young platoon leader, what I needed to be learning, and before anything else that I should be listening to my platoon sergeant. He modeled this ideal officer / sergeant relationship by having a great rapport with *his* counterpart, our first sergeant. Our first sergeant—one level above my platoon sergeant—is this crusty old vet with a ton of experience (and also one of the most energetic people I've ever met) but slightly subdued around the commander. The two of them run the company like a well-oiled machine, and between the example they set and the guidance I get from my platoon sergeant (who's seen platoon leaders like myself come and go), the platoon works just fine. I never pretended to know what the "right" way to do something was, I correct things that are wrong if I see them, and I always consult with the platoon sergeant to make sure we're both on the same page.

I spent Thanksgiving with Mom's parents back in 1996, you saw the pictures. One of the things I remember most vividly about Mom's dad, Fado, is the way he talked about his bombing missions in World War II. He kept a record of the basic mission details on a set of cardboard tags he'd tie around a bomb-pin, and after Sally-Mama went to bed one night he brought them out and described what the experience had been like. Maybe he understood then that death wasn't too far off—a knowledge he never acknowledged consciously, but why else share something like that with me? There was one story in particular, about how he'd been on the mission that bombed Innsbruck, Austria on Christmas Eve, 1944, that seemed to leave a deep mark on him. He talked about seeing the lights of the city—can that have been true?—and thinking that those were *his* people down there, Germans, his cousins—and he was bombing them. In a broader sense they were his people—they were people, many of whom didn't bear him any special or individual animus—and he was bombing them. War must demand a great deal of cognitive dissonance.

Well I've been to Innsbruck a few times and it's a lovely place, with lovely people. Being in the mountains gives me a sense of comfort and security that I don't get anywhere else, not in the ocean (what's beneath the waves?), not in the forest (what's behind those trees?), and certainly not in the desert or plains. The hills can be comfortable too, but there's still a bit too much sky visible—you can see the potential there—the mountains are different. You can put your back against a cliff and space reduces to known quantities. In Japan, every major city was surrounded by mountains. I liked that.

On that note, I'll sign off here with a promise to see you soon, over Christmas!

Love,
Adrian

Dear Teddy,

I got a chance to write again! Between training and learning how to do the administrative work of a platoon leader, I've had my hands full—luckily one of my best friends, the guy who pulled me into the 173rd, left. I was developing a totally undeserved reputation as an alcoholic before he went to Georgia for the Captain's Career Course (he's staying in to be a company commander).

This requires a little bit of background information. When I was a soldier, I thought that the company commander was God incarnate. Since then I've learned that he's just a really, really knowledgeable and capable officer, the lowest ranking officer entrusted to carry out the mission with "command authority." As a platoon Leader, I'm not a "commander," I'm the officer on the ground who represents the company commander. This is, I think, from an older style of warfare where platoons weren't really tactical entities so much as administrative groups; in World War I, a company went over the top together and was never much dispersed (at least not by design). Now, platoons could be ten or twenty miles away from their command headquarters—I think this was true of Vietnam as well. In the original French, the word "lieutenant" means, literally, "place-holder," which points to that truth—the lieutenant is the guy who's in a space that the real commander cannot occupy for some reason or another. He relays or delivers orders, or interprets them, but does not *issue* them himself.

We all have call-signs; my company, C Company is called "March or Die," so its radio call signs start with "MOD." MOD-6 is my commander. MOD-7 is the first sergeant, MOD-5 is the executive officer (ours, a former platoon leader, is not doing very well in his position—luckily the First Platoon's platoon leader has seniority on me and is next in line), and then the platoon leaders are, reflecting their platoons, MOD 1-6, MOD 2-6 (me), and MOD 3-6. Everyone has a call sign.

There was a training event at an area called "Grafenwoehr" in Germany that we all went to recently—three weeks, cold, already snowing, tough training, marksmanship and maneuver ranges. To do any good training requires German ranges, as the Italian ranges I've been to (a land nav range and a shooting range) were both informal affairs: farmer's fields in the mountains near a couple of small Italian villages, and a flat plain in the middle of nowhere with a couple of Italian Military

Police to keep inquisitive minds away. At "Graf" (which used to be an SS training facility in WWII) we did a ton of ruck-marching, eighty miles' worth (I only completed 40, as an officer I kept getting pulled away to supervise range setup details), a great deal of shooting, and some maneuver exercises. I got to maneuver my full platoon for the first time, and did a *comically* bad job; by the end of the exercise I was starting to get the hang of it, though. The sergeants in the platoon are all battle-tested and combat-approved vets, *extremely* capable and competent. There were a series of competitions at the end of the three-week period, and I came in second place in the battalion "best rifle-man" exercise. I won the shoot-out and the technical piece, but booted the written exam.

Beyond the traveling I'm sure Dad's told you about, I've been reading a bit about Venice and the history of the area, but nothing else—been pretty focused on what we're doing to get ready for Iraq, not so much focused on personal development. This is pretty disappointing, but I figure if I'm putting the rest of my life on hold while I do this, I might as well do it right, and I'm still working to overcome a knowledge gap between myself and the West Point / ROTC guys. They really are better prepared for this, though Ranger School and Reconnaissance School erased most of the substantial difference.

The officers here are a great group, and I've made some good friends. It's a lot like I imagine your society experience was—a bunch of outstanding individuals selected for an unusual distinction, serving together in the same place. There are a lot of generals' sons; I don't know if that played a role in their getting to Italy, but they constitute an unusually large percentage of the officers. I could name names but will not, and ultimately it doesn't matter because it's not like they don't deserve to be here—just odd, observing how the professional military is becoming more like Old Yale in certain ways. I don't even like thinking about it, makes me feel like I'm rocking the boat. And—to backtrack, these guys are really, really competent. My current CO came from nowhere, totally self-made, and never disparages anyone—I feel that he's the best officer in the battalion—but maybe that's the Stockholm Syndrome talking.

All in all, I'd say this has been a worthwhile adventure, and the fun I've had learning my job and getting to meet my platoon—a great group of guys, just one asshole in the group (who's now AWOL in America having defrauded some of his fellow soldiers of money)—

has really opened my eyes to what my country is like, why people feel compelled to serve. I have a confidence in the fiber and quality of our countrymen that I never held before. I always used to think people from the south were ignorant, and the rest of those tired stereotypes. Religion is a source of strength. My eyes are opening.

I'll write more soon, look forward to hearing from you (and maybe catching up over Christmas break)!

Love,
Adrian

6 December 2006

Mike,

I'm sorry to hear that neither you nor Bob will be able to visit me out here before you deploy. Great that you made time to meet up in San Antonio, though, I really appreciated you guys "including" me with pictures of all the fun you were having out there. It was a really nice thing to say that you'd be happy to attend my funeral if I didn't make it back from my 10th jump, that was thoughtful, and it didn't take a PhD in Comparative Literature to read between the lines later on and discover disappointment when you learned that I survived.

Well I don't know anyone in Al Qaeda, but if I did, I'd be feeding them as much info as I could about your unit movements in hopes that they'd ambush you. I'm sure your soldiers feel similarly; in fact, they're probably doing that as we speak. "The one with the big head—yeah, he talks a lot, he's always looking around to see if people are watching him—he's the one you want, make sure to rape him too." Well, I've got eight hundred bucks tucked away in case something happens to you over there and I have to fly back home with no warning... I have the story set for my battalion leadership, they'll understand, while in fact the only reason I'd be there is so I could dance on your grave after the ceremony... during the ceremony I'd be a model of sobriety, a real class act, everyone would love me... I'd deliver a stirring monologue about your dedication to Ayn Rand and her radical gospel of free market capitalism... people would be confused, knowing you, but unwilling or unable to question my revising the narrative of your life.... And you'd be powerless to stop me, up in heaven or wherever, just shaking that angelic fist impotently.

So the reason I couldn't fly out to San Antonio was that one of the other officers here, a guy I'm going to call "Dick Beau," decided to fly to Greece during a four-day weekend with no pass. No big deal, right? Everyone does this. Well, when other countries are involved, it's a big fucking deal, especially given our recall state. There was an incident, our dictatorial BC recalled the unit, nobody knew where this goofball Dick was hiding, and as it turned out he'd *shut off his cellphone* because each country in Europe has its own plan and calling into a different country racks up huge costs for everyone involved. I mean—don't get me wrong, I understand this officer's motivation, I've gone away for the weekend before without submitting a pass—but I was two hours away in Austria, I could make a recall formation, and my CO knew where I was. Nobody cares where you are so long as your boss knows your plan and you can drive back to post if crisis demands it. You know, our job. This guy goes to Greece and nobody knows where he is or how to get in touch with him, and there's a serious recall formation—boy, it stirred up a hornet's nest. Naturally everyone else suffered as a result, and flying to America became a big-deal thing all of a sudden, even on a four-day pass. No use complaining about it, that's life in the army. Fucking Dick Beau.

So instead, a couple of buddies and I got dispensation to take off to Slovenia. I'd actually never heard of Slovenia before I got here; the first time someone told me there was a great country close by called "Slovenia" where people spoke English and used sit-down toilets, I corrected them, "No, that's Slovakia, and that country is not at all the way you've described it, starting with proximity." But I was wrong, Mike. Slovenia is real, it's part of the Yugoslavia thing, which, as it turns out, is a lot more than just Marshal Tito, leader of the Non-Aligned States. No, it's like Hungry and Romania and Croatia and mountain people and witchy eastern-Europe-meets-Austrian-women and wine and the Dalmatian Coast, a weird country that's tiny and about three hours away from where I live now, past the ancient port city of Trieste. It was a blast, it was totally worth it, and I'll be headed back at the next opportunity.

Having said that, I really do wish I could've helped see you and Bob off, especially given that we've already lost three guys from our IOBC class in Iraq to IEDs. I'll just have to believe that you'll both come through it all okay. Why is it always either a stand-up guy with a wife and five children or a young couple who are expecting their first child? I remember me and you driving to Lieutenant M's apartment for the Super Bowl earlier this year, and running into Lieutenant L and his young bride-to-be; now she's six months pregnant and Lieutenant L is dead, in Iraq. He and I bonded when we both failed land nav, and then both made it through Pre-Ranger and Ranger School. Hurtling toward our individual destinies.

I'll keep you up to date on where I am and the possibility of getting together in the future. Still no word—rumor puts us in Afghanistan, on the border with Pakistan (which is getting to be a bad place to be, not that you hear about it on the news). By the way, when you and Bob go to Iraq and I get diverted to Afghanistan, expect to begin hearing a massive anti-Iraq propaganda campaign coming from my camp, about how Iraq is soft, and Iraq is bullshit, and Afghanistan's where the real shit is, that's where true heroic men go to get separated from normal heroic men, etc., etc.

Stay well,
Adrian

Journal Entry: 24 December 2006

I'd hoped that the second time Jessica and I met, it'd go better. Everything was as it should be—we met at the Yale Club, ate at great restaurants, walked, talked, spent time together like it belonged to us—and I still managed to fuck it up like a comic book villain. I'm with Jessica Benelli. Jessica Benelli says she loves me. I say incredibly insensitive things to her. I test her patience with curt comments and morally indefensible statements made to provoke disagreeable responses. Basically, the life I've imagined with a beautiful girl—fantasized about it since I was a kid—is slipping from my grasp. I am, it seems, a bottomless pit of insecurity and anxiety. I can conceal this from superficial relationships but am so terrified of judgment when it comes to opening up to the person who by rights should be the love of my life, I become my own worst enemy. And she still wants to stay with me.

22 January 2007

Dear Jessica,

Thank you so much for the cake and cookies, you know how much I love baked goods, and you pegged me right, you know just how to make a man happy. They were delicious, I shared them with my platoon leadership and everyone got a kick out of hearing our story. My platoon sergeant said that you're a keeper, which, of course, I knew before he said it… I can't believe my good fortune in ever having met you and in deserving the opportunity to build a relationship together.

At the same time, we can't ignore that things went crazily, terribly amiss again when we met in New York before Christmas. I've done some serious thinking about why that was, why that happened—what's wrong with me. Why I act that way when we're together. It makes no sense to me, it's not how I feel about you; I turn into this creature who's emotionally distant, even *manipulative*, a mask I've never worn before in any relationship. It's horrifying. I care about you deeply, and there's no reason to think that if I don't take this chance now, if I let you go, that you'll still be around later. Actually, I'm certain you won't be, that by putting you off I'm really saying that you and I won't end up together the way I'd like. I know how you think of yourself as the type who will wait patiently for her man to come back to her, but that analogy isn't right for us, we don't have a tree to bring us back to our connubial bed. It doesn't exist. On top of which, I don't know what I'm going to be like when I get back, if I get back.

I don't know exactly where I am right now, that's the only thing I've learned from all of my military schooling, from arriving at this unit. I didn't know that I wouldn't know, but everything I've seen suggests that war is going to be a transformative experience. Maybe constructive, maybe destructive. And I can't have you with me for that. I can't think about another person beyond the people in my unit, beyond myself. Forcing you to wait twelve or fifteen months for me to come back when I don't know what that will look like, what I'll be like. Then, the unspeakable question: what if I don't come back at all? I've already lost three comrades over there, and in this unit, the reminders are everywhere—how life changes for a society that loses friends and loved ones. I can't put you through that. I won't.

No, the best thing to do is for you to forget about me now, bid me farewell. We get our marching orders in the next couple weeks—it's supposed to be Afghanistan, now, the surge in Iraq pushed us off our normal rotation (which was supposed to be Iraq), and into a couple places in Afghanistan nobody's heard of, where some bad things are happening. Places where the Taliban movement never died, right on the border of Pakistan. If you're still around when I get back, if I still smile, if I haven't been changed to the point where you no longer recognize me, well, I'll look you up. In the meanwhile, live as though I'm already gone, because there's a decent chance I will be—if not physically, emotionally. Death is change, war is death.

I'm grateful for the moments we've had together, we owed it to ourselves to make an effort—there's nobody I've ever felt more in tune with than you, but life doesn't always provide the opportunities one would like, and the timing for us could not have been worse.

You won't be hearing from me again until this is over.

Love,
Adrian

★

7 February 2007

Brent,

Well, it's official: we're going back to Afghanistan. 1-503rd is going back to Paktika Province, where it will be OPCON'd to the 82nd Airborne, while the rest of the brigade is headed North to Kunar and Nuristan. Strange how a thing like a battalion could make such a difference… I'd be lying if I didn't admit that I wish I were headed to Kunar or Nuristan (your old company's getting detached to the cavalry squadron to help them cover down in Nuristan, and my company will be working alongside a cavalry troop we're getting from them in return), but I guess things are heating up all along the border. Just seems like a wilder place up north, that's where the action is. Getting sent to Paktika feels a bit like being put on the "B" team, actually. Maybe that's what the commandos in Burma felt like during World War II—fighting against the Japanese tooth and nail while most of the attention was focused on beating the Germans—I don't know. We search for meaning and ways to explain what's happening to us, fit it into a cohesive, but most of all, satisfying narrative—it's never enough.

Have you ever read Kurt Vonnegut's *Cat's Cradle*? A guy I used to work with on the Yale Record, Ian Dallas, sent it to me and I ripped through the book in record time while recovering from the Lasik surgery that fixed my eyes. If it weren't for the fact that my eyes get tired after a couple hours of reading I would've been done with it sooner, but as things stand now it took me nearly two days of reading, punctuated by breaks, to finish. Take a look, let me know what you think. I saw only truth in its pages.

We're headed back up to Germany soon for another Grafenwoehr rotation, followed by a Hohenfels rotation. Last time was fun, running around doing all that crazy training and weapons qualification, marching everywhere, stopping in at HHC CP to find you and Paul b.s.'ing about the last deployment—this time, with a mission focus, with the new lieutenants (now the old lieutenants), this is pretty much going to be the deployment set, the group we go with. It feels different. Quisenberry, Hepler, and Rufolo have been working late hours with the battalion XO getting their companies up to speed, and—the biggest change of all—I have a new CO. The old "MOD-6" is no more; he's helping out with planning on the BC's staff for now. Our new "MOD-6" is none other than Captain Dixwell, whom you remember as the "S-3 Air" on battalion staff. When my old CO left, he talked with me personally and said, "I know you're going to have trouble with this, Bonenberger; just remember that every commander is different and has a different style of leadership. Adapt to the change, follow his rules." Sure enough, I'm having trouble with it. It's been very difficult for me—it wasn't comfortable, but I trusted MOD-6 ancient, and Captain Dixwell—it's not his fault, he's just not the same. I guess I'll feel differently after Graf / Hohenfels 2007 version.

Our upstairs neighbor has not changed in the slightest; he's still making trouble for everyone in the building. The CID investigation into how he was monitoring our conversations shut him up for a while, so he limits his activities to calling the Carbs every time we throw a party, stonewalling our attempts to reach out to him in person and talk, hiding behind his mother's skirts. He's a slick one, and it's descended into a guerrilla warfare, each side doing what it can to bedevil the other. I grill on the patio every chance I get in order to smoke him out, knowing that he dislikes it; he sprays his hose (ineffectively) from the roof, and doesn't allow us to get a satellite dish for television. All very Italian.

Thanks again for bringing me out here. The debts are never forgotten. Let me know how you're getting on, where you're headed, and how life's treating you—I'll write again before I leave (late April / early May timeframe), and maybe catch up in person before we go.

> Humbly yours,
> Adrian

Journal Entry: 14 February 2007

I've never been a huge fan of Valentine's Day. Either you're in a happy, fulfilling relationship with someone you love who is inevitably disappointed in you when the misunderstanding arises over gifts or activities and that starts the argument cycle oscillating way out of control until there's no common ground anymore, or you're alone and surrounded by happy couples cooing over their good fortune. This time next year I don't suppose it'll matter much, one way or another. I'll be at war.

★

20 March 2007

Brent,

Man—a lot went down at Hohenfels. The BC totally creamed me during my live-fire. It was the second blank-fire iteration, and he screamed at me for the better part of two minutes. In the huddle afterwards—we had a half hour to get ourselves back together—old SFC Krause rallied the platoon, which had overheard everything. "Guys," he said, "The PL is *this close* to getting fired. Pull it together." They did, and I wasn't. SFC Krause was sent over to E Company afterwards to buttress their weak first sergeant. A really solid staff sergeant, Matt Carlson took over for him, just in time for me to leave. Our XO was moved up to battalion, and Matty Svennson went with him to be a battle captain instead of taking over as XO—and suddenly, bam, I was the new XO. I was replaced by one of those guys you sort of hate because they're such good dudes—I can't hate him, but goddamn do I ever hate this situation, XO right before deployment. At least 2nd Platoon is going to be in good hands.

The training was rough, it snowed half the time in Hohenfels, and it all felt really rushed and urgent. This guy from 10th Mountain came in from theater and was telling us about how their COP gets attacked every night and it's in a horrible tactical position so they've taken a lot of casualties. Their FOB gets rocketed almost every day. They have two companies worth of combat power and yet almost never patrol into the villages to their East because there are too many Taliban. The government is corrupt. Only the ANA battalion commander is any good.

Got some good times in with Quisenberry and Peters, bumming around Italy, hitting up Masi and Allegrini vineyards; it was a great send-off, but traveling isn't the same when you have a thing like deployment hanging over your head. We made the most of it, visited Venice—nothing like your send-off party in October, where we rocked it out properly—lots of farewells.

I'll write when I get to Afghanistan. Hope the Captain's Career Course is treating you well, my regards to Paul. You are missed here.

> All best,
> Adrian

28 April 2007

Dear Mom and Dad,

What a memorable trip! I'd never been to Rome before, and the ruins, the dinners, the tours—a special trip, the perfect end to my time in Italy before deploying. We leave in a week or so—Dad, the gear reached all the Goats, so tell the contributors that they're well equipped for a mountain fight, rather than the Iraq deployment we all expected. I'm settling into my new job as "XO" or "MOD-5" nicely, finally came to terms with the promotion. I have to see it as a vote of confidence in my abilities, rather than the loss of an opportunity to deploy to combat as a platoon leader. It is an opportunity, if I make it one. Just so many changes happened so fast—losing my old CO, the new dynamics within C Company, the old XO and the senior platoon leader getting moved to battalion staff on the same day—it's a lot to wrap my head around.

I look back on my time in training, how much I resented being turned out of bed on those days when the only thing I wanted to do was stay in and do nothing, having to run in the morning, going through the motions for days on end, and now with the responsibilities—it's up to me to accomplish tasks—those days when I had no choice whether to work or not, whether to think or not, seem idyllic by comparison. I fret constantly over failure, over making a mistake. The stress is all-consuming and culminative. This is the difference between having authority and having none—the grass is always greener. More latitude to do what one thinks is right with the former, less actual responsibility or expectations with the latter. I can understand, now, how a person could choose to be a soldier, or a shitbag officer with no real duties—it's so easy to simply workout, go to formation, eat and breathe; it doesn't require discipline or fortitude.

So bizarre how one action can have so many unintended consequences. America surges in Iraq, and a unit—the 173rd Airborne—gets bumped over to Afghanistan, to a much more complex and traditional fight. Alone on the border. It's almost as though my battalion commander, Eagle-6, sensed this, and that's why he had us read *This Kind of War*, a book about The Korean War. You have to be adaptable, unexpected things happen in the military, and if you get too attached to a plan or a way of doing things, you get left behind. I should also nod again to Jim Danly's wisdom in encouraging me to read the *Hagakure*.

Well—I realize this is a short letter but I have a few more to write—this is it, I'm the second in command for one of the best companies in the best unit in the army, joining the battle as I had hoped. I wouldn't have it any other way. Wish me luck, and I'll see you when I get leave.

Love,
Adrian

★

Journal Entry: 1 May 2007

Took a long run today with "Nasty" Nate Hepler, and John Intile down into Vincenza, through the square, up the stairs to Monte Berico, past the cathedral of the Blessed Virgin, down and then back up the winding "goat-trail" path then home the same way. One of our last before fifteen months of torture. Paused our workout after six miles to snatch a cappuccino at a local café, and I couldn't help recalling Jessica Benelli sitting across from me in a sundress; it was the café we met at last July, back when it seemed like we had a chance. John put his cup on the table and said "Andiamo, shitbirds," and Jessica vanished. Then the three of us returned to the road, to the aging town at the northern edge of the Po Valley, running between hills and along ridgelines, eleven miles into the run, beneath ancient bell-towers and medieval buildings rising out of the morning mist, and I couldn't help thinking to myself that I will never tire of this scene, this Italy, no matter how many times I run through the waking city, or look over the valley as it stirs from the night—this place, this experience is so unusual, there's no comparing it to other possibilities or potentials. I'm an Airborne Ranger infantry officer. This is my reality, my present. By the time we returned to the base, a group of Roman and Bolognese protesters had gathered at the front gate, and we had to duck onto the fort through a back entrance.

Went out in the evening with a couple officers who leave on my flight. We circulated through the usual places—the Argentinian Steakhouse, "Il Grottino," "Piazza Settima," and that wine bar by Palladio's statue—kept bumping into annoying American tourists everywhere, loud and generally giving us a bad name—eventually found a quiet corner to exist in without feeling typical or like stereotypes of ourselves. The Italians all know that we're leaving for war and give us an unusual degree of latitude. Regardless of their feelings about us or our presence in Italy, the fact that *gli Americani* are headed out—some never to return—allows us to sit and drink our *vino* and cocktails in peace.

4 May 2007

Dear Grandpa,

I'm headed to Afghanistan. By the time this letter reaches you, in fact, I'll be there—somewhere—either waiting on air transportation at one of the bigger FOBs, or at my home base, which will be FOB Bermel, in Paktika Province. We're supposed to take a mixture of planes and helicopters, hopping from FOB to FOB until we get to the final destination. In case you don't know what an "FOB" is—don't think you had them in WWII, they're a Vietnam War idea, the first time we muddled around with a counter-insurgency after the advent of the assault rifle (which allowed greater combat power to be massed, and increased the importance of platoons)—FOB stands for "Forward Operating Base," and from what I can tell is a logistical hub that increases in importance as the size of its occupying force increases but *decreases in relevance in terms of combat*. I've heard of company-, battalion-, and brigade-sized "FOBs." Bigger than that, Division-level, would be a Camp or a Base; Bagram, for example, is an "Air Force Base" that has resources for a Division-level command and control hub. Smaller than an FOB is the "COP" or Combat Outpost—that's for a platoon— and the smallest is the OP or "Observation Post" which is a little more than a squad. I think every army in every era has maintained "OPs" of between one and nine people. Despite the technology we have at our disposal, there's still no better way to pick up enemy movements than an awake and alert soldier.

It was great to talk with you before leaving. I'd never heard any of the stories you told me—Dad didn't seem to know about them either— but I guess it's one of those things. You try to tell someone what it's like in the army and if they were never in the army, they can only imagine. It frustrates me sometimes, thinking about that, the impossibility of telling someone outside this experience a story, of telling him or her what it's like. After a certain point they become either uninterested or simply cannot comprehend what's being said. I wonder if you and your buddies encountered something like that in WWII, when or how you decided never to talk with your family about what it was really like over there, participating in that event.

A little bit more about where I'm going, Paktika Province—the area's supposed to be rife with tribal disputes, which makes it a great area for the Taliban to exploit. I understand that Paktika has always been this way, certainly since America entered Afghanistan in 2001; our first permanent presence in the area beyond Special Forces was a unit from the 10th Mountain Division, 1-87 Infantry, which stayed in the area for nine months from 2003–2004. Reading the reports from back then and subsequent unit rotations through Paktika (including this battalion in 2005–2006), I am struck by the amount of violence, the outright gun battles between forces of Taliban numbering from fifty to one hundred fifty and a single American platoon. While we were training in Germany, an officer from the 10th Mountain Division (who currently have two companies in the area, from their 3rd Brigade, 3-87 Infantry, oddly enough) visited us and reported that if anything, it's gotten worse since they arrived, with greater numbers of Taliban making increasingly bold attacks against their FOBs and COPs.

I look forward to catching up in person when I get back for leave. Looking at an autumn timeframe, so let Mom and Dad know—it'll be great to see everyone again. Stay well, and be proud! I'm carrying on the family name with dignity and honor. I do not intend to disgrace our country, or my good name with despicable or immoral acts.

Love,
Adrian

GLOSSARY · SECTION THREE

FOB (Bermel): Forward Operating Base. FOB Bermel was established as a company (plus) FOB by the 173rd during their 1st deployment to Afghanistan in 2005–06. Owing to the relative lack of perceived threat in the area and in keeping with COIN doctrine it was not established with tactical considerations in mind, but rather proximity to a population and governance center. It was greatly expanded over the following two years as the area came under increasingly deadly attacks from Haqqani-affiliated Taliban.

Bermel District: Valley district on the border of Pakistan. Major population centers include Shkin, Bermel, and Margah. Foothills leading into Pakistan considered "Indian country." Scene of some of the earliest fighting with Taliban in Afghanistan following the conclusion of hostilities.

Orgun-E District: Valley district near the border of Pakistan. Home to an old Soviet fort that was nearly overrun by the mujahedeen (see "Siege of Urgun" for more details). Slightly more civilized than Bermel—driving around you feel more of a low and constant level of alarm, rather than the overt dread and certainty of impending ambush and doom one experiences driving around border towns in Bermel.

Paktika Province: A rural and comparatively isolated province in Afghanistan. One of the "big three" when it comes to violent activity, alongside Helmund and Kunar Provinces. Predominantly Pashtun mountain communities that are largely sympathetic to the Taliban, and resistant to government influence. The capital is Sharana, which is a decent-sized city that I saw a couple times—reminded me a bit of Mazir-e-Sharif. Sharana doesn't feel dangerous in the same way that much of the rest of the province.

Kyrgyzstan: Former Soviet satellite state that borders Tajikistan and China. Had a West-friendly dictator for a number of years until the people deposed him for the usual reasons—corruption, widespread human rights abuses, inflated sense of self-worth. He was still in charge when I flew through Manas on the way in and out—a crumbling former Soviet Air Force Base outside the capital city of Bishkek. Beautiful view of mountains and taiga to the East.

BAF: Bagram Air Force Base. Main logistical, administrative and transit hub for Afghanistan. Awesome chow halls. Hated by most infantrymen due to its restrictive regulations such as having to wear PT belts at all times and saluting, as well as the number of overweight civilians and franchise fast food restaurants. Indistinguishable in certain regards from life on "garrison" back in America.

FOB (Salerno): One of the first permanent bases established by the U.S. in Afghanistan. By the time I got there it was a fairly sophisticated tactical hub, and was not considered very dangerous. Older sergeants moving through commented derisively on its nickname of "FOB Rocket," earned during the earlier years when the insurgents took a more persistently aggressive posture against the base. These things move in cycles, though, and the base has come under attack again in more recent years.

Fobbit: Someone who spends their entire deployment on a FOB (pronounced like the part on top of old watches), but complains about how difficult it was in the 'Stan or Iraq and go out of their way to be seen as heroes by friends and family who don't know better in America. See "REMF" and "pogue" from earlier wars for similar meaning.

OP: Observation Post. Can be permanent or non-permanent position, manned from between one and twenty or so soldiers. Used for observing enemy troop movements or civilian traffic (for irregularities).

HLZ: Helicopter Landing Zone. The flat, graveled area where helicopters land to offload supplies or personnel. Without the gravel, in a place like Afghanistan, the helicopters kick up an extraordinary amount of dust—sometimes this dust storm can be so fierce, and especially in smaller valleys, that it creates conditions known as "Dust-off," or zero visibility. Helicopters normally don't land in Dust-off, and have to go around for another pass.

105mm / 155mm Howitzer: Artillery pieces. The 155mm Howitzer is a big, big gun that can shoot rounds over thirty miles away, and when it fires it sounds very similar to the noise a rocket makes when exploding nearby. It's much worse for the person / persons being hit by the 155mm round, though. Made me think about what soldiers must've had to go through in World War II.

TORCH Party: During a deployment or redeployment, it is impractical (and improvident) to move the entire unit at once. To encourage a gradual and largely seamless transition from one unit to the next, the transition occurs in phases. The first phase is the TORCH party, which is a minuscule portion of critical staff officers and sergeants (maybe 2% of the total unit strength), followed by the ADVON (advance) party. The difference in time between the first person deploying into or out from theater is usually between three weeks or a month (for a regular unit).

FLIPL: Financial Liability Investigation of Property Loss. Every piece of equipment is owned by someone in the army. When that equipment is lost, damaged, or broken, an "investigation" is initiated, to assign responsibility for the equipment's state, and to requisition replacement equipment.

ACU: Army Combat Uniform. This uniform succeeded the BDU / DCU (Battle Dress Uniform / Desert Combat Uniform), and preceded the Multicam Uniforms. Active Duty wore this pattern between 2006–2010. It was poorly manufactured and would frequently rip in the crotch area. The Velcro wore out after a couple months. Lastly it didn't camouflage you at all in most terrain; in fact, it made you stand out, the opposite effect intended. Sort of like the Redcoats in the revolutionary war. A widely detested uniform that gave rise to a hundred conspiracy theories about the acquisitions / procurement process, and who'd profited therefrom.

FSNCO: Fire Support Non-Commissioned Officer. The artillery sergeant assigned to an infantry unit to help plan missions and supervise the artillery soldiers' training. Generally speaking one of the three or four most squared-away sergeants in the unit.

A Bag / B Bag / C Bag / D Bag: Just like on vacation, when you deploy, you pack bags. The bags have to be packed according to a published list, to keep track of what equipment is in which shipping container. D Bag also sounds like a popular insult, which is funny.

Kandak: An Afghan battalion. They use the Soviet model of organization and consequently a Kandak has less combat power than an American battalion. I'm sure there are other differences as well of which I'm not aware but if you have a friend who's into Soviet military history he could probably yak your ear off.

TOC: Tactical Operations Center. At the battalion level and higher, this is the room where all tactical decisions are made by the commander with the assistance of his staff. Filled with phones, computers, flatscreen televisions streaming video from drones and planes and closed circuit cameras. When you're told to "report to the TOC" for no reason, it's a lot like being told to report to the principal's office.

Operation: A military operation is a big, planned movement of soldiers that takes days or weeks to complete. During my first deployment, the stated goals of most operations were not met, though we silently and collectively agreed to act as though they had been.

Meter to Yard conversion: A meter's a little longer than a yard. Most infantrymen are thinking in terms of kilometers (because of maps and artillery range) for longer-range missions or movements, and shorter range for tactical considerations (between fifty and 800 meters) such as rifle, machine gun, and RPG fire. There isn't much difference between 100 yards and 100 meters, it's about a football field.

CERP: Commander's Emergency Response Program. In 2004 this was a bag of money you got every month to do with pretty much as you pleased (as the commander). The idea was that it was difficult to clear money through bureaucracy, so this way a unit could go to a village and say, "What do you need? A well? Okay, I can build you a well." Or if you blew up a building, you could pay the owner. That kind of thing. Over time it became more and more complicated, with so many rules governing its use that it was no different from the bureaucracy it had originally been designed to circumvent. This was to prevent "fraud, waste, and abuse." In 2007 the bag of money had been reduced to $5,000 per month. In 2010, by the time I was in theater for the second time, it wasn't even available at the company level any more.

MEDCAP: Medical Civic Action Program. A doctor—major, lieutenant colonel, or colonel, sometimes male, sometimes female, flies out to your FOB. He / she is there to help you heal local farmers who don't have access to modern medicine. You go out for a day, take a few pictures of smiling kids with bandages and old people with a new cane or crutch, then report a positive interaction with the locals. Everyone feels good about themselves. Didn't seem to do much lasting good.

VETCAP: Veterinary Civic Action Program. *Way* more popular with Afghans than MEDCAPs, at least in rural pastoral communities where human life is cheap, pain is taken for granted, and a healthy flock or herd is almost as good as gold. There aren't many veterinarians in the military, but if there were we'd have had a lot more cache with the residents of Paktika Province.

PAKMIL: Pakistan Military. On this deployment, I'm referring either to their equivalent of Active Duty infantry, irregular infantry / militia (like our National Guard, but far, far crappier), or Special Forces.

FBCB2: Force Battlefield Command for Brigade and Below. The army's GPS computer system. It's state of the art as of A.D. 2000 or so, and the many glitches and technical shortcomings can be traced to hardware and technology limitations from that time. Features a touch-screen and many features we take for granted now, and is, in fact, quite a useful tool for a commander trying to manage a battlefield.

CDS airdrop: I think this stands for Combat Delivery System, and airdrop means that the delivery system is an airdrop. I'm putting this together from observation and experience—the CDS was a plane flying high or low, and kicking pallets out the back on parachutes. It is generally more accurate the lower the plane flies, but there's a trade-off when it comes to safety. Transport planes are not well renowned for being heavily armored.

ETT: Embedded Training Team. Same thing as the MiTTs in Iraq, a group of 10-12 officers, soldiers and sergeants who "advise and assist" Afghan units on how to function like regular, organized military units (and not militias). Some of those units were really "out there," and the best ones lived alongside their counterparts, often with no other Americans nearby—just 10-12 American service members and 200-300 Afghans. Took mettle.

Mefloquin: An anti-malarial medication with anti-psychotic properties, which I took for over two years.

Cipro: An anti-bacterial medication that also helps treat Anthrax, which I took fairly regularly for over two years.

TACSAT: Tactical Satellite. A form of radio that uses Satellites for retransmission, and is typically available in places that most other communication is not (deep in the mountains, far from radio retransmitters). The benefit of TACSAT is that you can talk to brigade or battalion when you have no other way of reaching them. The downside is that it's often when you're out there, way out in the sticks, a day's drive from any friendly base, when you find yourself confronted with messy moral quandaries—the kind of quandary where you really just wish you could talk with someone for guidance—but once you come up on TACSAT, you have colonels listening to you, so you can't discuss what's really going on.

District Center: This is where the mayor works, and often where he lives as well. Think "community center" in the town where you grew up, then add an elevated risk of suicide bombing, ambush, and getting rocketed, and you have the district center in most eastern districts in Afghanistan.

Shura: This is a tribal meeting. People often get confused when they hold regular *shura* and nothing happens, but one of the things I learned in Afghanistan is that shura is where ideas get thrown around and debated while *jirga* is a meeting where decisions are made. I saw a total of four jirga during my entire time in Afghanistan and countless shura. Seems to be a good way of integrating elder Afghans into the process of governance, and has within it the beginnings of representative democracy.

Wadi: a riverbed. In certain places, at certain times of year, a river. Especially in the mountains, when flash flooding could turn a stream into a legitimate torrent. The best way to travel in a convoy—used as roads by the rural Afghans.

Karez: a system of irrigation by underground tunnels.

Mosul: A city in Iraq that saw elevated fighting during the surge. Where my buddy Mike Carson was stationed during his tour.

Field Grade Officer: major, lieutenant colonel, and colonel. The name "field grade" is a holdover from a time when giant armies battled between each other on the same battlefield, and reflected the reality that these officers were the ones making decisions at the point of contact, which largely remained true from the Civil War until the end of World War I. Field grade officers were the command element of battalions and regiments. Beginning with portable, "wireless" radio, officers moved further and further back from the front. Now, the highest ranking officer at the scene of a battle is usually either a lieutenant or a senior captain, and even the lowest-ranking field grade officers are between twenty and seventy miles away.

ALOC: Administrative and Logistical Operations Center. This is the place where all the supply sergeants and officers coordinate between each other and with the requisitions departments to procure or guide equipment from higher echelons (division, brigade) to lower echelons that need it (battalion, company, platoon).

Ghazni: Home to "Task Force White Eagle," Poland's contribution to ISAF. My only exposure to this group was through the TACSAT—"White

Eagle" would come over the net regularly every afternoon, speaking in broken English, and yelling into his radio hand-mike as though he wasn't sure if it was working or not. I liked to picture an old man confronted by a piece of technology he didn't fully understand. "White Eagle" would do this regardless of whatever else might be happening on the TACSAT, so occasionally our unit would be in a fight, or getting rocketed, and, in the middle of a complicated report, our transmission would be interrupted by "WHITE EAGLE BASE WHITE EAGLE BASE THIS IS O-P EAGLE COME IN WHITE EAGLE BASE." At the time it was not amusing but has become so with time and distance.

DFAC (Bermel / Orgun / BAF): Dining Facility. The further you got from the big logistical hubs—BAF being the biggest—the less variety you have, the less "good stuff." It always seemed odd to me that you could get every type of soda and Gatorade conceivable on BAF, but when you got to Bermel there was nothing but water, diet Pepsi, and banana-flavored milk.

RAID: Rapid Aerostat Initial Deployment. A really tall flagpole with a massive camera at the top. The camera was incredible; allowed you to see for miles, had thermal capability, could shoot a laser to get a precise distance to a thing you were looking at, and possessed an 8-digit grid (important for shooting artillery or dropping bombs). We called it the "eye in the sky."

QRF: Quick Reaction Force. You're waiting in a tent with your equipment nearby, unable to get into a book or a movie because something could happen any time. Instead you're bullshitting with someone else in your platoon who's in the same boat as you, just trying to kill time. Finally, finally, it's 3am and nothing ever happens at three, so you all decide to catch some rack in your uniforms. You wake up. Someone's shaking you. It's 3:45am. Something happened, the QRF is rolling.

HMMWV: High Mobility Multipurpose Vehicle. The origin of the idea behind that awful gas guzzling monstrosity that rappers and tasteless nouveau riche Jersey Shore / Orange County wives both find irresistible, aka "Hummer" or "Humvee." Originally designed as a cold war recon and mobility vehicle, it was uparmored and repurposed to carry a turret for the initial stages of the counterinsurgency. In Paktika we still had a couple unarmored cargo HMMWVs, but most of them were 1114 and 1151 uparmored / turreted models. The heavy armor caused the vehicles to break every month or two, with constant axle and transmission issues due to the light recon vehicles being saddled with five extra tons of weight (for which the vehicles were not designed). Also—due to a quirk of the design—especially vulnerable to IEDs, as we discovered shortly after the insurgents began using that tactic against us.

AK: Automatic Kalishnakov. The Kalishnakov brand assault rifles ubiquitous in war zones. -47 variety is still widely used, though nearly seventy years old, and was very common with insurgents. -74 varient rifles were much less common, but still in use.

RPG: Rocket Propelled Grenade. The insurgents primarily used the "RPG-7," a Soviet-era, shoulder-fired bazooka that can be used for anti-tank or anti-personnel purposes. It can be reloaded, but isn't very accurate.

OBC: Officer Basic Course. Lieutenant training. Mine was "IOBC," because I was infantry. An artillery lieutenant might go to "FAOBC" or "Field Artillery Officer Basic Course."

MAM: Military-Aged Male. Amusing unofficial alternate acronym was FAG or Fighting-Aged Guy. Due to the cultural prohibitions around women appearing in public, as well as the overall danger of Bermel, we saw many MAMs, along with male children (future MAMs) and elders (former MAMs). Part of our general "siege mentality."

Charbaron Valley: A valley to the southwest of Orgun Valley. When we did a mission there in 2007, it was on account of the Taliban having burned down the district headquarters and routed the Afghan National Police from their fort. We went in to rebuild it all, made them a great new fort, a defensible and useful Observation Post, a new district center. Then we redeployed and I lost track of what happened. Until sometime around 2010, when the 101st (Air Assault) was deployed to the region. An article in the *New York Times* reported that they had just completed a mission in the "Charbaron Valley" to secure it from insurgents and build the ANP a new district center / fort, as the old ones had been destroyed.

APC: Armored Personnel Carrier. An armored, light-tank-like vehicle with a couple cool guns that can move troops around on the battlefield. Usually capable of resisting up to .50 caliber machine guns (where the round is bigger than a grown man's middle finger), but not designed to withstand antitank weapons.

Pashtun: The ethnic group and language of southern and eastern Afghanistan (they have influence in the north of Afghanistan, and there are some millions of Pashtuns in Pakistan, mostly in the "Waziristans"). Mentioned in historical sources going back to Herodotus as an aggressive tribal culture. Not much seems to have changed.

Sharia Law: A brutal and intolerant collection of rules that's probably better than no law at all, but not by much, based (totally incidentally) on apocrypha and historical events surrounding the Koran. A flashpoint for people who derive most of their news from radio talk shows.

Ghosting: When everyone in your unit (platoon, company) turns off their GPS units so you can drive faster than normal, or go into a place you're not supposed to without being yelled at by higher. Generally speaking, indicative of that age-old tension between company-level operations and below, versus battalion-level operations and above, and the weird pervasive influence of technology and its ability to let authority figures snoop on everything you're doing, not to sound paranoid or anything. *ALSO*, in more general terms, in a civilian context, "ghosting" can mean doing anything without wanting to be hassled by others: "Hey man, where've you been for the last week, nobody's seen you out." "Sorry, I've been ghosting—got the new Elder Scrolls video game and turned off my cell phone."

Bronze Star: An award that can be given during combat operations for service or as an impact award. Subordinate to a "Silver Star" but superior to an "Army Commendation Medal." Seeing the Bronze Star on an officer's chest means one of two things: either that the officer did a good job throughout his deployment without doing anything stupid to endanger his soldiers, or that he did something heroic in combat (this will be accompanied by a "Valor" device, a gold "V"). On a sergeant's chest, it usually means that he did something heroic in combat, but higher sergeants will also receive the Bronze Star as an End of Tour

(EOT) award, at the end of a deployment. The bronze star on a soldier's chest means either that he used to be a sergeant, or he's one heroic dude (or both).

Army Achievement Medal: An award given to soldiers for doing something really well in training. Could be getting the highest score in the battalion in a rifle-shooting competition, or being the strongest or fastest soldier in the company. Incentivizes hard work outside deployment.

Aviano: A small town in Northern Italy at the foot of the Dolomites that's also home to an Air Force Base by the same name.

IDF: Indirect Fire. Rockets, artillery, mortar—basically any big explosion where the enemy is so far away or behind a hill so that they can't see exactly what they're shooting at. We have computers and GPS systems and extensive training to help us with our IDF—the enemy doesn't.

The Dress Blues: The fanciest uniform commonly worn by army officers and senior sergeants at Balls and other formal events. They get their name from the fact that they are, in fact, blue. Blue is the infantry color, as I learned in Officer Candidate School when I was compelled to memorize the official meaning behind the crest of the 11th Infantry Regiment (which begins with "blue is the infantry color").

SECTION THREE

8

Dear Mom and Dad,

I'm in Afghanistan. FOB Bermel. The journey took six days by civilian plane, an aging jet contracted by the military to shuttle troops broke over Turkey. The tail rudder froze and the plane lost steering, so the stewardesses ran around asking us to move our equipment to help balance the plane, then the pilot maneuvered by increasing power to one engine or the other. He landed it in one piece, and we spent a couple days sitting around in near-empty barracks playing cards, making sure nobody had run away overnight, and generally doing a whole lot of nothing. Another barely-serviceable contract jet arrived a couple days later and flew us to "Manas AFB," an old Soviet Air Force Base in Kyrgyzstan, near their capital, Bishkek. We arrived late at night, had time for a quick nap (my blanket was not sufficient, it was freezing), then grabbed some food and piled onto a military transport plane. We have a very small presence at Manas, and everything looked deserted, ramshackle. I don't think we were there longer than ten hours, just long enough to see massive white mountains in the distance when the sun came up. It felt different and alien—I didn't expect anything, but standing there looking at the green conifers and the vast, quiet sky, it felt like a place well suited to the Kirghiz, or the Mongols, or the Huns, or any ancient steppe tribe. Beautiful but harsh. One step away from the image I have in my head of Lovecraft's *Mountains of Madness*.

Our C-17 military transport flew us next to "Bagram Air Force Base" ("Bagram" or BAF for short). The plane flew in using evasive maneuvers, including a steep climb, a bank, and a dive that sent everyone off their seats, floating in air—pretty fun, but I can't imagine jumping under those conditions. After finding our temporary quarters we received ammunition and were manifested to fly out the next morning, to a place called "FOB Salerno." The first sergeant was angry they weren't just flying us to FOB Bermel, he seemed to feel that this Salerno leg of the trip was unnecessary and wasteful. He was incredibly worried about soldiers mixing it up with the Military Police or losing a weapon, or incidents in general; luckily, we were able to avoid trouble.

BAF—I might as well say some words about the place, though I was only there long enough for lunch and dinner. Everyone who'd been to Afghanistan before hates this place. I learned the word "Fobbit" from listening to their conversations; a "Fobbit" is someone who spends their entire deployment on base, then comes home and brags about what a tough deployment they had. Our first sergeant went on a particularly memorable rant about Fobbits during a leader meeting with the new CO and the rest of the officers. The chief complaint about BAF seems to be that it's safe, from what I can tell. People take themselves very seriously here, especially mid-level officers and enlisted personnel, but the lack of direct and immediate fighting has lulled them into a sort of complacency—it seems like most people on BAF don't realize that they are still in a war zone.

Reminders of the last war still surround us—parts of BAF are fenced off, and during a morning run I saw dog-and-human minesweeping teams scouring one of the fenced areas, moving deliberately and scanning for buried mines. Over a decade after the Taliban put an end to the "warlord" period of 1989–1996, reminders of those lawless and murderous years remain buried, or hidden in plain sight. One of the sergeants remembered an earlier deployment (with a different unit), 2003 or 2004, where the Air Force had yet to clear dilapidated Soviet jets and helicopters from the runway. He also said that when looking for insurgent rocket OPs in the mountains surrounding BAF, his platoon found walls dating back to the time of Alexander the Great. Plenty of history in the area.

We were all relieved to fly to FOB Salerno on C-130 Hercules military transport planes. When they first established the base in 2002–2003, soldiers used to call Salerno "FOB Rocket" because its proximity to Pakistan resulted in routine rocket barrages from Taliban firing just inside the border of Afghanistan, then scooting back into Pakistan. In the beginning of the war, Salerno was (again, based on what the older guys like the first sergeant say) a dangerous place—four years later in present-time, it's primarily a helicopter base, rarely rocketed, home to a company's worth of guys from the 82nd Airborne Division. When we were taking the tour—MOD stayed at Salerno two days—I asked the first sergeant what he thought of the place. He looked around and sneered: "Fobbits." He has a very binary view of the world. I think it goes without saying that I don't want to be considered a "Fobbit" by him, or people like him; this is my goal in Afghanistan, to avoid being perceived as someone who'd rather stay on the FOB than go out and patrol. Maybe this means I've finally completed my transformation into a soldier, from a skeptical and largely unwilling citizen in soldier's clothing?

Well, we took some mandatory classes and did the country briefings, the medical briefings, the briefing after briefing after briefing about what to do and what not to do, until our eyes swam with boredom, and when it was all over there were a couple more briefings, and then we were given permission to leave. It was all anyone could do to keep our eyes open, such a waste of time. At some level, there's a general or colonel with too much time on his hands who says: "we should give people classes on how to walk, to make sure they don't accidentally trip and hurt themselves," and the idea for a critical, no-miss safety class has been formed.

The instructors "certified" us as country-ready that evening. The next morning we loaded all our bags onto pallets, and waited to board the CH-47 "Chinook" helicopters that would take us to our home base, FOB Bermel. While waiting—there was some confusion with the pilots, they'd thought the flight was scheduled for later, or hadn't had their crew-rest yet, something bizarre—I saw a bird fly into the jet engine on my CH-47. For some reason this image filled me with dread— it must've been the subconscious recognition that I was about to take a very measured leap of faith by getting into a thing that did not seem like it should be able to fly under any conditions, and here was this animal getting ready to nest in its *engine*—I played cat and mouse with it to the amusement of everyone behind me, but after driving it away several times only to see it return, I gave up. The pilots arrived, we boarded the choppers, and off we went. Presumably the bird left when the engine started.

Watching the brown Afghan countryside pass beneath us from the back of the helicopter, little pockets of civilization scattered in the valleys, isolated buildings on hills and mountains, I almost felt like I was just arrived in a foreign solar system, deep in space, and looking down at the surface of some alien planet. How anyone survives here, how civilization has hung on (certainly not flourished) is a testament to the fortitude of the people.

We landed at our FOB, which is a walled compound at the bottom of a long north-south-running valley, right on the outskirts of the "Bermel Bazaar," the significant marketplace of the district and seat of the local government. Once we off-loaded the helicopters, we walked quickly from the small HLZ or "Helicopter Landing Zone" outside the base through the front gates and into our new homes. Two 105mm Howitzers pointed east into the hills and mountains that make up the border with Pakistan. Further to the West, another range of hills ran north to south, and a big hill sat five kilometers or so to our North. The ground sloped gradually downward to the South, with no hills or mountains in sight. Barbed wire ran around the outside of the FOB, giving us a couple hundred meters of standoff in every direction. The FOB itself was made up of seven-to-ten-foot high "Hesco" barriers (giant felt boxes enclosed and shaped by steel wires, and filled with earth and stone), punctuated by heavily sandbagged guard towers where guards from the unit we came to replace, 3-87, 3rd Brigade 10th Mountain Division were pulling security, standing by their machine guns. We'd arrived in Indian country.

The next few days we sat through more briefings (surprisingly, given the negative associations with the word "briefing" we'd all built up at BAF and Salerno, these were useful) on how to use their systems, what to do if the base were attacked, or rocketed, or someone was hurt, how to liaise with our Afghan partners, who the tribal power players were, and the situation on the ground. The Taliban rocketed us ineffectively a couple times and we used the opportunity for "realistic" practice on how to conduct our indirect fire drills (I say that it was realistic practice but I guess actually it was just real, the real thing). Our equipment flew in on the next round of helicopters, and we found space for it, as well as quarters for ourselves. I supervised the handoff of the equipment from the 10th Mountain guys, then got to watch—from the FOB—as the platoons started going out on patrols with the 10th Mountain guys, then later as we took over the patrols. They saw a few minor firefights. The 10th Mountain guys got on helicopters and left, and now it's just us and the cavalry troop (basically the cavalry's version of a company, they have eighty or ninety guys to our one hundred fifty). Oh—and the artillery guys we have from the 82nd, the soldiers who man the artillery pieces, which get a lot of use. A very professional and reliable group, they are constantly running practice missions, if they're not called on to fire back at their unprofessional and disorganized Taliban counterparts.

Not much more to report; I'm probably in the safest place imaginable—the best-trained regular army unit, very capable leadership, motivated and competent "assets" like the artillery guys, haphazard and almost clownishly ineffective enemy efforts. I haven't been on any patrols yet, nor am I likely to run many, and the truly dangerous places—the COPs—are not places that I'd normally need to stay for any extended period of time. This worries me, I don't want to be one of the loathed "Fobbits," I came here to fight, not to sit in an air-conditioned office counting beans and ordering port-a-shitters, but it should make you guys happy. The life of the second-in-command, very dull, perfectly safe.

I should be coming home in September or October. Thinking of you!

> Love,
> Adrian

Journal Entry: 17 May 2007

During the week-long trip from Italy, all I could think about was getting here at any cost. I had this conviction that the FOB would be attacked in force, that I'd miss the big thing, and it would be quiet afterward—this thought obsessed me, dominated my waking hours. Like in a movie or a book. Then I arrived, and it's dirt and gravel and heat and waiting, and everyone from the 10th Mountain saying, "Get used to it."

The first officer I spoke with from the 10th Mountain was the HHC XO. He was wearing a DCU / BDU brown undershirt and a faded pair of army exercise shorts and sneakers, coming back from a workout. Clean-shaven, but his hair was long, way out of regs. When he talked with me about the area, what we needed to accomplish, he would look away, into the mountains, at the ground. Rarely made eye contact. At first I thought he was afraid, but the few times he did look at me, I got the sense that he was embarrassed, that something in me was causing this embarrassment. He was on his way to the gym so I let him go. The next time I saw him he was on the way back from a run. Then there was an XO meeting on an Internet-based chat system that broke down halfway through, during which nothing of any importance was briefed. During a rocket attack that evening he showed up with a new, clean undershirt / shorts combo, and his helmet. No more engaged than he had been when headed to the gym. Cracking jokes, bored, more irritated that he couldn't find a black-ink pen than that the Taliban were shooting at us.

I have to wonder whether this is what deployment does to a person—makes one jaded and wise and finished, utterly through with the experience—so much so that communication with anyone who hasn't seen it becomes superfluous or delicate, dangerous. I've wanted to be that person for so long without understanding why, and seeing it now—maybe I haven't fully understood what I signed up for.

30 May 2007

Dear Brent,

I'm here—went on my first patrol yesterday, as you can imagine it was over-hyped and everyone had a good time at my expense. First Sergeant finally "allowed" me to wear a combat patch, tons of jokes on the patrol, and then at the Combat Outpost we were resupplying. The area has three major tribes and like eight substantial sub-tribes, all of which hate each other, on top of the Taliban that live just over the border in Pakistan and rocket us nearly every day; the place on the Venn diagram where everyone unites or agrees is dislike or hatred for the American "invaders." Everyone sees us as at *best* an irritating nuisance to be exploited whenever possible, and at worst an invader to be resisted to the death. The previous unit didn't do us any favors; we have a poor reputation among the tribes here. I can't blame them, they got extended in the middle of their redeployment home, there were actually people from their TORCH party back at Fort Drum, most of the soldiers were in Manas or BAF waiting on flights—the surge in Iraq yanked them right back out to Bermel. Of course you don't hear about this stuff on the news—if you hear anything, it's just the sexy stories, the fighting. Not how thousands of soldiers and their families were jerked around in the worst possible way. Hey, they *volunteered*, right?

So, yeah, they checked out after their mandatory extension, started patrolling very aggressively in some places, and ignoring the COIN piece in others—visited a couple villages where they complained that American soldiers from "the last unit" kicked them or threw piss bottles at them—bush-league stuff. But we're talking about a unit here that has experienced days where the Taliban fired over forty rockets at them, fairly effective fire, platoons where every gunner received a Purple Heart for being shot in the head—when I got here there were two Purple Hearts being used as paper weights—like I said, checked out. I don't *condone* their actions, and like I said the heavy-handed tactics have made our job more difficult, but I can't judge them either, I haven't seen what they have. I'd like to think that as a combat leader I'd do something to make sure things like that didn't happen with the soldiers I was patrolling with, but that's all armchair strategist bullshit.

First Sergeant and Captain Dixwell have a different leadership dynamic than the one I was accustomed to under my first CO. The best way to describe it is that there is an "in" group and an "out" group, and everyone lives in constant fear of being in the latter. The glue that keeps everything together is the constant prospect of combat—we're manning this terrible COP in a village called Marghah—the enemy seems to use it as a training exercise for squads and platoons of Taliban moving further inland, an obligatory first stop, maybe their equivalent of a live-fire exercise. We've been attacked three times already, there just isn't much you can do to stop it, there's a wadi that runs from four km out and stops like 150m outside the base—whoever designed it, I don't know what they were thinking—maybe it was one of those things where you have to negotiate with the locals and they said, "Here is where we want you to build it," and of course the locals are in cahoots with the Taliban. There's a much better place for it just 400m north, on the high ground. Obviously I should be promoted to general immediately upon joining the military for my brilliant and intuitive insight.

I can already tell that it's going to be a long tour. Things are very hot here, but there's a joy in leaving the wire that, as I just mentioned, I won't have much access to—I can already see that most of my time will be spent liaising with Afghans, checking up on projects, doing Arms Room inspections, and chasing down logistical and administrative snarls. We just received our shipping containers, the ones they sent through Pakistan—our "D-Bag" container was pilfered (probably in Karachi), thieves (maybe Taliban affiliates) took almost everything—an entire company's worth of equipment, massive FLIPL (over $250k worth stolen)—we can expect to see the Taliban in ACUs, I guess. Apparently this is not an uncommon event. So I sit on the FOB and listen to patrols getting into heavy firefights, watch the tracer bullets in the hills, battle track (our FSNCO is a guy named Carpenter, he's a huge help, really dependable and smart too—one of those guys you're very glad to have around), eat rockets... leaving the wire is going to be a struggle, but I will never turn my nose up at a mission.

Our Afghan allies have been a pleasant surprise. There are three groups here: the army, the Border Police, and the Police. I don't see much of the Border Police as they're a newer project, so don't have much of a read on them, but there are serious concerns about their corruption (at least in our area). I think the idea coming out of Kabul is, "If you're a militia and you own the area, congratulations! You're now a Border Policeman!" and that always makes for peculiar leaders and situations. The National Police are very poorly funded and seem to consist of a lieutenant in his twenties, and a few teenagers with AKs and RPGs. Few of them have uniforms, and God knows whether or not they get paid—they patrol, though, and have some really high casualty rates. The army looks better funded and trained, but still ramshackle by our standards—the decisive element in the Kandak that works with us is its battalion commander, a full colonel who has that rare blend of courage and tactical proficiency. I'd always heard about how difficult it is to get the army to patrol, but these guys ask *us* to come out on missions with them, and are pretty much down for any mission that has air support. We're lucky to have such a good partner, and his men are understandably proud to be in his unit. Personality goes a long way out here, as I'm sure you remember, maybe it comes with the territory, the Massoud effect.

If it occurs to you and you have time, by all means put together a care package. Mouthwash is in particularly short supply here, so if you could send a bottle of the good stuff, it would be much appreciated and well employed.

Take it easy,
Adrian

10 June 2007

Dear Mike,

It sounds from your letter like you're in a hell of a place. Iraq is all over the news. I heard Bob hit an IED and got lucky—us not as much. I was getting ready to talk about what a shitty friend he's been at his memorial service—here it's just a battle with these turds in the hills who rocket us two out of three days. We had a company-sized operation where I got to man the TOC while everyone else in the company played cat-and-mouse with the Taliban—the last day of the operation the Taliban fired six rockets at our FOB just to spite them. I find it difficult to imagine what it must be like for you, in a city, constrained by roads and buildings. Our constraints are wadis, hills, and mountains.

I can't believe that you guys were locked down on base after a patrol hit an IED. That makes no sense to me—wouldn't patrolling less make it *more* dangerous to go off-base? If you cede maneuver corridors to the enemy—well, like I said, I don't know what it's like in Iraq. We've been patrolling aggressively (but intelligently), taking contact on terms that are usually favorable, but we haven't had to contend with IEDs. I suppose it would be different if we had to worry about what was in the road in front of us. Here it's the high ground, the terrain, and the enemy's ability to mass fifty fighters almost as fast as you can drive into or out of some village in the middle of nowhere.

There are two towns here that we know are bad, they've always been openly sympathetic to the Taliban and likely always will be. They're in the foothills that run into the mountains and the border with Pakistan, about 7km away. Standing in a guard tower, you can watch as trucks pull up to them from Pakistan—two wadis (not roads) cross the border, but there are no border checkpoints—I guess you'd have to be Taliban to use them, that's the policing mechanism. So strange to be able to look out at a place and know that it's hostile, that walking there with a patrol would certainly provoke a firefight.

Our solution to this problem is going to be to build a COP on a hill, in the hopes that it draws attention away from our FOB. Our CO has selected a really great location that's very defensible; it's in the hills, tough to resupply. It will test the Taliban by forcing them to respond to our challenge or risk losing serious credibility with the surrounding area. It will also reverse a longstanding trend where America builds forts according to the wishes of corrupt or hostile tribes; these forts are invariably built in the worst places one could imagine. At the bottom of valleys, right next to wadis, under cliffs, at locations where the Taliban can attack us more or less unopposed, near population centers: I have seen all of these forts, and unsurprisingly, they're attacked *all the time*. I think—not that this makes a difference—but I think that this new COP is worth the effort, that it might make a difference in the long run. The simple fact is that we can't check them by patrolling; it takes too much, a massive investment of personnel and logistics for us to assemble the necessary combat power to push into their area. Doing nothing just allows them to fire rockets at us unchecked as often as they like, which is an invitation to disaster as well as corrosive to the morale of the civilian population.

The mission's weird. We're an "economy of force" effort, essentially a strategic screen for Kabul and other areas deemed "safe" inside Afghanistan. The idea, I'm told, is that if we put the American flag up here, the Taliban will pay attention to attacking us and not tear up infrastructure projects that represent the real hope for a better Afghanistan. We aren't here to defeat the enemy; that's impossible with our resources. We're here to occupy them, to distract them from the women wearing blue jeans in Kabul. And frankly, I like the idea that women can wear blue jeans and mini-skirts; I haven't seen a woman since I got here. The few times I've been out on patrol, I've never gotten closer to a woman than 150m; they are colorfully garbed, and as soon as they see an American patrol they run or walk quickly toward their village. I want to tell them, "My friend Mike isn't here, it's me, Adrian, you're not going to have to endure endless awkward conversation," but I never get close enough. At least now I know, a little bit, how you and Bob must feel every minute of every day of your lives.

So—I don't know, man, I don't know. I can't think of any other way but a COP to solve our tactical problems out here, short of leaving (which isn't an option). The interpreters are mostly from Kabul, barely understand the dialect, are terrified of the locals (I feel that they really hate the people who live out here, and look down at them as backward, and maybe using people like that is worse than having no interpreters at all). Those interpreters that are from the area—mostly Orgun-E—take every opportunity to advance themselves when possible, to leverage their position to speak with the mayor, or the chief of Police—if you let them, they always have a "great idea" for a CERP project: a well in their village, or a power generator (they'll find a way to pay for the gas), or solar panels for their family… they don't think of these things as corrupt, although it says plainly in their contracts that this type of request is forbidden; they see it as the normal way to do business. And I'm sure they get pressure from home: "Abdullah, you work for the Americans while we are starving, I would cut off my legs for you, have you asked them about a road through our village yet? No? What are you doing over there while your sisters aren't married and your brothers have no job? Do you want to bring shame to us all?" At least local interpreters can understand what the local villagers are saying. One interpreter in particular has a knack for the poetry of the area—I'm learning, from him, how to phrase things in a way that make sense to the farmers, so I don't sound like a former commissar from the city. They're very fond of analogy and metaphor, heavily reliant on animal imagery, which isn't totally surprising when you think about it.

The CERP piece—I don't know how you guys are running it in Iraq, I hear you get tons of money for programs and initiatives to improve the lives of the people in your AO—here, not so much. The amount of need that exists for all types of aid boggles the mind; the crops are constantly failing, the infant mortality rate for children under five years old is around 50%, women have no rights as soon as they get their periods, effective literacy hovers between 5% and 10%—it's impossible for an institution to provide any kind of lasting help apart from building where and whenever possible (roads, schools, clinics, wells) and giving them as much seed as possible for planting (corn, wheat, apple trees, anything that has a chance of growing in this climate). The real change they need is social and must come from within.

Bottom line is that trying to fix everything will fix nothing. Our best chance at effecting lasting change here will be if we can focus on one or two ideas that will bring long-term benefits like infrastructure (the roads are a good idea) and education (the schools, providing they remain open, are a good idea—two of the four schools that have been built here are being used for other purposes, one of the four was destroyed by the Taliban, and the last one is still squeaking along). We're trying to get a veterinarian down here to provide a "VETCAP," which is like a MEDCAP except people will get to have their herds examined by a trained doctor. My gut tells me that this will be more popular than the MEDCAP—better to let a weak kid die than prop him up for a couple years with western medicine. Or so the logic probably goes.

I tackled *Moby Dick* and lost, again. One of the other officers out here, Dave James, has a copy of Borges' short stories—I liked it, wonder if you've ever read anything by him.

> Stay safe,
> Write when you can,
> Adrian

★

15 June 2007

Dear Elsa,

Thank you for the package, it was wonderful to have one—a lot of other people have started receiving them. I don't get many, enough to keep me going, but yours was one of the best by far; I hadn't read almost any of the literature you included (except for the Shakespeare, but thank you for that anyway, it must've been a hard thing to send those) so that'll keep me well occupied in my spare time. Denis Johnson's *Jesus' Son* was particularly appreciated—one of those books where after you read it you think, "How did I go through life without that, before?" The food in the package disappeared quickly.

It's "heating up" this summer—a lot of activity from the Taliban in different areas, and our area has seen its share of events and incidents—nothing terrifying, though. Not for me, anyway, I'm safe on the FOB sitting by the radios, typing up reports, sitting in on meetings. Just the occasional "milk run" patrol, nothing to worry about—the occasional rocket glides by our FOB in the morning or in the evening (they like this time of day for some reason)—it's a whole different matter in the hills, but I'm not going on those missions. Our commander, Captain Dixwell, and his first sergeant take the hard patrols—I sit here on the base, dutifully manning the communications platforms, recording the events I hear over the radio. In other words I'm usually close enough to hear the gunfire and watch the tracer-fire skip off the hillsides, but far enough away that it's all spectator sport.

I don't mean to suggest that this is sport, though there is an unusual and unexpected element of *spectacle* involved at a level absent from warfare for some time. Whereas in the old days civilians could go to a battlefield and watch the armies fight it out (and according to evidence this actually happened with battles like First Bull Run in our Civil War); nowadays it's the people in the TOC that get to watch everything in black and white on video feed from either attack jets or pilotless drones. We have a small 15-inch screen computer, like a laptop, that our Air Force liaison uses to control the planes—eventually we're in line to get a big monitor to hang up on the wall so more people can see—during a fight, or when these planes or drones "acquire a target," soldiers, sergeants and officers filter into the TOC to watch the action—it's like television. Either Captain Dixwell makes the tactical decisions, or—if the fight's very serious—he'll call back to the battalion FOB (thirty or so miles to our West, over a mountain range, might as well be back in America) and our battalion commander will decide. If the battalion commander can hear the same radio transmissions and watch the same video feed as Captain Dixwell—keep in mind he's separated from us by a mountain range, so this is a 50/50 proposition at best—he'll just run the battle himself.

So, you have a group of people standing around watching a television, one of whom has to decide whether or not the little white blips on the screen are enemies (I can assure you that most of the time we assume that they are)—if not, then we let them go about their business. Otherwise, we drop bombs on them or strafe them until the white human-shaped blobs stop moving. That's a significant portion of our interaction with the enemy, and it's as close as we get to having "eyes-on"; we might as well be sitting in the same seat as the pilot. You can imagine this gets to be tricky business on the border of Pakistan, where the PAKMIL stations their soldiers. To say nothing of the moral complexity of the whole process, the attribution and assignment of participation in a room full of people—one's obligation as an observer—I've seen it, I've seen one person in twenty say, "How can we be sure they're Taliban?" and that was enough to prevent us from dropping bombs that day. Of course we did get hit the next morning by rockets on timers, almost certainly emplaced by the group we'd been observing and convinced ourselves were simply woodcutters. But this is how it works: the first time you watch the screen, you say, "What am I looking at?" and someone explains that the white blobs are people, and the things on their backs are RPGs or rifles (or shovels, or who knows what). And you ask, "How can you be sure?" and the person says, "After nightfall, everything moving out there is Taliban. They know we shoot when they're in the hills, honest people avoid it." And, boom, you've just been conditioned to evaluate the video feed in the "proper" way, which is to say, in the way people seem to have been evaluating it for some time here, with a good degree of accuracy. We haven't killed any women or children by this means. But if we do, and, say, Captain Dixwell was the one who ordered the bombing, I feel that it's not *his* fault for issuing the command but that it's also each of *our* faults for not advising him not to if there were serious doubts about the target's identity.

I'm fairly certain this facet of war is unique to the current conflict—not since the old way of fighting went out of style (line up two groups of swordsmen or riflemen and hack / blaze away until one side capitulates) did commanders have the ability to visualize the battlefield at this level of precision, especially using battle-tracking systems like FBCB2, which plots the location of helicopters and vehicles on a map that updates in real-time (sort of like those fancy GPS car navigation systems you hear about). Even in what people call "Generation II Warfare" (two lines shooting at one another) the leaders, the generals surveying the battlefield from a hill safely to the rear, had a very limited ability to affect things, mostly (from what I've read) just a matter of "committing the reserves" at the right time. What I see is intervention at a very high level: colonels moving around teams and squads on the battlefield, directing individual vehicles. This is possible today, technology has made it possible. And it shifts the way people approach the war, how they think about it. So much so that at the officer level, there are substantial differences between today and even an occupation as recent as that of the Soviet Union. They maintained border forts as well, outposts of one hundred soldiers or eight hundred soldiers, but really couldn't hope to push those outposts too far from their main camp. And it was even worse with the British one hundred years ago; communication was impossible beyond the reach of a rider on horseback. That's not how we think any more, of course, there's less risk putting bases that can't really reinforce each other by ground.

So, overall, it's safer to be at war today than at any other time in human history. Which is great news for me!

Affectionately,
Adrian

Journal Entry: 24 June 2007

Couple of journalists have made their way to FOB Bermel, Tom Coghlan and Jason Howe (a photojournalist). I brought them in, showed them around, but before I could give them the full tour, the First Sergeant reminded me that I wasn't supposed to let them into the command post. I forget how I'm an army officer sometimes. What that means. Don't trust the media. Make sure they can't see the secret stuff such as maps of where they are. Don't let them see how many rockets have hit the base, let them ask the soldiers who will tell them. Establish an aura of impenetrable secrecy, because then they'll be friendly and not want to burn you.

Mr. Coghlan gave me a book called *Dispatches* by Michael Herr, in exchange for which I gave him one of my favorite books, and warned him away from *Absurdistan*, one of the worst books I've started reading and had no interest in finishing. So far I think it's been a fair trade. Pity we can't be proper *friends* though, what with the army and the media being enemies.

26 June 2007

Dear Jim,

Well, we're finally in it, old man, we're doing it. The dream of being at war together—didn't quite make that happen the way it might've—but why split hairs. In World War II I'd have been somewhere in the Pacific or maybe in Burma, and you'd be pushing hard against the Nazis—going off the relative importance and attention given our respective theaters—and both had our stories, which due to time and circumstance were (and are) not in competition with one another. You're in the heart of the Iraq surge, trying to stabilize or bring honor to a bad, bad situation; I'm on the edge of the empire, fighting ceaseless skirmishes with the barbarians just over the border, just beyond the reach of our power.

How are your ideas about war changing? What is happening to your civilian ideas about the proper use of America's overwhelming military advantage, about the limitations of our army and how it should and can be employed effectively? Have you begun asking yourself why cell phones and cities and iced coffee makes men want to seek death on alien planets? And whether that's simply part of civilization, part of the grand bargain?

I'm becoming skeptical that any of this is a good idea. I've seen good leaders, good people change when subjected to the pressures of war and decision-making under duress; even a choice that seems safe or innocuous like calling for air strikes or artillery on a suspected insurgent column from the feed off a drone or a jet fighter can lead to problems. No matter how many rifle-carrying insurgents we kill, they only seem to increase in numbers and proficiency. We've recently experienced a thing I'd only read about in accounts describing the experience of the German army operating in Russia in World War II: loss of operational mobility. It doesn't affect our combat units much—like the Germans—it affects our logistical resupply—like the Germans. Resupply trucks are no longer willing to make the trip over the hills separating us from our battalion headquarters, just thirty miles away over a single mountain line—this is a trip that was safe, for the most part, since 2003; at least safe enough for the truck drivers to make the trip in groups of five or ten trucks. After several convoys were attacked and burned the drivers won't come out here with less than fifty trucks, and an armed escort of at least one U.S. platoon. Up until this point this is how we've gotten our fuel and food. We are unable to stop the Taliban, and their operations have a direct effect on us.

We've started receiving food via airdrop, so, in a sense, we're cut off. Again, not completely—we can patrol to beef up our supplies, but there are over three hundred people on our base between our company, the CAV troop, and the ETT National Guard training group, and the food goes fast. We get some of it parachuted in from C-130s or C-17s, conventional "CDS" drops, which is a massive investment of time and effort (especially when many of those drops get scattered because the pilots don't want to risk getting shot down by flying low), some via Blackwater contractors who fly low in prop planes and push two bundles at a time out the backs of the planes from 150 feet—real daredevils—and the rest off helicopters, our own and a contract company we call "Jingle Air" (like Jingle Trucks) that uses former Soviet pilots *familiar with the area* flying Mi-8 transport helicopters to bring in two to three pallets per lift. The only way to get fuel is by truck, so we just mount deliberate operations for those supply runs.

So the trajectory here is not one of increased safety and security, it really isn't. We're building a COP next month that should give us a bit more standoff and make this area, our immediate footprint more secure; I doubt that it will have any serious or lasting effect in the district. Our battalion has started to take casualties—nothing significant in our company yet, thank God. Our brigade has taken worse up north, in Kunar and Nuristan Provinces, including a commander in the CAV squadron who I remembered from his time as a company commander with 1-503rd, Tom Bostick, a really great leader. There's a building sense of futility here that our new COP may help to reverse—again, we've had some very good tactical successes. My commander, Captain Dixwell, is a genius at this sort of thing, at finding devious and innovative new ways to kill Taliban—but when three or four Taliban spring up to take the place of each fighter we kill, what's it really accomplishing? Our screening mission?

Meanwhile, exposure to life at home is pretty damned depressing. The politics, the seeming decline of our culture, the ignorance about what happens out here every day—the reality of civilian life in America is probably the highest threat to morale we face. I've come to develop a real fear and hatred of *spotlighting*, and the drive for celebrity and fame—we've elevated it to a national pastime, it's become part of our patriotic, collective self-delusion. How do you explain the popularity of sports during a time of struggle? We Americans are too well entertained, too complacent. It's easy to declare war, or intervention, or whatever we call these things today—the politicians pursue their obscure goals, and everyone else watches the Oscars and the Super Bowl. Meanwhile, a man dies in Afghanistan or Iraq.

Of course we need sports; our society needs them to provide a spectacle, to offer us release from otherwise dangerous impulses. Life without the distraction of hollow heroes—do you remember that one running back with the Pittsburgh Steelers, I think it was Merrill Hoge? Or the baseball great for the Detroit Tigers, Hank Greenburg? Neither do I. But someone does, someone assigns importance to those things. Out here in *rural* rural Afghanistan, or in Iraq—maybe you see more civilization in Iraq—they don't have sports (at least from what I've seen—kids kick deflated soccer balls around, but no *buzkashi*, no cricket), they have *war*. They have martyrs. Their national heroes are those people who are good or effective at killing the enemy. I do feel that there's a connection, that sports provide a certain amount of release, like a safety valve, for the violent pressures generated by society.

Let your mother know to keep the packages coming, she's a wizard with this—my new best friend—just a wonderful, lovely supporter. Ripped through *Quartered Safe Out Here* and *The Complete McAuslen* in record time. Thanks for giving her my address. Stay well over there!

Affectionately,
Adrian

★

4 July 2007

Dear Mom and Dad,

It's been a little while since the last time I wrote, so I wanted to send a quick update! I'm in an unusually good mood tonight—it's the 4th, we popped some flares for the fireworks show, and the Taliban responded with rockets. On top of my duties and responsibilities—there's a big operation coming up, which will probably give me more chances to patrol—it's a lot of fun, getting off the base. I go to places that are safe, look at building projects that are underway, assess future projects, talk with elders, that sort of thing. A big operation means that I'm sort of running the normal show back on the base while the rest of the company is off in the hills or mountains playing hide-and-seek with the bad guys.

There's a lot to be grateful for over here. The Afghans live in unimaginable poverty; if you haven't seen it, you can't picture what it's like. Mom, I'm guessing it's *even worse* than whatever you saw on the Navajo reservation in the '70s. Except replace "alcoholism" with "the ever-present specter of warfare" as the proximate cause of said poverty (I'm trying to be generous and not suggest that anything else could be responsible lest others accuse me of cultural imperialism). Walking through the market recently with a dismounted patrol, we passed a butcher's shop, where they had skinned goats hanging—you could see the cloud of flies around the meat—the butcher's assistant slapped the corpse to keep the flies off when a customer walked in. That afternoon I had kabob with the mayor—probably the same goat. There's a medicine here, Cipro, that I take like candy to keep the pathogens away. God only knows what it's doing to my insides.

Our anti-malarial medicine is Mefloquin, which is a weekly pill (we all take it on Monday, which is called "Mefloquin Monday" as a consequence) that causes some seriously weird, super-realistic dreams. I look forward to taking it; the dreams fade in intensity as the week goes on, but Monday and Tuesday night are usually fun, almost spiritual journeys. I had one dream that was so much like reality that when I woke up, I wondered if I'd been to sleep at all, or if I'd just remembered the day before and had not dreamt at all—then I thought, "Ah, this is what they mean when they say 'having trouble distinguishing fantasy from reality.'" Although when fantasy is exactly like reality, that's not much of a problem.

We've had some strange personality conflicts brew up here of late, people going a bit funny in the head. We switched areas with the CAV (though we still live on the same FOB), so they have the North and we have the East—it's engendered some ill will between our units that nobody's dealt with. Seems sort of pointless to me, maybe even counterproductive—it's really because there hasn't been any kind of action the last week or so, and the stress of waiting. We're so used to competing with the Taliban that it's becoming a habitual way of interacting: when we're not competing with the Taliban, we compete with the CAV, when we're not competing with the CAV we compete with each other, and when there's nobody else around we're in the gym competing with ourselves. I'm still a fundamentally collaborative person, so I hate this recent development, I just want us all to get along and get the job done.

Well—that's it for the most part—settled into my role as XO, I've accepted my lot as the logistical officer, and play other roles as needed. It's satisfying to see the side of things where we help people and do what we can to bring a little bit of comfort to a place where people live in the dirt and mud, in awful, miserable conditions. Whether or not our ways stick out here at the edge of the world, we'll have done a little bit of real human good where we could. That makes it all worthwhile.

Deodorant is not in short supply, I was wrong. I got my advice from Iraq vets. It's baby wipes and laundry detergent, that's the thing here. Please send more. And don't bother with chocolate, it melts, and there's precious little refrigeration where we are. Maybe in the winter.

Love,
Adrian

Journal Entry: 28 July 2007

An engineer company has arrived and brought the comforts of Bagram along with them. I'd forgotten the simple comfort of a thing like fresh cheese or the texture and taste of ice-chilled fruit, ice in a soft drink, sauces beyond ketchup and French's mustard. I slathered a cheeseburger with Dijon mustard and Heinz ketchup and fresh lettuce, onions, and relish—took my time with it, didn't just bolt the thing, chewed every bite. Took me back to Japan for some reason—Hanami season—and, an unexpected, effusive and pervasive feeling of gratitude. Everything ends so quickly, without warning, even bad or boring experiences fade into the past almost without one noticing. Part of living well is understanding when you have it good, not taking fortune for granted. It's also important not to begrudge others their happiness.

I enjoyed another sublime Afghan mountain sunset today, sitting in the summer solitude of the last outpost of civilization before Pakistan begins, before savagery and murder replace law and order. Everything I learned in civilization has been reversed here—East is danger, and West is safety. The old religious models have it backwards. When the sun goes down it's safe—we can see them, and they can't see us. Sundown heralds peace and quiet, and, if necessary, victory; sunup—a renewal of the struggle. Maybe this is simply life in the desert, or life on the fringe.

1 August 2007

Brent,

By the time this letter reaches you, you'll have already heard about Major Bostick's death—probably already attended the funeral. Just wanted to send my sympathy and condolences, I know you had a chance to work for him, and held him in high esteem. I was in the TOC along with Captain Dixwell and 1SG and was tracking the battle as it unfolded over the army version of AOL instant messaging and sporadic TACSAT—hell of a thing. I'm sure you'll hear all about what happened and how at the funeral; I won't go into details here.

The event made me think about Camp Keating (1-91 was at Kamu), which is where Legion Company is posted this deployment. I saw some pictures, and it looks hellish—a tiny valley surrounded by giant hills—nearly impossible to defend. I complain about Bermel's location sometimes—we're constantly getting rocketed from foothills that are too far from us (and too close to enemy strongholds), we're in the middle of a big valley—but we're at the far edge of the effective range of those rockets. There's a COP here that I may have mentioned already, the "Margah COP," that we started manning and then handed over to the CAV troop that's stationed here—it's a lot like Keating, in *tactically* one of the worst places anyone could have put it. They threw it up in 2006–7, I think it was a 10th Mountain installation. One of those places that was supposed to increase our ability to live with the population and develop better ties to them, and as time has gone on, really only serves to offer the Taliban a convenient target whenever they want to fire off a few rounds without serious fear of reprisal.

It's so weird, though, man: Iraq is all over the news, and here we are, just kind of squeaking by in silence. You know where I'm coming from—sometimes I just feel like it's so senseless. We don't have the assets to make this strategy work, so everything turns into a "screen" or a "holding action" or "economy of force" effort—everything is circular, our reason for being out here in the bases is to be out here in the bases, to protect ourselves and the outlying COPs (which are there to protect the FOB, and vice versa). In situations like this, what's right: to hunker down and do nothing, ceding the area to the enemy, or patrol aggressively and lose American soldiers while pursuing a doomed strategy that has no immediate and very low long-term prospects for success? What's it worth? And then to lose a guy like Tom Bostick. Fuck, man.

Adrian

Journal Entry: 5 August 2007

Three of the interpreters asked for emergency leave today. It's times like these that I really hate my impossible position—forced to read selfishness into my fellow-humans' behavior, to question motives and seek subterfuge. Out here, in my role as XO, my first thought was that they have huge families, so naturally someone is sick or dying once every week or so—they only use that as an excuse to go home when they don't want to be here. I then quickly assumed that they'd gotten wind of the upcoming operation, which is bound to be long and fairly dangerous. Despite their being humans, as I have to remind myself, and some of them really fine, patriotic humans with whom I'd get along really well under different circumstances, I'm forced here to look at them and think things like, "As a group, the interpreters are the most narcissistic and cowardly pack of scoundrels I've ever encountered." That's being generous with my ungenerous thoughts. I've had much worse.

Perhaps they understand the system, which dictates that we take them out on patrol with us. Even though most of the terps can barely speak the dialect here, they give us a certain stamp of authenticity—if something were to go wrong because a lieutenant forgot an interpreter, it would be the lieutenant's (and captain's) fault. If, on the other hand, something went wrong but the interpreter was there—he simply failed to interpret something correctly—that means it's not the lieutenant's fault. Even though the interpreters rarely interpret anything correctly, and we know that, and can't do anything about it.

So even though they do nothing for us save as the bureaucratic symbol of how things should be done a certain way, the interpreters must stay here, regardless of their sick and dying cousins and siblings and grandaunts. Hell, my grandfather's sick and old, and I don't get to go home to see him. This isn't even my country. This is why Afghanistan's going to fail—people who are making three times the average income don't want to stick their necks on the line.

I guess that could go for back home too, come to think of it.

10 August 2007

Dear Teddy,

I'm writing from our newly constructed COP, a marvel of modern engineering. We picked the most defensible hill: an engineer company came out and terraformed it, we cut down the forest for 150m in every direction, built an HLZ, improved a couple trails leading up to it, and now there's a triangular fortification with three towers that is wholly capable of resisting all but the most dedicated enemy attack. It would take hundreds of Taliban to overrun our base, maybe all of the Taliban in the area (they're really Haqqani out here). I doubt that they'll risk it.

Best of all, it means a stop to the rocket attacks that have been a regular part of my experience on FOB Bermel. The COP overlooks the best places to fire rockets at us, so now the FOB with its huge fuel tanks and food and ammo depot will be safe while there are no easy ways to hit the COP... pretty small, and well designed to resist fire... no overlooking high ground from which to shoot... unpredictable wind patterns because of the mountains... genius. Most of the FOBs and COPs I've seen here were established as contingency outposts, part of presence patrolling that assumed (as we all did) in 2003–2004 that the Taliban were gone—as a result they're in *terrible* tactical locations, but often easily accessed by roads or helicopters.

We've been having trouble getting regular food shipments, which has reduced the menu variety to a Mexican dish, a chicken dish, a shrimp dish, and reheated pizza when we're not eating MREs. The Taliban have mastered the art of ambushing our "jingle truck" food resupply convoys, so I'd become fairly accustomed to "want" until the major operation recently, when the engineers showed up. The additional security on the only road between us and our battalion FOB in Orgun-E allowed for several large resupply pushes, and consequently, for two weeks we enjoyed a menu we hadn't experienced in months. Spaghetti, hamburgers, actual chicken, a soup I'd never seen before. Daily helicopter flights brought in fresh fruit and vegetables (and—importantly—cheese for cheeseburgers). Credit to our cooks and the conditions they work with. Anyway, that's all memory now—the engineers have gone, and with them that delicious "Bagram-quality" FOB food. The working refrigerator is stocked with Diet Pepsi and water again, no more fancy sodas such as Mountain Dew and Dr. Pepper, and we're on our second straight day of "Shrimp Scampi," also known as "Shrimp Butter," or just "Melted Butter with Shrimp Flavor and Rice." How the Taliban know to leave the Shrimp Butter truck alone is a mystery, but that one always manages to make it through the ambush, just like the spaghetti truck always gets burned. Why?

The few times I've been out to a COP and had dispensation to spend the night, the food has been better—most of the steak and hamburger goes to the units that have to spend a week or two without access to showers and exposed to constant risk of attack—they get first choice of dinners, of soda / soft drinks, of everything—and they all have cooks. Dinner is almost always "grill" or meat cooked on a BBQ. If I could live on a COP I would; it's also cut off from the constant, nonsensical demands of "higher" (probably located somewhere in BAF, an office dedicated to bedeviling us all), and I'm sure I could go without a shower for a couple weeks (that doesn't sound great, actually).

During the construction of our new COP, we took a trip down to the base to our south, FOB "Shkin," which is on the border with Pakistan. America and Afghanistan have a couple of OPs there, manned mostly by the ANA with some army advisors. The Taliban attack these OPs from within Pakistan nearly every day. FOB Shkin itself is home to a group of Afghan commandos that receive training from a Special Forces team. They're about twenty kilometers south of us, but they could almost be in another country—the only way down is through a wadi, which floods periodically (sometimes with us in it). Traveling at ten mph and stopping or slowing down at points to mitigate risk of ambush or IED, the trip takes between one and two hours. We made the journey for a "white flag border meeting" with the Pakistani military—an event that was so far as I can tell largely unscripted, with no State Department supervision—an unusual event that was long overdue.

We stopped at Shkin briefly to pick up our SF counterparts, then drove to the ANP compound by the border, parked our vehicles, and left for Pakistan. It was the first time I'd seen the official border crossing from Pakistan (the village of Angorada) into Afghanistan (Shkin) in our district this one time, and it struck me as remarkably representative of the problems Afghanistan faces. On the Afghan side, twenty or so Afghan Police lined a strand of triple-strength concertina wire (razor wire), with a group of four Afghan Police by a dilapidated mud hut. A small line of tribesmen waited to cross into Pakistan, and the ANP were busily waving individuals through. On the Pakistani side, it looked like around 100 soldiers lined the same wall of concertina wire, with several trucks mounting heavy weapons, and a compound of buildings near the gate. A long line of tribesmen snaked back into Pakistan. The Pakistan military were performing diligent and meticulous checks on people—I only saw one car allowed through while we walked toward the crossing.

As soon as the Afghan police saw us, they stood up straighter, and the group at the checkpoint began checking for passports and looking through the car in front of them—felt sort of bad for the station wagon, hated to be the cause of their holdup in the line, the agent of misfortune. The group at the wire turned around to face their disciplined Pakistani counterparts; now that the Americans were here, the Afghans had to pretend that things were being done a certain way… I assume they'd been punished in the past for lax security, or poor discipline. Don't get me wrong, I didn't want a suicide bomber killing me and a bunch of other people that day, but—I don't know, my feeling was, "Do your own thing, don't let me dictate how you get the job done right, doing things 'the way the Americans like it' will probably infuriate the locals, do it however it works, period." Sure enough, the line on both sides of the border erupted in honking and gesticulation as all progress ground to a halt.

We arrived at the checkpoint and were met by a delegation of Pakistani officers, who told us in English that we should follow them, which we did. Our Afghan officer delegation—an ANP lieutenant colonel and a couple lieutenants—remained behind. We entered Pakistan, and our hosts led us into some nondescript concrete military compounds where we met the battalion commanders (or their representatives) of the regular PAKMIL units on their side of the border (the 6th Punjab, and 13th and 21st Sindh—sounded like something out of Kipling). These were all uniformed officers, and we had a somewhat fruitless but broader-scale useful trust-building session where we marked our respective unit locations on each other's maps, and tried to come up with better ways of communicating cross-border to stop rockets and Taliban patrols from attacking our bases. There's no point in bringing proto-militias like the Frontier Corps into these discussions, most of those organizations are wholly supportive of the Taliban. After the meeting we had food, and I chatted up a PAKMIL captain who talked about playing polo at some school in England. One of the PAKMIL LTCs said that I looked like a Pakistani, which made me an immediate source of entertainment for all and sundry. Then we left, without incident.

I've sat in many of the routine district shuras, with the mayor of Bermel and influential elders representing the various tribes. The elders attend in greater or smaller numbers depending on recent events or a perceived threat of attack (the Taliban will sometimes fire rockets at the meeting—it's held at the district center, directly adjacent to our compound). Since arriving here I've become fairly disillusioned with the immediate promise of progress through dialogue and diplomacy. I had a sense that having been certified through Charlie Pillsbury's mediation licensing course in New Haven, I could solve everyone's problems in a day (I'm not suggesting Charlie taught me to expect that it would work—on the contrary, his course taught the opposite, that mediation was a process)—and the lack of measurable progress has been disheartening. Whatever gains we make here through dialogue—and there is a utility in staying connected through communication, in developing relationships, even in a place where relationships are measured in decades and centuries rather than months or years—will be the gains that last, much more so than those transient changes we see on the battlefield. The border flag meetings are an integral part of that, because talking with the PAKMIL is the closest we get to communicating directly with the Taliban (apart from the "talking" we do with guns and bombs).

My job here—that of any combat officer, platoon leader, executive officer, company commander or above—is, in addition to everything else, that of a diplomat. Everyone has their own idea about what that entails—mine is that as a representative of the United States of America, I'm making a good-faith effort to do as much as I can for a country that's much less privileged than mine, filled with people no different from me. This attitude, I hope, will carry me through the overwhelming amount of resistance, frustration, and setback I (and everyone) encounters at every turn. It also seems like it should be the proper attitude to hold—it feels right—why would anyone not want to treat others well, if we all agree that Jesus' Golden Rule is the standard (and eminently achievable).

Love,
Adrian

Journal Entry: 22 August 2007

Another mission into the hills. Another scheme. A plan to terraform and fortify a hill so that hill can be attacked. Clear the trees. Set in the Claymore mines. Establish sectors of fire for the machine guns, and target reference points for the mortars and artillery. Separate the groups into people who live at the COP—the cool kids—and people who don't—the uncool kids. There won't be enough platoons left to patrol effectively, but we weren't patrolling effectively before, either.

You could pour ten thousand soldiers into this valley and it wouldn't be enough.

We are just here to attack and defend. The logic of our presence doesn't extend beyond this valley. It's pinyon trees and scrub, and ripped plastic bags hung up on strands of concertina wire at the bottom of a hill, and poor children trying to steal enough to survive, and nights so hot you can feel it weighing down on you, the whole empty sky.

★

27 August 2007

Dear Dad,

There wasn't much time to react or talk when I heard the news, so I wanted to write more after I had a chance to let it all sink in. Now that it has, there isn't much to say. I'm so sorry I wasn't there to help with Grandpa's funeral, or be more available in general. The CO, Captain Dixwell gave me some time off the day I heard the news—I did my immediate grieving then, got back to work, and this is the first chance I've had to sit down and process everything. I'm very good at compartmentalizing.

I didn't write him enough, I didn't see him when I could. That's the first thing. I was waiting until I got back—I guess in my mind it would've been a pretty short visit, a matter of hours, but I'd see him, catch up, hear him talk, swap war stories. I'm sure as the night went on I'd have gotten bored, and looked for ways to scoot out, find a bar, go drinking. It never really occurred to me that he wouldn't be around—and now he's gone.

He was tough to be around. I haven't met many characters like him in my life, and they were mostly from his generation. Mom's dad was similar, curmudgeonly, cussed, set on getting their own way, but also deeply in tune with hardship, suffering. Maybe it's what they saw in WWII, maybe it was growing up during the Great Depression. Or both, plus the fact of life before medicine and technology made it safe to have children, or cured polio, or all other diverse forms of sickness and malady that were probably quite familiar to their generation. Mom's mom losing all of her siblings to horrible accidents. Your mom dying in childbirth. A certain type of personality—a guy like Grandpa

Wes—I feel that when you experience enough pain you just kind of "button up," stop trying to put yourself out there. You do just enough to survive, to feel good, and nothing more. That was him, always *aggressively* nonchalant about society. Opinionated and gruff. Also a kind man, trapped in a prison of his own construction.

I wish I could've been at the funeral, at least, but the only dispensation that they grant to leave a war zone is the death of an immediate relative (brother, sister, father, mother). I think even then I might not leave—if the choice were up to me I'd have to think about it—it would be surreal to be home and away from my allotted time, and I'd be worrying constantly that I was creating hardship for the unit, that my absence would somehow be responsible for other people dying. I'm so far inside this experience right now that anything that smacks of the personal, of the "me" seems selfish, unfair—like I'd be "getting over." I guess they'd probably make me come home, and I'd be glad that I did—but it would be a difficult thing. I wish that I could have attended the funeral.

When I'm back for leave—that makes it even tougher to think about, the fact that I was so close to seeing him again, a little more than a month—I'll grab a bottle of scotch and remember him, remember the good times, sitting around the table as a family, with him as the smiling patriarch. Well, wherever he is, at least he doesn't have to deal with a lot of *people* now—at least, the type of people he always professed to dislike!

Hope you're well, and going through your own process; sorry I had to miss everything. Your dad was a really unusual guy, which caused you and your brother a lot of hardship growing up, but it turned out all right in the end. As it always does, inevitably. He'd agree with me there.

    Miss you guys,
    Love,
    Adrian

30 September 2007

Dear Mike,

 I'm writing from Bagram Air Force Base, more commonly known as "BAF" or "Bagram." Haven't been writing much of anything lately, or reading, just working a lot—operations, the grind—my last remaining grandparent died recently, before I had a chance to see him on leave, and it's been easier not to think about anything than to correspond with people. I'm going on leave now, but I don't really want to—did you have that experience? Is it some bizarre perversity in me and my area, or is it common to everyone? This fear that something big will happen while I'm away, and I'll have missed it?

 I hope all's well for you in Mosul. It sounds like things are just miserable over there, but that the surge is working. At this point, I know enough about how things go in the streets to understand that nothing gets reported exactly right; the news is always flawed when you're hearing it from a field grade officer or above (with very occasional exceptions—great read I found recently called *Toxic Leadership* that some LTC wrote in 2004, it probably doomed his career but he tells a lot of truths to which I've borne witness), and the administration is essentially run by propagandists. So, I sure fucking hope the surge is working, because over here it takes two weeks to get replacement parts for mission-critical equipment because of "Iraq."

 It's a strange thing, to think that a surge of some tens of thousands of troops could bring stability to a country as populous as Iraq—the cities: that makes it seem feasible, the concentration of population, the concentration of power and politics—I can say for certain that such a surge would fail here. The only cities in Afghanistan worth mentioning are Mazir-e-Sharif, Kabul, Jalalabad and Kandahar, and even if we were to provide 100% security in them, which would probably take more than the 30,000 soldiers we have here now (or at least every single one of them—and you know as well as I do that only a percentage of the "30,000" are actual combat troops), securing those cities (which I think was the Russians' plan) would essentially cede 90% of the population and the entire agricultural output of the countryside to the Taliban, who would then run wild. To "secure" Afghanistan militarily would require, on average, a battalion per *district*—not sure how many districts there are in a province, but there are thirty-four provinces, and our province has nineteen districts, of which our battalion of six companies (A Co, Anvil Troop, C Co, D Co, HHC, and E Co) is responsible for, I think, nine. PRT has a couple, 82nd has five or six, and the Polish and Romanians have a couple. So in one of the most dangerous places in Afghanistan, the place where a whole number percentage of the TICs occur, the place where one would logically station an infantry battalion, rather than a "surge" you see massive swaths of terrain uncovered, and, unsurprisingly, the Taliban are all up in this shit, swarming.

I'm not second guessing the generals—but if you have a mandate to "secure" Afghanistan without ceding an inch of territory to the Taliban, and 30,000 soldiers to do it with, what *can* you do? What are the options? Other possibilities would incur the possibility of failure—*different* failure, which is much riskier than the accepted form of failure we have today, which we call "conditional success." No general would sign up for something like that. And what's the point, the rate of failure here has been acceptable, for the most part—nobody wants to preside over something catastrophic. So—as I think through this—that's it, we've hit upon a very comfortable way to preside over a slow, not-precipitous and inevitable decline of power and *influence* here.

Of course nobody can say that publicly. It'd be pointless and destructive to talk with one's soldiers about that or topics like it; the only thing that a frank discussion would accomplish would be to brand me as a defeatist, or pointlessly negative. You can't talk about how *nobody knows why we're still in Afghanistan* or *if things continue on the way they are now we will certainly lose and the Taliban will win* or *Pakistan is Afghanistan's enemy*. This is all heresy. So instead, now that we lack an official department of the censor, I consign it to personal correspondence. It's what everyone's going to be asking me when I get home for leave, right? "Are we winning?" "So, what do you think our chances are?" "How's it going?" And I'll have to trot out the same tired smile, talk about the rights of women, educating little girls, blue jeans, bubble gum, and how most Muslims are just good ordinary everyday people, just like you and me.

I flew out to BAF on leave pretty early so I'm here for a few days. Luckily the head of the ALOC up here, a guy named Dave Palmer, is a friend of mine, we were XOs together before he was put in charge of the ALOC. Former marine, soft-spoken, really good guy; it's great spending time away from Bermel, walking around on a base where I don't have to worry about eating a rocket every morning and afternoon. Helping him out with little tasks. Seeing my supply sergeant, who gets 90% of the logistical legwork done for our company. If part a of thing's to be had in Afghanistan, you can find it on BAF. We have nothing, and a huge percentage of the really good kit we get is stuff my supply sergeant wrangles through what we call the Supply Sergeant Mafia. He's one of the best—I can't thank him enough or provide him with enough praise and credit—just a top-rate guy. I'd look like a total incompetent without him. Or if I had a bad supply NCO, like some of my fellow XOs.

It was an unusual trip to BAF. We had a really important border flag meeting a few days ago where we got the PAKMIL liaison to IS-AF—a guy I'll call LTC T—to come out and help us make progress with our cross-border counterparts. A PAKMIL infantry officer. His presence at the meeting helped us to make some progress with our PAKMIL counterparts, but nothing decisive; meanwhile, the Afghans probably think we're all spies, or in cahoots.

After the meeting and back on FOB Bermel, LTC T got his own Blackhawk to pick him up, and I hopped on board to grab an empty seat. It was a little on the early side, I didn't need to be in BAF for a couple days, but air is pretty irregular. If it were a matter of me jumping on one of the "jingle air" helicopters, I'd have no trouble reaching BAF or anywhere else, they fly almost daily. But "rotary wing assets" from the U.S. can go up to two weeks between turns. People have gotten stuck before, missed their leave dates, which fouls up the system. I got to see some pretty weird places, and speak with LTC T in person—fascinating guy. The point he made, during a stopover in Ghazni at a base manned by Turkish soldiers, when I asked him point-blank why Pakistan wasn't doing as much as I thought they should against the Taliban, was that what we see as a Counter-Insurgency, they see as a civil war, and not many people in Pakistan's army wanted to shoot or fight people they saw as first and foremost their countrymen, especially not at the urging of a foreign power (us). That makes sense to me on a human level, I don't know why more isn't made of it, rather than the litany of complaints one hears about how they aren't doing enough to pursue the Pakistani Taliban. I can't imagine how I'd react if the roles were reversed, and I was being told by a foreigner to hunt down and kill people from my town of Branford, or East Haven, or Guilford—or Texas. It would be difficult for me to rationalize acting on behalf of any other country, or even my own, if the lives of my countrymen were at stake (no matter if they were deluded by some awful medieval ideology).

I'll leave the thought train there, before it derails into the bog of whether or not a citizen—or a soldier—can actually imagine having to defend the constitution from *all* enemies: foreign *and domestic*. The Korean chow hall closed here recently, which had been where I was taking lunch—fortunately there's a small DFAC here called "The Rib Shack" that does decent BBQ and has a small cult following. As with everywhere, the taste of the food is improved by the knowledge that it is a secret taste, that most transients at BAF never learn about it… stay well, and look forward to seeing you next time.

        Faithfully,
        Adrian

Journal Entry: 1 October 2007

The difference between my life in Bermel and my life on Bagram Air Force Base is almost unthinkable. There's a massive gulf—here, people are well fed on discipline and the order of their various procedural obligations. Back on Bermel, there's an unspoken urgency behind every action. I find myself frustrated, almost violently so, when I sense that things here are largely carefree. I wonder how this will translate in the civilian world.

I was sitting at a table for dinner tonight with DP and AG. We were talking, and two females in Air Force PTs walked by. Very fit, both of them, a blond and a brunette. Painfully attractive. They walked to a refrigerator, and the brunette opened the door for the blond. The blond bent over, low, to retrieve drinks. Apparently the drinks she wanted were in the far back of the refrigerator. I watched her perfect legs fold in on themselves, noticed how clean and tan and taut they looked against her light-gray and blue exercise outfit. Her socks were short, not tube socks, but they covered her ankles. She could have been five-six, maybe five-seven. She leaned in, reached back, way back. Life seemed to slow down to a crawl, and I felt myself break out into a cold sweat.

Good to know that I still have some reaction to females.

2 October 2007

Dear Jim,

More thanks to your mother for being the best care package commissar ever. Each one of them is perfect, containing a mix of great British snack treats, DVDs (movies or TV shows (*Arrested Development*)) and literature. A couple of packages arrived just in time to rescue me from existential crisis. It's strange how depressed I've become out here—maybe it's spending too much time on the FOB getting rocketed to no purpose, or that there's no victory in sight, or just the great spaces of the sky and mountains—it's maddening, to feel trapped within infinity. One could go anywhere here and it would be equally useless. There is no action that I could take that would make a difference.

It sounds from your last letter as though you've made substantive changes in your area. If it were anyone else I wouldn't believe it, but knowing you as I do I'm not surprised in the least; if anyone could outface the enemy, it's you. I don't need to preach to you about this, you understand me completely, but an overlooked and dangerous component to our current efforts—the component that will effectively doom our efforts here—is the simple truth that in order for one to wage a successful COIN struggle, one must *love* the culture one is trying to defend. I'm sure with your knowledge of Arab culture and your expansive, romantic personality it's no great trouble to *love* your Iraqi allies—which on a basic level incentivizes your allies to work hard to justify that love, not to disappoint you. I can say that here, nobody loves the Afghans. Quite the contrary—I even find myself looking down on them—hating myself for it, but looking at their rural antics, their ignorance, their awful corruptions and immoral predilections (institutionalized pedophilia and polygamy) and despising them. The educated interpreters and government representatives from Kabul who wear designer glasses and quote Marx have a similar dislike for their rural cousins, and I fear that these are the people that our ambassadors and diplomats listen to for assessments when they visit. Things are bad here, and the impossibility of *love* and respect for the Afghans are at the root of it all. We dictate the terms of culture and progress to them—the urban, literate Afghans love us and what we promise, and the other 90% of the country rightly understands that for them to have to change in the ways we insist must mean that we perceive them as evil or wrong.

This reminds me of an incident that occurred before I left for leave, in August. It was late—one or two in the morning—and our RAID tower (we call it the "eye in the sky," you probably have one, our outside-the-wall security system) picked up three Afghans near a road about 3km to the north of our FOB. Our CO spun up the QRF and they went out to apprehend what everyone assumed was an IED gang. They came back a few hours later, no shots fired, having successfully apprehended the group—my CO was convinced that they were up to no good, but the platoon sergeant on the QRF was skeptical. Having been asleep myself, I was curious as to what happened and asked the platoon sergeant point-blank.

"When we got there, the guys were just standing off to the side of the road. They didn't try to run. They were digging a hole in the desert and setting up nets, and had some old-ass boom box playing bird sounds on it. They had shovels and wires, but no explosives—the whole thing was just really, really weird Afghan shit."

I asked the terp what he thought happened. "I tried to tell them," he said, "the people often break curfew to catch birds at night." He explained that there was a particular type of desert quail that lived in the area and only came out at night. It would sell at market for fifty bucks, and people would buy them as pets. "It's a good way to make extra money before the harvest."

They were in prison for a few days, then released before I went home. My CO certainly wasn't wrong to go with his gut and snatch up three Military-Aged Males who were digging by a road where we've hit IEDs before, with electronics, well after curfew. On the other hand, besides the curfew bit, these poor guys weren't really doing anything wrong.

I'm in Kuwait now, battened down while a sandstorm blows outside. What a process this is, waiting for the flight! Everything seems more organized here, better laid out. More space, more systems, better bureaucracy. If I were to lose something, I might never leave "Ali Al-Saleem Air Force Base," instead condemned to wander between drab tents as the wind howled. Things in Afghanistan are necessarily more chaotic. The card-swipers work here; in Afghanistan, if anyone has a card-swiper, there's a chance it's broken, so everything's done by hand. The refrigerators work (I don't know how what with the oceans of sand that get on and in everything). New aircraft depart and arrive every day.

An odd consequence of leaving Afghanistan, of coming home, is that for the first time since the very beginning of my deployment I've been thinking about Mefloquin and the role it plays in my life. Partly, of course, because I'm supposed to continue taking the antimalarial pill regularly—and partly because I'll probably be drinking and must therefore consider the likely damage done to my liver. I'm assuming that you know what I'm talking about and take the weekly antimalarial pill yourself (or its daily equivalent). I'm one of those people who gets affected by vivid dreams, especially on the nights immediately following my taking the pill—Monday, Tuesday, and Wednesday (it's worn off by Thursday) are my "dream-walk" days, where I can look forward to an entertaining night's sleep. I find that the dreams are most vivid on the FOB—one recent dream stands out as a particularly representative example. In the dream, I had to fill out the fuel and ammunition consumption report, submit it, and then attend the morning XO meeting, after which I got up to go to lunch—I woke up, shook my head, filled out the fuel and ammunition report, submitted it, and then attended the XO meeting, after which I went to lunch. People predisposed to violence or depression should not take this drug under any circumstances. In the field, though, the dreams never bother me—the only time I even remember dreaming at all was near the end of a week-long mission, when I dreamt intense memories about a woman I left behind. This woke me up at 4am, and I couldn't get back to sleep—the dream itself was lovely, but waking up from it, lying in the dust of Afghanistan by my HMMWV, was almost more than I could bear.

In any event, I've tried many different types of drugs—in college, of course (where I learned to blaspheme and was brainwashed by the left, etc.) but Mefloquin might be my favorite. I've only ever had one nightmare on the drug, and without Mefloquin, nightmares usually plague my sleep. It was the most conventional nightmare I'd ever had: I dreamt about stabbing my CO with a butcher's knife, and I could feel the blood—it was hot, sticky, wet—this was back in May, when I was still "fresh" in theater, nothing like it has happened since. If it were a regular feature of my evenings, I'd be really worried. As it stands, though, usually I can visualize the things I need to do during my Mefloquin dreams, then wake up and do them. The only possible drawback is an eroded ability to distinguish between fantasy / dream and reality. It's important to acknowledge that certain borders are not quite so distinct as we all might like to imagine!

Well—after this, it's nine months of deployment before I'm back home. By then you'll know whether you're staying in or getting out, and we can meet up for a good steak dinner somewhere—New York City if it's in the cards. I pray that your efforts with the surge pay dividends, and that you keep safe. IEDs scare the shit out of me, more than ten or even thirty guys with AKs and RPGs in the hills. And it sounds from the news as though the Iraqi insurgents are surgeons with those things. Stay safe—and we'll lift a glass together in fellowship when this whole ridiculous, doomed misadventure is over with.

Much love and respect,
Adrian

9

15 November 2007

Dear Brent,

A month goes by, and what a difference… It was great seeing you in New York during leave, but—lord, I came right back into the frying pan. Hard to write this stuff. Lost four people I knew personally, two of whom I actually liked and cared about on a personal level.

Well, back up. So, after leave, after my whirlwind tour of New York, Connecticut, France, Switzerland, Italy, and Connecticut (again), I flew back to Afghanistan and played the waiting game for three days, standing by for helicopter lift assets. The future D Co commander used to be in the Rangers and knew some MEDEVAC pilots so we were able to jump on a swap to Salerno, then another flight to Orgun-E; I landed and had eight hours to pack my bags for a two-week mission. We rolled out on October 31st, and were chasing ghosts in the mountains for the next ten days. Just got back to Bermel yesterday, fell dead asleep in my bed. Hadn't seen Bermel since September 29th or 30th, whenever I left.

I don't even know how to write this. I've known guys from OBC and OCS or soldiers I'd interacted with briefly who died, but it was an abstraction, they weren't sharing my particular challenge—I grieve for their families, but part of it is seeing a person in training, in their youth, with dreams and ambitions, and not being able to imagine them gone. These deaths out here are more intimate, it's the same death that I face; I knew their laughter, their anger, their frustrations, their fear— the details of their deaths are pictures to me, I can see it, I know how it happened. That doesn't make sense, though—why I should care more about the deaths of some people I liked versus others I also liked…

Well, the company commander for our sister unit here (a CAV

troop) died while I was on the operation. A/1-91, 173rd ABCT, CPT Dave Boris. As you know, CPT Dixwell and I have never been close *personally*—I respect the hell out of him professionally, he's a clever tactician and terrific warfighter, but we don't really click as friends. Part of this is probably the lingering resentment I never dealt with between losing my old commander and being elevated to XO and taken away from my platoon. CPT Boris provided that human element, he was a good guy, a legitimately good human being. I was thinking about that when I was going home on leave, and looking forward to seeing him when I got back, catching up, watching a movie or something—none of that is possible, now, our social opportunities have been reduced to a permanent zero. Of *course* he's married with a couple kids. I knew his gunner too, a sergeant with a great sense of humor whose name was also Adrian; the details of their death, according to the guys that were with him—I can't write it, man. I'll tell you about that shit when I get home. It was senseless. It always is.

Let me walk that back. I'd wish it tenfold on my worst enemy. I hope we can track down the fucker responsible and really hold him over the fire. Let him die slow.

Meanwhile, up in Kunar, a guy I hung out with in Vicenza a couple times, a lieutenant, got ambushed coming back from a shura and died along with six of his soldiers. Massive ambush. Really solid guy, one of those West Pointers that you meet in Italy, not like some of the more wobbly offerings from lieutenant training or Airborne School—the future of America types. What a waste.

Just to take my mind off this shit—don't know how to discuss it, except to look forward to a big bottle of Maker's Mark whiskey when I get home. Ah, hell, man. This sucks.

Hope all's well,
Much love,
Adrian

P.S. Have you heard from Jacob recently? I've sent him a couple emails and a letter, and he never responded. Is he okay? Didn't see him on leave, because he's "ghosting"—just hope the guy's alive!

16 November 2007

Dear Mom and Dad,

Sorry for not writing sooner, I promised to give you word of my safe return, but before I had a chance to do so I got wrapped up in a "battalion mission" in Orgun-E—didn't even get back to my home base, FOB Bermel, before we had to leave. The mission lasted two weeks and saw me traverse some very interesting places; I have fun stories to relate that will give you a good idea of how much entertainment there is to be had on even the most routine, benign mission.

The first thing that happened—apart from getting roped into a long mission with no warning (I was happy to go and be off the FOB, don't get me wrong) was something I didn't see, but the 2nd platoon leader told me about. Apparently, as they were driving the three hours from Bermel to Orgun-E (the battalion FOB where I met up with C Company) they passed thirty or forty Toyota Hilux pickup trucks with something like three hundred "Military-Aged Males" or "MAMs" in the back—everyone assumed that these were the Taliban that we would be fighting, who saw us coming and decided to move into our district while we were walking around in their home hills. So—the prospect of us encountering any fighting, not great to begin with (which should make you happy); the Taliban hate cold, and also prefer not to attack forces that outnumber them—was reduced even more. There really is safety in numbers.

After the first phase of the mission was complete, in the North, we drove back to the battalion FOB and then, with an engineer RCP, southwest into the mountains. There was this one valley, Charbaron, where the previous unit had built a fort for the Afghan National Police (ANP) and the mayor of the district, and the Taliban had burned it down. The engineers were going to rebuild everything, and the ANP were going to reoccupy another new facility—we'd have a big party, and try to convince the locals to help the ANP and not the Taliban, then stop at a couple more villages; try to use the absence of the Taliban to expand our footprint. It was a good plan, and it worked out more or less exactly the way it was supposed to. The fort was built, the ANP occupied it, we held a big party, there were three whole companies there (I got to see Justin Quisenberry and Marty Peters, which was great fun—I basically live for those moments of communal friendship that happen randomly or as the result of processes that are wholly outside my control), and then our company moved out to another valley to meet up with villagers and another company (A Co).

This was where things got a bit fun—funny—after we did everything we were supposed to with the villagers and achieved our reconnaissance objectives. The next day, we were supposed to drive back to the Charbaron Valley. The trail was so difficult on the way in that we'd broken one vehicle and looked likely to break others. The 1SG decided we'd go north instead, to "PRT Sharona," a massive brigade FOB, bigger than Orgun-E (like, ten times bigger, with an airfield and everything). This was going to take us along a road that nobody had traveled—we were with an MP platoon (they had these weird Russian-looking APC vehicles with slated windows and gun turrets) and they assured us that the road was fine. Someone—I don't know where or how this rumor got started, but the 1SG bought into it immediately—said there was a paved road that we'd link up with that would take us into Sharona directly, and that the drive would take no longer than three hours.

The whole thing was a massive clusterf***. The MPs got lost almost immediately, wasting an hour of daylight, and we had to rely on our own maps and GPS systems to discover the way to the road, which involved driving down a narrow trail through a mountain pass. It was terrifying, and we nearly lost two vehicles in the process, wasting another hour and bringing us to sunset. We finally made it through, and began following the MPs toward a road that was always "five minutes ahead," until that magical moment when they realized that we were in a completely different area than they'd thought, and that the paved road had therefore never existed in the first place. At this point we turned north in the darkness and drove between fifteen and twenty miles per hour through the open desert until we found PRT Sharona sometime around 11pm. I checked my email, grabbed a bite to eat, and nearly busted a gut when the 1SG came into the tents and said that battalion had ordered us back up the pass into the valley we'd just left. We didn't have to go, thankfully, and were cleared to return to base the next day, but it was too funny.

The rest of our mission passed without event, and after two days of driving and one sleepover at Orgun-E, we made it back to Bermel. Back to my home-away-from-home. There are some small differences—and there were some personnel changes, so the captain that I told you about, where it's me and him in the picture with General Pace, he's gone—but other than that nothing remarkable.

Well, nine more months of the grind. Miss you guys already!

All my love,
Adrian

Journal Entry: 28 November 2007

Definitively back on FOB Bermel—soon to be renamed FOB Boris. The memorial service was difficult. A civilian photojournalist was there taking pictures of the ceremony, and each of the soldiers and leaders while they made their peace with CPT Boris and SGT Hike. The event, the day, it felt like I'd been walking through a Mefloquin dream, but I didn't wake up. Saw a couple officers talking with the photojournalist afterward, looking at his camera, at their pictures. Life goes on. In the evening I ate a full meal, and played Grand Theft Auto "San Andreas" in the first sergeant's hootch. Everyone back from patrol, everyone settled in, no patrols imminent for a week or so. The room at the end of the hall our last remaining reminder that a captain used to be with us, and has gone.

There was a suicide bombing in September; a lot of people died. That scene, the bodies, the blood—they didn't have the same impact as this has. And even this hasn't—I can still sleep. I can still function. Which seems pathetic, or depraved. I was more broken up in college when some girl broke my heart. Shouldn't this be at least as bad as that was?

19 December 2007

Dear Mom and Dad,

Thank you for the Christmas package. I'm writing thank-you letters to everyone who sends me or any of the guys from C Co a package—for each package—this is something that feels right. I've never been great about sending thank-you notes; the whole process of gift-giving has always struck me as a little bit off, like you're obligated to find someone else the perfect gift because they're doing that for you. This has been particularly frustrating in relationships, where my dislike of gift-giving has time and again exposed me as some sort of sociopath or narcissist—in this situation I have not asked for any care packages, and friends, family, and well-wishers are sending them anyway. To avoid expressing gratitude would disgrace the communal and patriotic nature of our efforts here, it would betray our cause more completely than negligent patrolling or tactical failure. In a very real sense, the wars in Afghanistan and Iraq are battles for the soul of America. So it does me great good to write thank-you notes, it feels like part of the effort.

Things are quiet now. The snows moved in, it's deep-winter cold, and everyone would rather hunker down than go out and stir up trouble. There was some discussion about possibly flying down to Kandahar to take part in a big attack that's going on somewhere between the city and Helmund Province—apparently there's a dam that the Taliban took from the British that needs recapturing—anyway, the whole thing fell apart, and so we've just been planning for a mission that will take most of the company into some weird, faraway village. The idea is that now that the Taliban are all in Pakistan it's easy for us to show up and get some easy credit from the Afghans for helping them, improving their lives.

So, snowball fights, care packages, fat living, no rockets, no ambushes, none of the bad stuff that could happen. I know you guys heard about some of the incidents that occurred earlier, and I'm sorry for that—they didn't affect me personally. In fact, I was nowhere near them—quite safe, far away from real danger or harm. There are 1,500 fighting soldiers and officers in the 173rd Airborne—every time you read about something awful happening, it doesn't mean that has anything to do with me! Most of my time is just typing on computers, writing thank-you letters (ha ha), and checking to make sure the fuel deliveries are coming on time. Walking around the FOB counting sensitive items, making sure we haven't lost anything valuable. Managing the guts of the war, not fighting in it. Actually, the most troublesome part of my life recently has been trying to figure out how to do the SI (sensitive items) checks without standing for hours in the cold—it's brutal here, and of course our good cold-weather equipment is on back order. I'm sure it'll get here in time for the Spring Offensive.

Sorry, didn't mean to get nasty, there. Dad, we should've gotten some good gloves with the Gear for the Goats purchase—these army-issue gloves are pretty terrible. Of course, nobody can wear gloves or any other piece of equipment that isn't "army-issue" on the FOB—off the FOB on patrol is a different matter.

Well, have a merry Christmas and a happy New Year. I'll be thinking of you guys—I'm sure some soldier will get suited up as Saint Nick and run around getting into trouble—things are as well as one could hope out here at the edge of the world. My love to Christina over the holidays!

Love,
Adrian

Journal Entry: 25 December 2007

I dreamt last night that something important was about to happen. A helicopter landed and Lieutenant General Petraeus jumped out. He handed the CO a huge bottle of Jack Daniels, and he, myself, and the 1SG spent the next couple hours drinking it down. In the dream, he was a hard man, but fair—his eyes radiated calm and resolve, the sort of leader one would follow into hell just to spit in the devil's eye. It felt significant, his giving us hard alcohol to drink like that—in the dream, he was apologetic, like "sorry I couldn't bring more, boys, this is all I have, so you'll just have to make the best of a bad situation." LTG Petraeus. In my dream!

This time last year I was wrestling about what to do with Jessica. Haven't spoken with her since April, and miss her presence in my life. It's futile to think about what might have been—after all, going into this process solo seemed like the right thing at the time.

God, I could use some booze. Fuck this Merry Christmas.

2 January 2008

Dear Teddy,

Thanks for a wonderful and unexpected Christmas care package! *The Tunnels of Cu Chi* was a great read, top five stories I've ever heard coming out of Vietnam, the Petzel headlamp is boss and will get heavy use, and the Malcolm Gladwell reminded me why it's important to step outside the box every once in a while and look at things from a different perspective—I wish someone like him would take war metrics from various conventional and non-conventional conflicts and come up with unorthodox explanations for how to win—feel very strongly that we assign so much value to "the gut" and other similarly deceptive and harmful methods of evaluating "progress" in war that the system *needs* an overhaul. Of course it's also possible that the military has conducted such analyses, and what they discovered was so horrible that they immediately shelved the reports, like something out of a Lovecraft story. Unlikely, granted, but possible. Your choice of what we call "lickies and chewies" was similarly inspired, and therefore well received and quickly devoured by hungry paratroopers. It didn't occur to me to expect that you'd send anything, frankly, and when the package showed up it was a very pleasant surprise. I treasured it.

Christmas itself—well, you can imagine, it was full of a sort of bacchanalian mood of excess and abandon. The Taliban fired two rockets at us, completely ineffective; it felt like a desultory nod to the religious component of our conflict. A couple of the soldiers dressed up like Santa Claus and ran around handing out gifts and generally making a welcome nuisance of themselves, and everyone gorged themselves on holiday sugar cookies, candy, and goodwill.

I couldn't help but think of the European experience of World War I—how during the first Christmas the British, French, and German soldiers went "over the top" to play soccer matches and celebrate Christmas together—the generals on all sides immediately put a stop to that sort of practice, as it was deemed to be "bad for morale," as though on top of everything else one has to do as a soldier, one also has to preserve the fiction that one's opponent is something inhuman. After all, it doesn't take an emotional Einstein to put two and two together and realize that if you're capable of treating your enemy like a human and he's capable of treating you like a human, then the direct inverse must also be true. And the direct inverse, I think, is very difficult to return from as a human, once you've crossed that line. I worry about that, I worry about hating the Afghans, seeing them as something less than equal. There's no chance of us playing soccer together, that's for damned sure.

The moment that came closest to insanity, for me—there have been a few, and I'll just touch on one of them—occurred during the last big operation I went on, in November. It was just after my mid-tour leave, I arrived at the battalion FOB and hopped straight into a HMMWV for a two-week mission. While there, we were in this one valley—the "Charbaron Valley," where an allied Afghan National Police (ANP) base and the district mayor's residence were burned. I went on several mounted and dismounted patrols with some of the platoons, visiting little villages along the sides of the valley. They had their little primitive economies: camels, pine-nuts (it was the season), flat-bread with dirt baked into it, woodcutters—smoke curled up out of a few mud chimneys, the overall impression was one of extreme poverty, warmth and comfort, and insulation from the outside world.

After visiting two of these villages we came upon a third, much smaller village, up by the treeline. As an elder and two Military-Aged Males (MAMs—I'm really into emphasizing this acronym—endlessly amusing for some reason—and much better than the informal acronym that many of the soldiers, sergeants, and officers use instead to describe likely enemy fighters: Fighting-Aged Guys, or FAGs) walked down from the village to greet us, and we walked uphill into the cluster of compounds, past a burned-down ruin of a compound, we could clearly see two villagers running into the woods with bandoliers of ammunition and rifles slung over their backs. We talked with the elder and two of his fellow-villagers (and relatives, of course), and when they brought out tea, the two villagers who'd run off into the treeline walked down to join us, now unarmed.

After hearing that the village had no active Taliban (they'd left a week earlier for Pakistan, due to the winter), and no weapons, we played our trump card, which was that we'd seen two of the people there run into the woods. We threatened to search the village and surrounding area if they didn't bring the weapons down (we had soldiers pulling guard, we were not worried about a draw-down). The elder acknowledged that he had weapons, and begged us not to take them. We didn't promise anything, just told him to bring the weapons. Ruefully, he complied.

His nephews brought down three immaculately oiled and maintained Enfield Rifles, and hundreds of rounds of ammunition *stamped with the eagle of the Third Reich and the year 1945*. We told him that he was allowed to have rifles and ammunition, that it wasn't against the law, then returned everything to him. He was absurdly grateful, and ordered more tea, more cookies, insisted that we stay longer.

During the unforced candor and dialogue that occurred, we became curious about the state of the village, and its problems. We asked about the ruined compound slightly downhill. He told us that the compound had belonged to a rival family, and that one night during a thunderstorm the family had attacked and killed his mother over some sort of land dispute. His family had retaliated, killed two of the family's women, and drove them out, burning their compound behind them and leaving the bodies for the dogs. He held up one of the Enfields, and said that it had belonged to that family, but now it belonged to him. He was proud of this, describing what sounded a great deal like the plot of a horror movie. We took our leave shortly thereafter.

Murder and savagery in the hills. That's what waits for us at every turn—there's no *understanding* these people, their lives are so completely different from our own. I'm losing my capacity for empathy, at least intellectually—on a human level I can still get by—but it takes a greater and greater effort on my part to remind myself that they're people too, that I'd act the same way they do under similar circumstances. That thought, of course, is the real mind-bender, because in order to be truly empathetic, in order to *love* your enemy on a certain level, you have to *love* every enemy, you have to just sort of love people in general, love the brutal impulses in yourself, and suddenly you find yourself loving the Mongols, and the Japanese and Germans in World War II, and the Russians and Chinese during the Cold War, and all of them, because on a certain level they're all products of their time, representative of certain visions for humanity that on a certain moral plane are just as valid as our own.

Now I'm going to black out, like any good H.P. Lovecraft narrator who has seen too much, and must live with forbidden knowledge for the rest of his days...

Don't encapsulate COIN in doctrine, it's too dangerous! Leave it be!

Love,
Adrian

Journal Entry: 27 January 2008

I can no longer picture the future. Everyone's supposed to have a purpose or a motivation but I can't find one, don't know where mine is. This winter seems to drag on forever. Went to a district security shura with the Civil Affairs guy and a fire team for security in a couple of "gator" class John Deere vehicles. Six Americans and an interpreter among a sea of Afghans, maybe two hundred. I'm losing my perspective of what's safe and unsafe—becoming accustomed to life here, to the fatalistic attitude toward everything. The interpreter obviously lost and confused. The Civil Affairs captain alone in a room with ten Afghan tribesmen. Is this progress? Maybe the Taliban really are gone.

I guess so long as we keep feeding certain of these elders business contracts, we'll never know. This is how to rule in a society that depends on violence to keep order: maintain the hope for money and influence, no matter how small, and the population will remain compliant. Once that hope disappears, heaven help you…

The money keeps us safe. Worst case scenario: the elders take part of the money we give them and use it to bribe the Taliban—so it's in their best interests to leave us alone too.

Last year at this time I was receiving baked goods from Jessica Benelli, great buttery pound cake and cookies. Useless to think about that now.

3 February 2008

Dear Brent,

It's winter here, deep winter. Outside, the mountains and valleys are covered in a persistent blanket of snow and ice. The air's sharp and crisp, our breaths freeze when we step outside. Everyone's smoking or dipping, peeing in bottles they store in their rooms and then run out to the garbage only when absolutely necessary. Conversation is limited, people stay in their rooms off-duty, socializing only when compelled by professional necessity. Christmas and New Year's came and went, and afterward it seemed as though something had changed in the dynamic—the boredom forced people to make choices simply for the sake of choosing. People have gone away on leave and come back;

it feels like things are building up to some kind of decision—when the snow melts and things begin to grow again, we will learn what that decision was, what's happened in Pakistan while we've been sitting here.

I'm starting to go beast-mode with my fitness, running daily on the treadmill and lifting almost daily—there's not much else to do beyond playing video games—have you ever heard of *World of Warcraft*? I played this for about two weeks until it became too much of a burden on my professional duties, as well as several other computer games. That's winter deployment in Afghanistan in the east: nothing to do but kill time. Reading a ton, taking my journal-writing very seriously, and of course the video games. Other than that nothing much to report.

I have to admit that war is both exactly what I expected and something completely different from what I thought it would be. I suppose it must've been the same when you deployed here with the 173rd in 2005–06; you never know what to expect. We received two 155mm howitzers to replace the 105s we fell in on, and they're employed at least twice a day, every day. It's dangerous to drive around, the Taliban (a nasty breed of them called "Haqqani") are very willing to ambush us or put IEDs in the road. But none of that is the thing that really gets to you—I mean, you have to adjust your understanding of danger, sure, you can't be cavalier about leaving the wire—the things that have scrambled me up good were incidents of extreme cultural disconnect, such as the casual approach of the rural Afghans to murder and death, or those incidents where I was responsible for another's death or injury. There was a mission recently where someone put an IED in the road *two miles* outside our FOB—killed a jingle truck driver. I'd spent four hours haggling with him and five other drivers, one of which was his brother, to convince them to drive out to our COP (they must've known it would be dangerous), appealed to their patriotism, offered them money, had the mayor talk with them—all because there was an HLZ that needed gravel to prevent dustoff—when his truck hit the pressure plate IED he was sent flying like thirty meters. The platoon sergeant on the patrol and one of the soldiers sort of kneaded the dead Afghan driver into a body bag, his bones had been pulverized by the blast and being thrown through the windshield—his brother, still alive, wailed and fainted. I will *never* forget that scene. I guaranteed their safety.

In January we caught 150 or so Taliban surrounding our COP, and CPT Dixwell organized one of the most effective Generation 3 warfare strikes I'd ever seen. CAS, CCA, artillery, mortars, and direct fire systems—we mowed down fifty of them, most of them didn't even get a single shot off, or were killed running for the border of Pakistan—the only odd part was watching much of it from the company CP (with the CO, the 1SG and about twenty mixed soldiers and officers from the other units on FOB Bermel), and exalting in the deaths of people on a screen, other humans who were running for their lives (granted, people who'd desired the deaths of my fellow C Co soldiers). Who knows, maybe they were thinking about going to school to study physics or Persian literature, they were done with war; there's no glory in a war where you get massacred without getting a chance to shoot back. I don't know. If it had to be done again, of course it would happen exactly the way it did—it wasn't until the second group of Taliban (Haqqani) were bombed that I started to realize that, hey, they were people too. You know.

Another one of those moments arrived in autumn. When we first got here a few people actually tried to learn Pashto from the interpreters. This stopped quickly, once we realized that none of the interpreters had a sufficiently nuanced grasp of the local Pashto to perform their jobs well, let alone teach us anything useful. I'm sure it was worse when you were here—I feel somehow that we have more assets than you did, or at least the institutions have had more time to adapt to the challenges over here. At this point everyone understands that sending interpreters from Kabul out to the hinterlands is useless at best, and counterproductive at worst—people from Kabul are from the same general honor culture as the rural Afghans, and therefore loathe to admit when a job is outside their capabilities—rather than just telling us, "I can't interpret, I don't know the language," these guys will just say that the local villagers are lying or complicit with the Taliban, when the picture's often muddier. On top of which, the Kabul and city-educated Afghan interpreters here loathe their rural cousins—the feeling seems to be mutual on the part of the rural Afghans, who see the urban Afghans as weak and foolish—and dialogue under these conditions becomes nearly impossible. We had a CAT-2 terp here in September while the battalion commander was swinging through—a guy who legitimately spoke Pashto, originally from Orgun-E—and the difference was astonishing (terrifying if I took the time to think about it). I learned more from him in two meetings than I had over months, struggling with the other CAT-1 interpreters hemming and hawing (no wonder it's difficult to stay awake during long meetings—I can only hear "he's bullshit-ting, sir" so many times before I think to myself that I'm wasting time). In the meetings where I had the CAT-2 terp, I was amazed to hear the speeches of the Mayor and the tribal elders almost word-for-word—it was a revelation. They spoke in proverb, allegory and fable, making heavy use of animals and nature—each story a lesson as well as an example of why a certain policy was succeeding or failing. I felt for the first time that I was able to speak with them, instead of delivering yet another doomed, pedantic lecture to the wall.

I'm hearing rumors that I may get moved over to the Easy Com-pany XO slot, which is technically a promotion, but also a step in the wrong direction; the battalion commander is convinced that I'm not cut out for the infantry, and does not want me to be out on combat pa-trols—I shit you not—luckily Captain Dixwell knows better. If it were up to the BC I'd probably be in the ALOC in Bagram. It's wild—his dislike for me is irrational, wild. Maybe I offended him somehow in Italy, or he saw me drunk during one of our expeditions to Il Grottino or Piazza Settima? Well—at least he doesn't think that I'm a *moron* or useless—still, it's tough to swallow, my boss thinks I'm weak. My reac-tion to this, of course, is just to resolve to take advantage of any and every opportunity I have to prove myself—I know that he's wrong. It's not irresponsible leadership—if you think someone doesn't have what it takes and lives are at stake, you should do everything in your power to remove that person from a position where they could make harmful decisions. But that *can't* be it with me, I'm still granted enormous au-thority and latitude to make choices that carry serious consequences. Maybe it's a physique thing—there have been officers here who have committed such fantastic blunders of judgment that they lost their pla-toons, but they get second chances because they can lift a lot of weight, or look like what one expects an infantry officer to look like—I can bench my body weight, but put more stock in the power of intellect to solve problems than my muscle density. So, it's just that my boss, a dis-tinguished warfighter in his own right, is "absolutely" convinced that I am not a combat leader. Which of course is "dead wrong."

I'll leave you on that note—winter—I've neared the end of myself several times, this place could drive a weaker mind mad—the moun-tains call to you, and it *almost* seems like it would be a good idea to just… walk, walk to the closest village, put the old life behind and start over as an Afghan farmer, anything to get out of the same dull rou-

tine. Of course that's not really an option, some Haqqani sympathiz-
er would truss me up and have my head off on YouTube. Still almost
seems worth it to take my chances—some days I yearn for an end to it
all. The cold, the solitude, the Taliban.

    All best,
    Adrian

10

Dear Mom and Dad,

Good news from Afghanistan; I've left C Company after twenty months, which is the usual amount of time to be with one company in my battalion. There's a lot of officer movement, and I've been given a *second executive officer position*, which is a great honor, and entails new challenges and a change of scenery. It's also, for your purposes, good news in that I won't be patrolling nearly as much, and the patrols I do lead will be in a very secure area. The social situation here at Orgun-E is almost ideal—there are many other junior officers like myself who've washed up here through the most recent spate of roster moves in the battalion. Everyone's in the same boat, and consequently after a long day of work there's usually a good conversation at dinner that I can look forward to, or an after-dinner cigar-smoking session.

My new XO routine keeps me busy. The CO is a guy who's really precise and methodical—I like him, he's not egotistical, just focused on providing services to the soldiers out in the dangerous places with no refrigeration. We have a good 1SG, and my "XO team" is a couple of *females*—a female soldier who's married to one of the soldiers in another company—HHC, I think—and a female sergeant, my new supply clerk (I'd call her my right-hand man but that would be inaccurate for obvious reasons). She has a real knack for administrative work, and her talents complement my own perfectly—I'm not quite as organized with paperwork, and tend to focus on getting things done through consensus and shady back-room deals, or simply by any means available—she's totally by-the-book, and that makes me a much stronger XO than I was before.

For the first time in months, I'm starting to see the daylight. It's nearly the end of March—that means we have April, May, June, and July (most of July will be consumed with loadout and moving home, presumably, although as the E Co XO I'll likely be one of the last to leave)—we're short-timers! Here's food for thought—we'll have spent fifteen months deployed, which is a typical army "surge" deployment. The marines do nine-month deployments. Most Air Force and Navy units do six-month deployments (they call them "rotations," which makes sense when you think about it). Special Forces and Ranger units seem to do three- or four-month deployments / rotations. From my perspective, six months really is the most time a unit should spend doing this type of thing. I remember the 10th Mountain Unit we replaced out here, how burned out they seemed—I understand now, civilized humans were simply not designed to spend this kind of time in a war zone. It wears you down. Then again, I'm compelled to feel "lucky" to have even deployed, to have had the opportunity to serve with this unit, the 173rd Airborne, surrounded by Rangers and heroes. And I do! But I'm also looking forward to getting home for leave, and visiting you guys, spending time in Branford, maybe taking a couple trips up to NYC. No—can't think about that now—have to keep myself focused on the job at hand, not on that joyful moment when I'm reunited with friends and family.

>   Miss you all,
>   Love,
>   Adrian

Journal Entry: 13 April 2008

I've been sleeping more and feeling less rested. Working out does nothing. Writing, working, watching movies, eating, reading about brewing beer—nothing makes a difference here. More meetings with the Afghans—different faces, same story. They smile and nod in their security shura while I take notes and act as the first line of defense against actual Afghan complaints. The primary gripe here? What else. Land disputes.

After one recent shura in Orgun we conducted a patrol in the bazaar. Some of the guys bought local food, and as we picked our way through town a sizable crowd grew up around us. More evidence of the separation between American and Afghan cultures—this shouldn't have been an exceptional event, what with our living maybe a half-kilometer away, but we might as well have been from Mars. Many of the Afghans spoke English, and it felt like a good interaction. Like peering behind the curtain—what life would be like, down here. It was good for the soldiers too, who leave the FOB about as frequently as I do. Made me wonder about the Afghan army / Afghan Police again—what their thoughts on this struggle are. We rarely talk to them, or visit their part of the base, nor they ours. Parallel realities.

Back on FOB Orgun I returned to my room and nothing had changed. Played a video game with my roommate, climbed up to my bed. Never knew fatigue and depression could be so *angry*, so aggressively impotent.

3 May 2008

Dear Brent,

I haven't been writing much lately. My work with E Co has kept me busy—we switched commanders recently, the man you remember as Easy-6 has gone to take a Master's Degree and then teach at ROTC (I think)—the new Easy-6 is more convivial, more my kind of leader—which could be bad, as the old CO kept me in check a bit. He also bent over backwards to get me out on patrol, and the new guy likes patrolling. Used to do logistics work for SF. He just got off an MiTT assignment in Iraq, and used his "I can go anywhere I want to within reason" chit to get to Italy. Not a bad deal.

We've got two more big battalion missions in front of us—now that the snows have melted the Taliban are up to their old tricks and then some, really coming at us across the AO. I can't talk about this with my family, of course, but you know the score—it's getting hairy here. There are reports that put the number of active Taliban in our section of Paktika Province at somewhere between 1,000 and 1,500 fighters after accounting for Afghan math (our allies would have us believe it's between 10k and 15k, which is obviously absurd).

I'm going to have a small role in the next big battalion push—I get to act as a liaison officer for the battalion with an ETT team that's driving to Bermel. The old Kandak commander, the guy I knew while I was still XO of C Co was seriously wounded by an RPG, and his replacement was a political appointee from Nuristan, a short, blue-eyed little shit who must be one of the worst leaders ever. Seeing him do business (never around, always shirking responsibilities) reminds me that great military catastrophes of the past often had this component of patronage on one side—a general or leader who had no business being in command of anything, least of all thousands of soldiers. That's this guy—LTC M*****. I happened to see a copy of the mission, which sends this weak Kandak into the heart of bad-guy territory, and, certain that it would see serious contact, I raised a red flag. In this case, the bias against lieutenants worked to my advantage—they disregarded my advice, and allowed me to volunteer for the mission. This means I'm set to spend ten days outside the wire, and I'll have a good chance of getting into serious trouble.

As the days are getting longer and we get closer and closer to redeployment, there's a special urgency to every patrol and mission. Whatever we hoped to accomplish here is just about finished. It's warming up; in the spring light, shadows last longer, the golden minute is turning by phases back into the golden hour for photography, and I can hear Rachmaninov announcing the end of history in B-flat, before every patrol. All I can hope is that history will judge us all fairly—it's written by the victors, and the great thing about being an American is that America always wins, even when it's losing. Afghanistan won't write the history of its victory or defeat; America and the West will.

We've expanded our footprint, and the only thing this seems to have accomplished is that the Taliban were motivated and incentivized to expand their tactical footprint in response—and they've done a much better and more thorough job of it (wouldn't be much of an insurgency if they couldn't recruit heavily in their own back yard). I don't blame anyone—every leader I know is working their ass off to come up with good solutions, to bring their soldiers home in one piece—but if there are no easy *or difficult* answers to be bought at any price, isn't it really sadistic to leave us out here? Is this how the Italians or Austro-Hungarians felt when they realized the jig was up? That it had all been some other country's mad obsession, that in the end it had nothing to do with any of them? That the only thing they'd done was to hasten the end of an old order, and replace it with something new and unrecognizable? I feel a certain simpatico with them, with their doomed mission. Benazir Bhutto was killed by extremists in Pakistan over the winter. We've lost freedom of maneuver. Kabul is more corrupt than ever.

Jesus—I'll stop feeling sorry for myself and expressing defeatist sentiments. Apologies for getting all morose on you. Never mind it all. Can't wait to see you when I get back for post-deployment leave, gonna be a great time.

Much love,
Adrian

5 May 2008

Dear Jim,

I hope all's well on your end, that you got out of your deployment more or less unscathed—twelve months into my own I'm ready to go home—if it weren't for a ten-day operation in the high places of Afghanistan I'd be completely checked out. I'll tell you what it is—being the XO of a maintenance company—our E Co—with all the battle around me, I feel wholly uninterested in doing the basics of my job. I do it—E Co has all of its SI and will redeploy with everything it needs to get home—but the fact remains that I need an attitude change. I think what I really need is a new battalion commander—this one has been convinced that I'm something very different from what I am.

Have you been following the primaries at all? The first time this has been really interesting in eight years! How weird for the Democrats, after years of boring and unmotivating presidential candidates, to have two appealing candidates—I'm especially curious to see whether we pick a strong woman or a black man to represent us for president. I'm putting my vote with Hillary, think she'd make a great president—obviously be the best person for the job—a strong and willful leader who has experienced great suffering and hardship who'd govern us well. Obama reminds me of some of the worst examples of narcissism from the Yale Political Union—those grasping personalities whose identity in life could be summed up as one massive tendency toward ambitious actions and goals—detached from any desire to wield the fruits of ambition, or any understanding of what one does as a leader. No, give me Hillary—she quite clearly does not give a fuck. I wouldn't be surprised if she dropped the axe on Iran during her first term. And why not? If we're going to offer the world the old Imperial Guarantee of safety, we might as well knock out all of our rivals. Let's make this into an old-school democratic crusade. I've always wanted to die at fifty, with an eye-patch, a grizzled colonel on the edge of the empire... then we can give it all to big business, *Bladerunner* style, and let them take us into space.

Now you see how I entertain myself out here.

I don't know if this is just a Persian-culture thing or if you've seen it with the Arabs too, but there's a saying about the Afghans (I learned this from a couple locals), that roughly translated (of course) means: "If a neighbor becomes king, everyone wants to knock him down so they can be king instead." The joke that goes along with it is considered a Pashtun joke: "A Pashtun farmer is digging in his fields. He unearths a dirty lamp. Wanting to clean it up, see if it's worth anything, he rubs it with the hem of his tunic. With a 'bang' the genie of the lamp appears and says: 'Thank you for freeing me. As a reward I will grant you one wish. There is a caveat, though—whatever you get, *your neighbor will get double*.' The Pashtun farmer wrestles with this idea for a while, before responding: 'I've made my decision. I wish... that I lose sight in one of my eyes.'"

How can you build a coalition under these circumstances? We'd have to be here for seventy years at least to educate successive generations in proper civic habits, whereby a neighbor helps build his neighbor's barn and generally wishes that good behavior and altruistic acts of kindness be rewarded (or at least abets that fiction for the benefit of all). I want to believe it's different in Iraq, which hasn't been plagued by three decades of fighting. The antiquity of the joke leads me to believe that things have always been like this in Afghanistan, it wasn't just the constant warfare that hardened everyone's hearts. The generational warfare has destabilized their culture in the sense that it privileges people set on vengeance or opportunistic profit-schemes. So long as selfishness and retribution are rewarded, so long as the ungenerous, the fence-sitters and double-dealers get ahead, the Afghans will never see any real progress against massive social and even existential threats.

I think that the Taliban are going to be the real and ultimate victors here—they're going to come back and impose Sharia law, and it'll be awful for kids and women and non-Pashtun, but it will serve as a vehicle for some kind of stability and progress. What we have now ain't working.

At the same time, I see how things are here, and I'm filled with a feeling of nostalgia and possessive love for my own country, which, jokes about democratic crusades and the presidential primaries and impending election aside, is not in great shape. How long can we go with crumbling infrastructure, an education system that consistently shows up near the bottom of the middle of the pack of first-world countries in every important metric, and these ceaseless foreign military interventions? I'll tell you what—either we manage to hang on for another couple decades, or our children look back at this age as the moment before the fall, when all the signs were clear, and we failed to act. Combination of greed and hubris. The greedy say, "Well, I've got mine so I don't have to worry," and the proud say, "We'll never fail, we can't." What our Republic needs is less Empire, and more responsible citizenry. Maybe togas and term-limits for congress?

All best,
Adrian

Journal Entry: 18 June 2008

I led a patrol yesterday. It was supposed to take us an hour north of Orgun-E, to a village in the hills—one of those places that we don't frequently visit. A place where the stakes are higher, where you can stumble into an ambush. Beautiful old mud-and-thatch buildings worked into the side of a hill, each one a fortress—a *karez* on the outskirts, gurgling with clean mountain springwater, orchards, sullen tribesmen. Anger at people who come from the city with a different culture, or who don't come with anything. Felt like a mission worth being awake for.

Twenty minutes into the patrol, ten minutes north of Orgun, just within radio contact, we were called back to the base. Suicide Bomber threat. We drove back through Orgun Bazaar, past the district center, under the great Russian gate. When we arrived, another patrol had returned just before us—the cloud of dust they'd kicked up in driving up from the south was still hanging over the road like a haze. We took our place in line behind them as they waited for permission to "RTB" or drive back onto the FOB. A truck drove past the rear vehicle in our convoy, bouncing along the road to Orgun-E, headed north. Everybody watched him go.

★

3 July 2008

Dear Mom and Dad,

I've just done my last patrol! Before leaving, each unit has to provide a "handover" to the new unit, which includes conducting joint weapons and equipment inventories and passing along the accumulated knowledge of more than a year's worth of systems and habits. This "handover" also serves to introduce our replacements to those officials in the local Afghan government with whom we've built significant relationships. The Afghans are such skillful dissemblers, I could almost believe them when they claimed that they would miss our unit. If there is any remorse at our leaving, it's probably over the hassle of needing to relearn all their tricks: how to manipulate us, how to predict leaving the base on patrol, when to expect supply drops—reestablishing communications patterns with their Taliban buddies—it's going to inconvenience them. The new unit seems pretty competent, so I feel confident that they'll be able to pick up where we left off and keep making forward progress here.

We're full of big patrols now—I went on one at the end of May and had a few adventures—was in the middle of a massive fight between the ANA and the Taliban, where the ANA (Afghan army) was routed so completely that it took us nearly five hours to rally all the troops—leading the charge away from battle was their "Kandak commander," which is sort of like "battalion commander" for the Afghans. To give you some idea of the danger we were in, the leader of the patrol characterized it at the time as "comedy hour." We found some enemy weapons on the operation, and got to hike around in the hills a bit— that's what I thought I'd be doing the whole deployment, of course, and things didn't work out that way at all, so I was happy to get some fresh air "off the FOB." My time in the gym working out paid dividends—we had some steep climbs. I loved it.

The tribes around my FOB had a bit of a brouhaha last month, shooting at each other and fighting over (what else?) a piece of land. One tribe claims that it was granted them by the British (they have the scrap of parchment to prove it), another tribe claims it by rights of occupation since before "The Time of The King," and the last tribe asserts that it was granted to them *by* the King after some land-redistribution program in the '30s (they have the piece of paper to prove it). In short, everyone wants, everyone deserves, nobody can compromise. The deal that my old CO had worked out with the tribes and the Afghan government was simply to claim that the land needed to be empty because of its proximity to the American FOB, for the safety of the people. Apparently that logic is no longer sufficient.

It's over! My last patrol is done! Can you tell that I'm happy and excited? The only things left to do involve sending equipment and people home; this event involves every "XO," and will totally consume my future, until it's done with, at which point I'll be that guy I encountered when I first arrived at FOB Bermel in the beginning of last May, who went to the gym twice a day, ran, and ate at the chow hall in his PTs (not in uniform), burned down to the very nub of his ability to care or self-motivate about anything or anyone. *Relieved* at the end of direct responsibility at last. I should be back in Italy by the end of this month, and back home for post-deployment leave early August. So—to answer your question of whether or not to throw me a coming-home party, please do by all means—I can't wait to see everyone—I think putting awards on a welcome home banner would be tacky, so please don't, but to satisfy your curiosity I received a Bronze Star and Army Achievement Medal. Both of those awards were for doing my job. Not to take anything away from the awards, it was a tough job—but it's not an award like you think of one, where you charge uphill throwing hand grenades and killing people. I didn't get one of those awards.

That might sound a little regretful—I suppose it is—I'm more or less happy with the work I did over here, I suppose most people probably feel the same way, like they tried the best they could. Still, it felt—this will make you happy—that because I was never in much direct danger, I never had an opportunity to prove to people that I am courageous and valorous. I know I am, I was tested a few times and came out all right—but there's something about having that ribbon, the public confirmation of heroism; I feel the hole where it would rest on my uniform, the absence of the ribbon is a physical weight. Don't worry, I won't be taking stupid chances to force something—as I said, I'm on the FOB now, getting ready to come home.

I'll be happy to share some (abridged) stories of action and adventure when I get home, but for now, can't find the words to describe most of the things I've seen. The cliché one hears about this sort of thing, the reason your fathers never talked about most of the things they saw in WWII—I'm pretty sure at this point (not to equate my experience to theirs, but it is comparable) that it's a language thing—you learn the words to describe your experience in training, then you see things, and if you don't know the hundreds of shorthand expressions that sum up a whole range of emotions and reactions, to say nothing of feeling able to participate in the morally compromising jokes and observations that are the social currency of a unit in combat, there's no point in talking about it.

Make sure there's plenty of booze for me when I get home—think food during Ranger School—I'm reading about how to brew beer, this is how I keep myself entertained. I have a powerful thirst for the stuff, scotch, wine, anything I can lay hands on—I'm looking forward to this like a fat man looks forward to second breakfast.

Love,
Adrian

Journal Entry: 20 July 2008

I was standing by a giant connex today as it was lifted up by a crane and secured onto the back of a jingle truck. The cranes, the trucks, the wild-eyed Afghans hopping from corner to corner with great metal cables—I wearing my helmet—in retrospect the whole thing was extremely dangerous. I feel a newfound respect for construction workers and people who work around heavy machinery. So much squealing and clanking—the humans were a small but important part of the process, the guiders, the fasteners. Great vehicles that would barely have noticed if they squashed me like a bug grumbled and shrieked about their business as I stood there, arms crossed, oddly content.

With the last shipments inventoried and secured, there's nothing left for me to do. Flights are leaving regularly now, just a few of us left.

Nate and Justin fly the day before me, but we'll meet up in Manas. It's okay to think about Italy now—it's better to think about Italy, and home—over here, the news is too awful, the failures too obvious.

26 July 2008

Dear Jim,

I'm writing from Manas, a small AFB we rent from the Kyrgyz (I think that's what they call themselves). This is the last stop before Italy, we'll fly into Aviano then take buses home, but this is where we grab our civilian jet. No stopping in Kuwait (there might be a refuel stop somewhere along the way). Nothing changed on my end since the last time I wrote, but in Afghanistan—I don't think this is being covered in the news, but across the *brigade*, on our way out, nearly every company came under some kind of vicious attack. Three of these attacks occurred against our battalion weeks before we left, hitting A Co, C Co, D Co and HHC; two attacks against our sister battalion. There might be multiple Medals of Honor or Distinguished Service Crosses coming out of them; the C Co (2-503rd) in Kunar Province had a platoon nearly wiped out, seven or eight KIA and I think another fifteen WIA; they got pulled off the line and sent home early, which is how I found out about it. I was sunbathing yesterday (there's really nothing to do here and the weather is magnificent, mid-seventies with no breeze) in the glorious mid-summer sun, killing time (our flight's in a couple days) and dozed off—woke up after a half hour, grabbed my pack of smokes, pulled on my shirt and walked in my flip-flops over to a cupola where some soldiers I didn't recognize were smoking. They were from 2-503rd's C Co, the one that got hit hard, and were telling stories. I asked a couple of questions, but mostly listened.

Each person has their own vision of the war, proprietary of their own experiences. The idea that someone *equal* to you might've had a more authentic experience was intolerable—their PL had been killed (I didn't know him—he replaced another PL I did know who was killed earlier in the deployment), and without anyone with whom to feel a sense of competition or rivalry, I was free to empathize with their experience. I did not mention my own, which wasn't worth mentioning, or those of the 1-503rd Companies, which weren't mine to mention.

All in all, watching the Taliban go on the offensive everywhere—helping us leave—I didn't want to go home. Felt like our job wasn't finished. The next unit (which has 70% of our combat power, and our power was insufficient to secure the area) will have an even more difficult time of things; I suspect that they'll reduce our footprint, abandon some of the forts we built, hunker down in the bigger bases and cede much of the territory we were contesting to the Taliban. What else are they supposed to do? In Vietnam, people were allowed to "re-enlist" to stay in country longer—I would have considered doing that if it were an option. Not sure why it wasn't.

Another thing I noticed while looking back on the whole of my time in Afghanistan, how we did things (how they might be improved)—was it this way in Iraq too?—was that we quickly reset the PowerPoint slides describing progress in our area to yellow or yellow-red when we arrived (though they had been yellow or yellow-green). In June, most of the slides were yellow or yellow-green; the incoming unit has, looking at what's happened recently, reset them to yellow-red. The cycle continues.

There was an officer who didn't get along with me—a peer—he wasn't an infantryman. The two of us would argue, and it finally occurred to me why we had such a difficult time with one another: he's a Fobbit. I've come to the end of my deployment, and can now tell the difference between someone who legitimately doesn't want to be here, thinks the whole war is bullshit and to be avoided when and wherever possible, and myself. I'm not a Fobbit, I'm not a coward. This guy, on the other hand, breaks his back looking for opportunities to sham. He's a waste of space. *He* sees himself as a freedom fighter, resisting "The Criminal Bush" and his unjust war. Everyone else thinks he's an idiot, a joke. I'm half-convinced that he joined in order to subvert the military, that he existed simply to make our lives more difficult—he sure made my life more difficult by generating a massive amount of extra work for me.

My godfather sent me a book for Christmas by Malcolm Gladwell. You've probably heard of him—it's sort of brain candy, not substantial but fun and thought provoking—COIN could definitely use more of that "new approach" and no-holds-barred approach to solutions. It sounds like the techniques and tactics you used in your AO worked; we just spun our wheels. I think part of the problem is that the military relies heavily on the dialectic of *progress*—if the security situation isn't improving, then something's wrong with the leader in the area—so if the leader wants to make sure he keeps his job, he simply reports that the security situation is improving, regardless of whether or not there is any evidence to support that. And in this case, the shit flows uphill, because if a fact is true for a company commander, it becomes true for the battalion commander as well, in his security reports to his higher command. Our greatest advantage over the Taliban—robust and capable institutional capacity—is also our greatest weakness. And no matter how much the generals, colonels and lieutenant colonels would like the soldiers to believe it's the civilians' or politicians' fault for not supporting the military better, if the buck stops somewhere it should stop with them. Or maybe the peacetime military, which encourages people to *talk* like they're risk-takers, but actually act conservatively. Think about it—we built four wonderful, massive COPs in our AO, which will never be overrun by the Taliban. The only result of these COPs has been for the Taliban activity to increase by at least 100% in our area, and a shift in their tactics from IDF on big FOBs to massive attacks, IEDs, and ambushes. We've stepped on a long balloon, and seen as the air rushed into another section of it—nothing more.

If we're not willing to put more soldiers into Afghanistan, we should pull out. And if we are willing to "surge" here, we'd better have a plan. I hope that it doesn't involve security assessments or anything with red / amber / green flowcharts. If so, it's probably bullshit. Meanwhile, I think America's probably going to just pull out of the Korengal after the next unit finishes their rotation (1st ID—all due respect to them, they're going to have a beast of a time up there).

As for me, I'm done. If you can make it down to my house there's going to be a welcome home party in mid-August, and I'd love for you to be there, meet some of my other buddies—Adam, my freshman year roommate, Brent, one of my best friends (and the guy responsible for bringing me into the 173rd, he's on track to command with the 101st Air Assault) and Mike Carson if he can make it. If not, or if so, we've gotta get dinner together in New York before you leave the army—we'll rock the blues.

Miss you much,
Adrian

GLOSSARY · SECTION FOUR

Skirt / Split-tail / Bang-tail: Popular terms in the infantry for a woman, which, when you think about them, make it less surprising that sexual assault is a significant problem in military culture.

MCCC: Maneuver Captain's Career Course. A six-month course on writing "orders" or plans of battle, under varying conditions of stress. Something of a gentleman's course when I went through, owing to the war. Still, very useful, and graduates are more highly regarded than their peers.

MiTT: Military Transition Team. The name for the small teams (10-15 soldiers, sergeants and officers) that would embed with and advise Iraqi military and police units. The scam with the MiTT was that because it was seen as a bad career move, a waste of time, you'd get preference on your duty position of choice afterward. While the shooting was still going on in Iraq it was an easy way to rack up a quick combat deployment before heading back over to Afghanistan (or taking some time off).

Post: The army fort / unit to which you are assigned. I was assigned to an infantry battalion with the 173rd ABCT, so my post was Caserma Ederle. This term goes back at least as far as the British Colonial Empire.

Light / Airborne / Mechanized / Ranger Infantry: The different classes of infantry. Light is dismounted, classic infantry, and includes Air Assault (helicopter), Stryker Brigades (that use Stryker Armored Personnel Carriers) and Mountain infantry. Airborne is infantry with the capability to jump out of airplanes. Mechanized infantry use light tanks. Rangers are the most elite infantry in the army, multi-purpose and savage.

Old Guard: The army unit in Washington D.C. responsible for ceremonies. Also a light infantry unit with specific duties in the event of D.C. itself coming under attack. Generally thought of as a good postwar assignment—they give you high-quality dress uniforms, you get to live in a great area (exceptionally unusual for the army).

IRR: Inactive Ready Reserve. Every officer signs up for a certain obligation to active duty—three years, in my case—more in the case of West Pointers and ROTCers—this was extended to six years when I signed up for another three years in order to command a company. At the same time, when you receive your commission you incur an obligation to the army for a period of *eight* years—the difference between your active commitment and that eight-year period is the amount of time you are then vulnerable to being "activated." I served six years, ten months on Active service, leaving one year two months of "Inactive Ready Reserve" time. This means that until September 1st, 2013, the army can call me back to Active Duty service. Of course, if we were in a situation where this was necessary, I'd be at the recruiter's office before they could recall me…

Inshallah: an Arabic term that means, generally, "if Allah wills it." A tenet of the fatalism that seems to pervade Afghan culture—for better, for worse.

The "Q" Course: The yearlong course that Special Forces candidates must pass before donning the fabled Green Beret. Mike and I gave Bob a lot of shit while he was going through the process but it's actually very difficult.

OPORD: Operation's Order. "Five Paragraph Operations Order" is the Ranger / army-standard approved way to make and then brief your subordinates on a mission. Takes about five or six hours to put together a decent plan with no prior information about an objective.

CONOP: Consolidated Operations Order. The PowerPoint version of an OPORD, and genesis of much aggravation. Many feel that the CONOP has led the officer corps away from the precision of earlier wars (Vietnam, Korea, WWII) where we would only use the OPORD and no condensed version.

OCONUS: "Outside Continental United States." Any duty station (Italy, Hawaii, Alaska, Germany) that isn't in one of the forty-eight contiguous continental states. Also could mean Iraq, Afghanistan, or any deployment.

S3: The chief planning officer in a battalion. You would think that the battalion commander would make his own plans for battalion operations, the way it happens in a company, but there's too much for one man to do. Hence the S3.

AS3: "Assistant S-3." The Maneuver Captain's Career Course—graduate captain who helps the S3 organize and write plans for the battalion commander. A thankless job that is feared and hated by all. See "story-time."

The Game: Yale / Harvard football game. I'm tired of Yale losing.

UCMJ: "Uniformed Code of Military Justice." The specific legal code that governs the military, and operates in parallel with civilian courts. So, for example, if you're a soldier and you stab someone to death, you'll be tried in civilian courts as a murderer. You'll also be charged under "UCMJ" with whatever article governs murder. If you're not charged in civilian courts, you can still be charged under UCMJ. And—yes—there's a regulation for *everything*.

AO: Area of Operations. This is a practical way to designate where one unit's responsibility ends, and another begins. That way you don't have duplication of efforts, confusion over the radio, or fratricide. My first AO was "AO Eagle," in Paktika Province. My second wasn't called an AO, because some general thought AO would encourage the idea of ownership in subordinate units, and we don't own the terrain, the Afghans do, so it was called an "AoI" instead (Area of Influence) but it was the same thing. That was "AoI Summit," in Kunduz Province.

Scott, our FSO, had the brilliant idea of calling it AoO Summit, or "area of operations," but this convenient idea didn't make it far.

RPG: Rocket-Propelled Grenade. A shoulder-fired anti-vehicle or anti-personnel grenade. The Soviet version is reloadable, and carried by both Afghan and Taliban forces. Our version is a "fire and forget" bazooka called the AT-4, not much good for troops in the open.

Rocket: This is what you hear about when you read that Israel has been rocketed again by Hezbollah or Hamas. 107mm or 122mm Chinese, Iranian, or Soviet rockets that can accurately hit targets up to 5km distant (107mm) or 10km (122mm).

CAT system for interpreters: CAT-1, CAT-2, CAT-3 where CAT-1 is the least able, and CAT-3 is the most. The increase in skill seems to be exponential, as each company typically receives between four and eight CAT-1 interpreters—for a total of somewhere between twenty and thirty total CAT-1s across a battalion—but the battalion receives at *most* two CAT-2 interpreters, and no CAT-3s. The ranking system seems to describe how well the interpreters can speak English—unfortunately, it does not track how well they speak dialect in Dari or Pashto, nor does it track how well they can interpret. Consequently a good interpreter is like a *gem* when you find one, a coveted resource. Also, a human being!

SEABEES: Navy "combat" engineers. Name apparently comes from "CB" or "construction battalions." That's what a garrulous staff sergeant (E-6) told me once, anyway.

CHEMO: Chemical Officer. Because this person typically has nothing to do, he can either be a great asset to the battalion staff by doing work others don't have the time for, or a huge fuck-off dickweed who only cares about himself, like Dick Beau in 1-503rd. God, *everybody* hated that guy.

TIC: Troops in Contact. For some reason nobody says "battle" any more, they say "TIC." "A Co is in a TIC, send them reinforcements!" I didn't think about it at the time but in retrospect it seems strange.

CAS: Close Air Support. Typically describes any airplane that arrives to strafe or bomb the enemy on your behalf. Could be awesome (B-1 bomber, Specter Gunship A-10 anti-tank plane) or a totally lame and massive disappointment (any fighter jet).

CCA: Close Combat Attack. Typically describes any army helicopter that arrives to strafe or rocket the enemy on your behalf.

F-22: A fighter jet. See CAS.

CH-47: A transport helicopter with two rotor blades that looks like it shouldn't be able to fly. Nicknames include "Chinook," "Shithook," and "Bumblebee."

(Army) Staff: The group of soldiers, sergeants, and officers who help the battalion commander run the battalion through planning and organizing.

Toxic Leader: A military leader whose presence makes his organization (squad, platoon, company, battalion, brigade, or higher) worse. Usually characterized by an inflated sense of self-esteem and self-importance, vulnerability to flattery, and the reedy, high-pitched tone of their screams (delivered whenever their whims are not immediately met with full agreement). Often have conventionally attractive girlfriends / wives. Also known for reading and professing admiration for Ayn Rand past their twenties. Understand that they have to appear to be sympathetic to their subordinates or they will be punished or miss promotion, but do not actually possess the capacity to sympathize or empathize with other humans. Have the ability to charm attractive women and superiors, while remaining viscerally detested by almost every one of their subordinates.

EOD: Explosives Ordnance Disposal. The guys who blow up the enemy's bombs and clear out minefields.

Mid-tour leave: The mandatory vacation you get during a deployment. Fifteen days for a twelve-month deployment, eighteen days for a fifteen-month deployment. It's never enough, and always too much.

DFAC: Dining Facility. The place where you eat, aka "chow hall."

Drones: Also called "UAVs" or "Unmanned Arial Vehicles." Robots that we can use to spy on people or kill bad guys.

Thermals: Thermal sights that allow you to see a person's heat signature (rather than the visible spectrum of light). On thermal sights, people look like white blobs, and colder areas are black.

SECTION FOUR

11

29 November 2008

Hail, Brent Old Friend!

Thirty-one years old, and I'm on top of an unthinkable decision: whether or not to extend my commitment to the army for three years, which would guarantee at least one more deployment. If I got out now, I'd feel incomplete, like I hadn't really tested myself. I'd make a good company commander or "CO" after everything I saw during the last deployment, and I think I understand COIN in a way that most other army officers don't really get. Overall, though, the thing that's keeping me in is an idea my first CO gave me, talking about why and how he was making the army a career: "Keep doing it if it's fun, stop when you start hating it. Otherwise it's not fair to your soldiers." I'm still having fun.

Haven't written much to anyone since getting home—been busy boozing, cruising, and carousing. Having a lot of that good, mean-ingless fun, bouncing around Europe, hitting clubs from Germany to Hungary, dating exotic dancers, burning through my deployment cash and living beyond my natural means. Here's the schedule—you know it well: leave work between four and five, meet up at someone's apartment, pre-game with beer, switch to cocktails, dinner and drinks, drinks, chasing skirt, drinks, hit the sack between two or three, show up for work at five or six in the morning, run, muscle through the day, then rinse and repeat. I've gone days—weeks without being fully sober, just various shades of drunk or hung over. Better off that way. Every-one seems to agree about that, if little else. I've got my MCCC date for January, so I'll be heading out with Rufolo and Peters. Looking forward to the change of pace.

Meanwhile, you're headed to Iraq, scene of the surge. And—what are the odds that your new battalion commander would be our old battalion executive officer? I remember you speaking very highly of him, and while I never had a chance to endure his legendary, marathon XO meetings, all of the stories I heard and the limited opportunities I had to see him in action or listen to him speaking left me with a deep impression of intelligence and capability. I'm very curious to hear what you think of Iraq. If I can I'm going to try to volunteer for a MiTT in Iraq right out of the MCCC, then request another light post, or possibly the Old Guard. Let me know if Iraq as a theater is worth the trouble of getting there. After I get my second (or, if I'm lucky, third) deployment in, I'll probably call it a career.

I haven't done too much thinking about Afghanistan since getting home in August. It was a weird time—the Russian / Georgian war went down during leave, and I thought about buying a ticket over there, and might've done it, save to fight alongside a foreign military (even that of an ally) means to forfeit one's citizenship. Most of the thought I've put into what happened, the significance of it all has been tied up in superficial observations. For example, have you come to the conclusion that an officer needs to deploy more than once? Soldiers tend not to have a choice, but the way officers make commitments, unless they're being activated by IRR for duty on a MiTT (or anywhere else) they can usually figure out ways to avoid a second deployment—especially if they get out after one hitch. I think you've got the right idea, taking command of a company and deploying again—I can't imagine fifteen months being the sum of my experience. Going *back* feels like it elevates the significance of what I've done as a man to a higher level—I didn't just go, I *went back*.

Don't think I could do SF (no junior officers from our BN have gone to Ranger Regiment, but fifteen (I think) guys went to SF selection, and nearly everyone passed), that'd be too much—four or five years' commitment takes me to thirty-six or thirty-seven, at which point I might as well make it a career, and a career in SF doesn't sound great unless you're doing the tactical stuff, which I wouldn't at thirty-seven. No—I feel that staying infantry is best for my situation. Knock out the Career Course, and then head to a light unit (no interest in Mech), command there. Keep fingers crossed that I don't have to work for a toxic-type battalion commander.

On a slightly different topic—have you ever noticed that in attempting to remember the things you've seen in the military, the catalogue of people and events that were significant at the time, regularly outpaces your ability to transfer them to the page? Even a thing as trivial as basic training—I used to know everyone in that platoon, intimately—now, oddly, I remember only the exceptionally irritating or exceptionally good people. I couldn't name or even picture everyone in my platoon. I know this because when I was back home on leave in August I dug up a picture of my basic training platoon, and while I recognized the faces, I couldn't put names to all of them. It's similar with lieutenant training, and much worse with Airborne and Ranger training (Airborne was so quick, and then I sleep-walked my way through Ranger School, I'm not surprised that I can't remember them)—I wonder if it will be that way with my memories of Afghanistan someday. It seems so—unnatural, somehow. This is supposed to have been the most important collection of events and human interactions in my life—that's what the movies and books say, that's what my grandparents implied—and it was strange and unprecedented in certain ways—it wasn't, by itself, the end-all be-all. Maybe I expected too much. How much of a high school yearbook does anyone remember?

Oh—I had Thanksgiving in London with JQ at the Danlys' house—met a friend of Justin's, an Italian lady named Giuliana—the first time in a long time I've felt like actually reaching out and pursuing a relationship. We'll see how it goes. It's nice to feel something beyond animal lust for a woman. We should make plans for the holidays, for New Year's—then, when I'm in Benning, I'm happy to talk about coming up to Nashville. I'm sure you won't have any problems justifying driving down from Clarksville.

See you soon champ,
Adrian

P.S. I'd been thinking about Jessica before I met Giuliana, considering writing or calling, getting back in touch (I think she was in or near London), and I noticed on Facebook that she was (is) in a relationship. I had this idea that if she were still available when I got back from Afghanistan we could give it an honest try—things were so colossally fucked up when I left, and there was no point in exposing her to variables that I was certain would only lead to our not being able to stand one another's company and totally dooming any chance we had at a future—then, of course, there was the whole going away to war thing—we'd really left things unresolved, and that weighed on me. Seeing that she'd moved on, that she's living her own life now, realizing that and internalizing the truth that the world had spun on its axis while we were off in the hills—understanding that on that deep, gut level, I was able to let it go. And the second I did that, life presented me with this new opportunity.

30 November 2008

Mike,

Bob tells me you two were living together in Georgia earlier this year. Now that he's gone off to do whatever it is he does, and his room's empty, you should let me move in with you. I'll even pay rent, which I'm sure Bob refused to do on some pretext or another. I'd move in sometime in January, and leave—well, as soon as possible, obviously—but probably no earlier than June / July. By then my "Captain's Career Course" will be finished, and I'll be headed off to my next duty station. I'm sure we can stomach each other's company for that long, and who knows, maybe it'll even be good for our intellectual development—you can listen to my good ideas and hear about books you should read, and for my part I can practice delivering monologues to an adoring audience.

It's worth mentioning that I've been boozing pretty hard in Italy—recently stopped (or toned it down) because I became legitimately worried about the health of my liver, and maybe just my health in general. When you drink continuously without break, it does something funny to your sanity—things happen much closer to the margin—I feel like at first maybe it was recreating that sense of chaos we had on deployment, but the longer it goes on the more detached I get, the less stable I feel. The stats on drinking more than ten drinks a night regularly and—whatever we drink on the weekends, fifteen or twenty drinks—you know, the getting back from deployment norm—are shocking, "sobering" (why is it that "sobering" information is information that makes you want to get blind, staggering drunk?). This is all to say, in a brief and embarrassing moment of honesty, that we should consider making some kind of "let's not drink" pact, understanding that, bit by bit, that pact will erode, until one fateful Friday, with no prior coordination, we'll each have brought a couple of bottles of wine back from work, and then, bam: right back into the spin cycle.

> Respectfully,
> Adrian

Journal Entry: 5 December 2008

Back in London, visiting Giuliana. It's been so long since I felt like giving a relationship an honest shot—a lifetime—every detail is precious. The greens of the plants here are greener, the colors and textures of fabric stand out, the weight of the air—everything feels significant and substantial. Giuliana met me at the airport and led me onto a bus, then down into London's subway system, up to another bus, and finally into a residential neighborhood that reminded me of something out of Sherlock Holmes. Londoners washed around us on the street, by the supermarket, but Giuliana herself outshone them all, I don't think I looked away from the moment I caught sight of her. Upon arriving at her apartment I was unceremoniously directed to my quarters—an air mattress in her living room. Experienced a moment of doubt and fear, then remembered that I wasn't in London to seduce another woman—I was there to keep Giuliana's smiling face in my life for as long as I possibly could. Inflated the air mattress with my own breath, spread the sheets and covers, and when the time came, lay myself down to sleep by the floor like I did for the last year. Alone, but not lonely. This is a good reason to drink less.

8 December 2008

Dear Mom and Dad,

I'm set on my next step—moving to Fort Benning, GA. I'm going to live with Mike Carson, who I don't think either of you have met—he's applying to History programs to study for his Masters and PhD—he'll make a terrific professor, he's got a sense of humor that is, like mine, deranged—his experience in Iraq may have unhinged him a little bit, but in a good way. It's going to be a great time living together—he's better read than I am, and I look forward to tempering my ideas in the fire of his criticism (he and I do not see eye to eye on things most of the time, but both value dialogue and are willing to concede points to the other when we're legitimately wrong—would that the rest of the country were like this). It may be a renaissance of sorts—years from now I could look back and think, "So that's where it all started!" Whatever "that" is…

My stay in Italy's nearly come to an end—too soon on the one hand, and not a second too soon on the other. I feel like I just went through this, leaving home, when I left Afghanistan, and now I'm transitioning back to Fort Benning—from there who knows where. This is life in the army, always on the move. There have been no really bad events here, and a lot of great memories to tide me over. I'll never forget the trips to Venice, or Rome with you guys before deployment—trips around Europe with my friends, feeling like these lovely, incredible old cities were my back yard—Asiago, Padova, Traviso, Trieste, Verona, Vicenza—to say nothing of wine country, Lake Garda, exploring those small towns on the periphery. A time when I had few real responsibilities, most of it occurring before I even understood "responsibility." Such an incredible treat and privilege, to live in a place like this—to live quite well in a place like this—I know Mom's dad would've understood and approved.

At the same time—I never complained much about this to you at the time because what would be the point?—the Italian people seemed not to want us there, a sentiment that arose from dislike for a proposed base in "Dal Molin," or involvement in the Middle East, and even a crazy conspiracy theory about nuclear missile silos in the hills around the city of Vicenza. Agitators periodically organized and held numerous, large (25,000+) protests against the American presence (and by proxy "the criminal Bush"). It reminded me a bit of Japan, of that "world outside America"—all the non-Americans chanting "America go home" with little real understanding of why we're there, and how much we'd all rather *be* home with our families and loved ones. But in keeping with the Japan experience, the only real consequence of their passionate anti-Americanism was a sort of persistent low-grade nuisance—the inconvenience of having to avoid protesters while jogging, or having my routine or schedule disrupted, or encountering superficially hostile individuals in cafés.

The one actual piece of information that I learned as a result of the "disagreement" over our presence in Italy was how much money we pump into the Italian economy. With regards to the new base—we're paying Italian contractors to build entirely new facilities on land we'll rent from the Italians—*American taxpayers* are the ones who should be protesting this, not Italy. It's basically a "right-to-work" program for Italian construction! I looked harder at the issue, and it turns out that we lease our existing base from the Italian government as well. It's occurred to me, moving my car back to the States, my household goods, the money I'll get for moving, the stipend I receive for living in Italy, on top of all of the other costs and fees for living in Europe—as our economy implodes, it seems to me as though we spend a LOT of money on operating costs for people living outside America. Substantial sums of money.

Why are we spending so much money to maintain bases in Italy and other foreign countries? To project power? To maintain foreign economies? Tradition? I can't think of any unimpeachable reasons. Well—what do I know?

I hope that things aren't really as grim in the States as I hear in Italy—Ireland and Spain are certainly experiencing a fair degree of real-estate-related turmoil, and I'm currently surrounded by people in what looks right now to be a "recession-proof" industry—I have yet to see what it's like on the ground, such as it were. The combination of an unprecedented election and a once-in-a-lifetime "market correction"—how does that look on the street? Shuttered businesses? Less people eating out at restaurants? I just can't visualize it.

Obama's election has had an interesting effect here in Europe—officers and soldiers have all noticed that suddenly it's cool to be an American again! They really did hate Bush and Bush's administration—I don't think many people at home understand this, how far he drove many of our long-standing allies away from us. Of course, the way we've been embraced after Obama's election points to Europeans having always liked *Americans*—or at least been prepared to like them. Anyway, it's been interesting to live over here—different from Japan, communication's easier—and seeing America from a more or less neutral political standpoint, from our economic and military allies, but without the nearby threat of China or North Korea, people feel happy to speak their minds.

My last day here will be the last day before winter break, and you can expect to see me home before Christmas. I don't need it to be a white Christmas—it's fine if it is, though last Christmas I had more than enough snow to last me a lifetime.

Love,
Adrian

12

Dear Jim,

It was wonderful to see you and Frankie over the holidays and get an overdue meal together; I'm also glad you could meet Giuliana. She remarked on you and I drinking three cocktails in the space of an hour—this was the first time she'd been exposed to the way we vets do things, and she didn't immediately bite my head off, which is either a relief or a bad precedent. We'll see. Thanks for keeping mum about the timeline of my obligations to the army—I could see the gears turning when Giuliana brought up her version of events, which is that I was *already* committed to an additional three years when I signed the papers. I'd only known her a week, we'd never even *kissed*, and how was I supposed to know that she'd become such an important part of my life? The truth—the truth is that I was committed to this course of action before I met her. I didn't choose the army over her, there was no choice to make. But Italians are so hot-tempered, why risk it?

I'm writing from sunny and chilly Fort Benning, Georgia—you remember it well—*inshallah* it will be the last time I'm stationed here for any reason. I've heard wonderful things about the "Maneuver Captain's Career Course," but have no way of knowing firsthand if the rumors are true. I'd say about a quarter of the class are officers from various branches who've made it through Selection and decided to go "Special Forces"—after MCCC they will disappear to Fort Bragg to attend the "Q" course and, if they excel, lead A or B Teams. The rest of the officers are a mix of infantry and armor officers; some foreign exchange officers as well (we have a Japanese infantry officer in our group, he teaches at their equivalent of Ranger School); as with my lieutenant training, many of the officers come from the National Guard.

The first day of training, our instructor—an armor major with a combat record stretching back to Panama—told us that alongside learning the material, this time, this moment would be about us getting healthy and recuperating from our last deployment. It seemed that way for the first week, but I can already see students raising their hackles and competing, taking the course way too seriously and forcing everyone else to follow along, stay late, all that rot. I've decided I'm going to abuse a 4-day that's coming up to go visit Giuliana—totally against regs—I can sense the push-back building—so much for "taking a knee." And all because a small group of self-anointed go-getters are intent on dotting every notional "i" and crossing every (for the purposes of training) "t." Don't get me wrong, there's a lot of material, and I definitely need to learn it. It's just that if there's one thing I've seen from my life to-date in the army, it's that the learning can't be forced, and the more work you do in a vacuum, the more work you have to do when you get to the real world. Learning the theory is great, but until I get to the point where I'm being forced to write and re-write operations orders, I'm not going to know how to produce an OPORD or CONOP.

You have to let me know where you end up for law school. It's inspiring, you and some of my other friends (I'm sure you've seen the same thing) getting out into the real world to pursue your dreams—and secure America's future. I wonder if our grandfathers felt a similar sense of excitement in the years following WWII… When I think about the challenges we face—these days they're obvious, financial, political, cultural—the only thing that allows me to sleep at night is knowing that vets like you are taking the lessons we learned on the battlefield and drawing on them for motivation in the civilian world. If Congress were made up of combat vets, there'd be no worries about nonsense like you see today, the political posturing. You'd see a return to civility, and outcomes-based legislation (rather than this constant maneuvering for points, to gratify the egos of Washington insiders). You'd see a return to the golden age.

I'm living with Mike Carson, I don't know if you ever had a chance to meet him—he's an alcoholic and a cynic, one of the most cynical people I know, you can barely have a conversation with him about certain topics, he believes in nothing—then, when it comes to other topics he's an idealist and a dreamer. In other words a dangerous drinking companion. Maybe someday you'll get to meet him, you and he can have a love-fest about how much "realer" it was in Iraq than Afghanistan. Unless I get to Iraq (I've got a buddy heading over there soon, and Brent recently came back—said the violence against Americans has been dramatically reduced—I guess the surge worked—put that in your pipe and smoke it, liberals).

To sum it all up: having signed my extension paperwork, here I am at Fort Benning again, starting another three years of service in training, although under slightly different circumstances. I did drive by Sand Hill—didn't stop to see what was going on at "Charlie Rock"— everyone would be different there by now anyway—it looked smaller, somehow, less intimidating. Did I tell you that we slept in D Co's barracks for two days after Ranger School, to keep us separate from the people at Darby? Did our laundry, "all that crazy stuff," as our basic training first sergeant would have put it... *that* was wild—even then, Drill Sergeant Y was already gone. How quickly the army forgets the contours of its soldiers' faces, the details of individuals' service—no trace of us remains there, Jim, we're totally gone—and in three years' time, there won't even be a person to testify that we were ever there.

> Stay well,
> Adrian

Journal Entry: 23 February 2009

Just had ten days with Giuliana. It's so strange to live with a woman—to have her share my space, to cook with her, allow her access to my life—to grant each other rights to intimacy. The day before she arrived, I looked around my room, really saw it for the first time. Papers scattered everywhere. Two books lying open near the door, their spines creased with careless neglect. Clothes unfolded. Military gear spilling out of bags in my closet. Desk undusted. Computer keyboard sticky from my beer-and-wine-stained fingers. *This* is the mess of my life— liking a woman enough to invite her in is one thing, but scrubbing the bath and toilet, wiping down the blinds, using a steam-vacuum... once again, I had no idea what I was getting myself into. Luckily the trips north to Nashville and east to Savannah helped balance everything out. Still, I was a little relieved when we said our good-byes in Atlanta.

MCCC has been a great class, but no matter how much I try to get myself enthusiastic about the prospect of a career in the army—I just can't. Moving all the time—raising a family on the run—I don't have whatever constitutional or emotional reserves that requires. You see it in some officers—they start to go funny—can't describe it better than that. They start to check out *in garrison*—that's when you know it's time to quit. I'm not there, but I could see myself getting there as a major.

15 March 2009

Dear Teddy,

I'm writing on the Ides of March: my four year anniversary in the army. On this day in 2005, Mom and Dad dropped me off at the recruiter's office. They spilled a few tears, and then sent me on my way. Two days later I was in Fort Benning, and since that time I've been kept busy with training and deployments. Now I'm back at Fort Benning, a little more than halfway through my "Captain's Career Course" (MCCC)—this will qualify me to Command a Company. Yes, I want to go back. Yes, I didn't get enough of it last time. Yes, I know, it seems like a stupid or maybe at this point deranged decision, based on emotion rather than logic. Yes, I'm condemning my friends and family to another deployment of annoyance and irritation. It's a selfish act. It's also counterproductive in the sense that I'd like to start a family soon. I met a great woman recently, an Italian girl who lives *damn the luck* in England—this makes the deploying even less responsible from a certain perspective. Nevertheless, this is the way it has to be. Having seen the difference between a lieutenant and a captain, between a platoon leader and a company commander, I have to go through with this. Beyond company commander there's no reason to stay in—thankless staff work, lack of social opportunities, a thankless job with no opportunity for interaction with soldiers or any of the "leadership" responsibilities that make one's job worth getting up for in the morning. After this hitch, I'm done.

Up until now, Ranger School and RSLC (the Recon School) were the only useful schools I'd attended—the only places where I really felt that the army was taking my training seriously, the only places where

I felt that I'd improved as an officer and also as a man. MCCC hasn't pushed me physically (this is very much a "gentleman's" course, so I've been pushing myself—such a welcome change of pace, growing from internal motivation rather than in response to a sergeant or officer screaming at your face to move faster), but learning how to make a plan has challenged me intellectually and emotionally. My instructor for the first phase, a former Ranger, broke a very complicated process down to its essence. He realized that so long as you develop a plan for the enemy, you *have* to develop a plan for yourself (which is a bit more difficult than it sounds). Anyway, I spend about forty-five minutes developing a solid plan for the enemy, and once I've charted out where I'd put my forces if I were the bad guys, it's easy for me to see where to maneuver my soldiers. Works like a charm. Brilliant!

In other news, I've applied to my next unit. When the "Branch Manager" came around earlier this year—this is the major who is responsible for assigning captains to their next unit, and as you might imagine occupies an outsized space in the imaginations of young captains like myself awaiting their fate in Fort Benning—he made several statements that turned out to be guidelines, rather than strict rules. This is the trick in an institution, figuring out what they want you to hear, versus what the actual rules are regarding a thing, then finding the person who can accommodate your desires. He said, for example, that if one were in an Airborne or Light unit (I was Airborne), one would go to a Mechanized unit. He said that if one's first post was overseas or "OCONUS," one would not be offered another post overseas (excluding deployments—everyone expects to deploy again). He emphasized the need for instructors at Ranger School, where one can teach as a captain, and various other training jobs at Fort Benning, such as teaching at OCS where I commissioned, or the lieutenant's course. He told us to fill out a paper with our top choices, submit that paper, and that he and two captains that worked for him would be back in a month to hand out assignments.

Well, only two of the ten or so people I knew who went out for one of the training jobs got a slot, the rest were filled from outside the MCCC. When the time came for me to fill out the paper I did so, more or less dutifully, but I pulled a bit of a sneaky move; knowing that I didn't want to go "Mech" as that would almost guarantee that I would deploy to Iraq (and if I have to deploy anywhere, it might as well be the place I know, Afghanistan), I selected all "Light" units. I didn't put

"Airborne" units down as I figured that would be too obvious. Two weeks later when the captains came around, and I sat down to talk with one of them, I was told that there were really two options for me if I wanted to stay "Light"—which was an option—a posting in Alaska (OCONUS), or a post in Fort Drum, upstate New York, with the 10th Mountain Division. Boy, I tell you—it was a no-brainer. I'm going to the 1st Brigade, 10th Mountain Division.

Here's an odd coincidence, though—the day after I learned where I was headed, we switched from the "company" phase of instruction in the MCCC (where you learn to plan like a company commander) to the "battalion" phase of instruction (where you learn to help make plans on battalion staff), and one of the guys I was in Italy with, Greg Ambrosia, was in my section. He lived down the street from me—was in the other battalion, the one from Sebastian Junger's book and the movie *Restrepo*, where he earned a Silver Star *and* a BSM-V—he and I were in lieutenant and Ranger training together, were both made XOs very quickly at our units (he after five or six months, I after eight), are at MCCC together, and are both headed to 1st Brigade, 10th Mountain Division. In other words, he and I have lived this weird parallel life, our career *timelines* (if not accomplishments) a direct mirror of each other—now, it seems, confirmed by this last act, my final post in the United States Army: Fort Drum.

If I never mentioned it before, it's worth mentioning now—after basic training, I learned not to imagine that I'd made friends, because you know that everything changes. People move around, it gets painful. You only learn this after your first post, I think. I made some great friends in Italy and that's all behind me now—not to suggest that they're not friends, but they're not here. I'd see Greg down at this local pizzeria (Vesuvio's), we'd exchange a few lines about how difficult it was to be XO, then go our separate ways—no rancor, no particular friendship either—this assignment gives that all meaning and context. This in spite of the fact (and he'd be the first to admit it) that *temperamentally* we have almost nothing in common—just very different people. Now we're going to another same post, again—maybe even the same battalion—if that's the case, there'll be a good reason to invest emotionally in this person. He'll have become family.

I've had some time to read recently. *Slaughterhouse Five*, *The Golden Bough*, and *Germany: Jekyll and Hyde* were the first books I finished during the course, and I'm currently working my way

through *Extraordinary Popular Delusions and the Madness of Crowds.*
The book you sent me for Christmas, *Blink,* was terrific in the way
it synthesized various seemingly disconnected studies, then used sta-
tistics and economic models to draw new conclusions from them—it
was while reading *Blink,* though, that I realized that I wanted to read
some of the books that Gladwell referenced. I wanted to read *the things
themselves,* rather than the books that merely collected others' argu-
ments and improved upon them, I wanted to close up the loopholes in
my education, especially when it came to Anthropology and Sociology
(which are fields of study, I think, particularly well suited for military
officers). So—here I am. *Slaughterhouse Five*—well, I don't know how
I missed that one in the first place. I've also got a book by a German
from World War I by a guy named Ernst Junger called *Storm of Steel.*

All this reading—it's like I'm making up for lost time. Well, I did
spend the last four months I was in Italy drinking like it was my job,
"quaffing" large amounts of wine, knowing that it'd be a long time before such an opportunity came my way again. I've been a "good boy"
here in Georgia—living with another intellectual / alcoholic, and it's
just too good an opportunity to waste by pouring it literally down the
drain (of my throat). I could write you a dissertation of the ways in
which I feel the books I've read so far have expanded my mind, and
have more to go—I need to lay hands on some Levi Strauss—thank
God for all this material.

Thanks for keeping me rolling in the ideas, keeping my brain lim-
bered up with reading material! Gotta stock up before I head north in
June!

Love,
Adrian

12 May 2009

Dear Mom and Dad,

I'm not writing with any particular purpose—just realized I hadn't
written in a while. I haven't been writing much since getting back to
America, for a number of reasons. I might've written to Grandpa if he
were still alive, but he's not—haven't had anything worth writing for

Brent recently—don't need to reassure you guys that I'm all right—going to Elsa's wedding in a month or so, haven't had any correspondence from her otherwise, and Giuliana and I don't really have a "correspondence-based relationship" (we talk via Skype, which, for reasons that defy my understanding, is free, making inter-continental relationships possible)—then, I live with Mike, so correspondence with him is just yelling.

He's got a strange life down here—it seems like he's constantly trying to get into things that appeal to him aesthetically about the South, like fishing, or seeing places that he thinks one should see. He's right to do it—everyone should know how to fish, and should like it—but it leads to certain ridiculous situations like spending four hours on a lake with a bunch of people from the very rural areas of southern Georgia and eastern Alabama, drinking and "existing," which despite our best efforts really means watching others catch fish and rebuff our attempts to make conversation. I'm sure he'll figure it out; he's a quick study when he sets his mind to a thing. He's applying to colleges now for History, might end up in Connecticut, so eyes peeled.

The class I'm in here is useful and good, and I feel that I've learned a lot. Even this second phase, which many people dread, seems relevant. A lot of the guys here talk about how if we'd had this instruction as lieutenants we'd have been better prepared to do our jobs—I'm not sure that's necessarily true as many of the lessons in planning we're learning here rely on the knowledge that comes through experience. If the exercise were merely intellectual, it might not be the same. Just trying to figure out how one set of training experiences could feel so trivial, and this seem so good and important.

The "alcohol-free" experiment has gone back and forth, but overall I've been happy about my limited boozing. Even living with Mike, which could've been an unmitigated disaster, hasn't broken my resolve (though the resolve's been shaken several times)—the weeks of overindulgence from Italy have been replaced by occasional Friday or Saturday night romps. That's more appropriate, right? There isn't time during the week, one can't be late for morning workouts or class (or doesn't want to be). It's nice, I feel that the ship's stable, that I'll be well positioned to move on to the next post—Fort Drum, New York—with all of my faculties intact, ready for the next series of challenges. My head certainly wasn't right for it when I left Italy—felt really disoriented from everything, the deployment, all of it. This is a failing of my over-intellectualized, sensitive background—the thing that actually makes me effective at COIN, a balanced approach to things, would make me look weak to fellow infantry officers who tend to take a much more binary approach to problems. I think about this while walking through the WWI / WWII type problems we have to solve through plans in this course. What good would I be in a fight with planes and ships, where the enemy has helicopters too? I'm not sure—it's a different thing, fighting on the defense. We're very capable on the offense, where it's a matter of coordinating different weapons platforms, but when the pressure's on, I imagine it would be stressful in ways that we don't typically encounter. Unless I had access to alcohol, of course. I imagine in that case I'd end up being like Nixon from *Band of Brothers*—the Yale grad who's always on the lookout for more booze. What a character!

You can expect to see me sometime in June as I make the drive from Benning to Drum; I'll be spending some time with Giuliana in Oxford, but other than that I don't expect to have any serious travel responsibilities. I look forward to relaxing at home, during everyone's favorite time of year—summer! I'll be escaping the "Deep South" just in time...

Love,
Adrian

Journal Entry: 22 May 2009

Spring came and went so fast I missed it. The overwhelming proliferation of vegetation here—green everywhere, tendrils creeping over walls, sprouts driving concrete slabs apart, the reek of pollen choking up my sinuses—and now it's summer, when you throw heat and humidity on top of the smell. Last time I left Benning, I left in July—it was a blissful escape—this time I'm leaving in June, and by God, let me never come back.

I considered eating at the OCS chow hall once for old times' sake after one of the Building Four lectures or tests, but something always distracted or interrupted me. I'd walk into class in the morning with everyone else, coffee in hand, thinking "today I'll do such-and-such," but after a three-hour lecture I don't have patience for anything beyond a nap in the car or a quick run to Subway for a sandwich. The thought of sitting in a regimented training facility with people in miserable conditions shoveling food silently into their mouths would not inspire me with any kind of productive nostalgia, and the White-Ascot chow hall isn't good enough to justify going there. I used to fantasize (in OCS) about coming back when I could outrank or outface most of the instructors—but now, having acquired that power, the only thing I want to do is to stay as far away from it as possible. Grabbed a beer at what used to be the NCO club, which was a much better nod to progress and the future.

It's regrettable that the only way to transcend the effects of hierarchy in the military is to achieve rank—because the more rank I've picked up, the more beholden I've been to it—the deeper into the system I go, the more enslaved I become to expectations and the burdens of responsibility. I was most free when I was just a rankless specialist in basic training.

2 June 2009

Dear Jim,

Here we go again; another trip on the merry-go-round. As I leave the South (for Fort Drum, the far north), I have yet more cause to reflect on how time passes, the changes in my life. Things are still going very well with Giuliana, a terrific woman, and I'm really confident about our future together—maybe I'll even be engaged before the year's out! Fort Drum's another light infantry post, and the way the timing works I should be taking command of a company as we deploy to *Iraq*—how cool is that? I'll have both theaters under my belt—then redeploying in time for me to submit my paperwork. And once I've submitted my paperwork, well, I look around and see guys like you and Brent and Mike all pursuing your dreams—*that's what it's all about.*

I'm looking forward to being the company commander. Sometimes I think about it and worry—none of my company commanders seemed to get much sleep, or have any free time; it was an incredible amount of work and investment. On the other hand, I'm confident that I've got what it takes. I just hope I get a hard-working 1SG. I'll never forget my first day as XO: we were training at Hohenfels and a colleague of mine, the XO of another company (I was C Co so I'll leave that detail to your imagination) came up to me and asked what I was doing about trash details before we left to drive back to Italy. I told him that our 1SG had taken care of it, that it wasn't really my lane, and asked him what his 1SG was doing. He told me that his 1SG was asleep. It was 2030.

That's what I saw in Afghanistan: if everyone pulls their weight, the company works well together and can be a good place to exist. War sucks, there's stress and pressure, but overall if you have a sense of being part of a community, part of a team, then everyone gets ahead and only the real scumbags sink to the bottom (or float to the top depending on the analogy). I'm sure I can foster that environment. On top of which, I have a very good idea of what one needs to do to manage a COIN environment; my model, Captain Dixwell, was a tactical genius, and beyond that I spent so much time managing the Mayors and tribal elders of Bermel and then Orgun-E Districts that I feel like I could run my own shura if I had to. Actually got to enjoy it a bit by the end. It can't be too different in Iraq, and it's even possible that by the time we get there we won't be doing any meetings, in which case it would just be training and joint patrolling. You can be certain that once we learn more about where we're going I'll beat you up for any advice you have on how to make a good impact on my Iraqi partners.

I wish you luck in all of your endeavors, and look forward to the time that we can lift a glass of scotch together. It's always too long, and never long enough.

Much love,
Adrian

13

Journal Entry: 13 July 2009

Settled in at Fort Drum. The friendship circle here is a little close—I've spent time with Greg Ambrosia and the C Co commander, John Principe—beyond that, there isn't much to do but work. We go to Louisiana for Iraq trainup for the month of August. The summer here is less humid than in Fort Benning, but substitute gigantic, aggressive horse flies for the swamp mosquitoes of the South. Not sure which one's better. The club here is certainly more accessible and amenable to drinking, though the MPs and constant low-level fear of drunk driving is sure to keep my more serious sprees limited to the apartment. Every Friday night there's a parade of officers and sergeants carrying twelve and twenty-four cases of beer up to their bachelors' / bachelorettes' quarters. Then comes the rap music.

Drum used to be a camp, and is home to the 10th Mountain Division. There are two gradual hills on post—beyond that, it's a two-hour drive to get to any mountains. Reminds me of the situation in Italy: an airborne base that's two hours away from the closest airfield. A mountain post that's two hours away from the nearest feasible mountain training. Or FOBs and COPs at the bottom of valleys infested with insurgents. Why when I look at how things work do I always have the feeling that a high schooler could've done things better?

Missing Giuliana; it's going to be a lonely post, here, nothing like Vicenza.

Journal Entry: 24 August 2009

After having vowed never to return to the South, I found myself at Fort Polk, the deepest part of the South. Little time to read or relax, just worked my tail off for three weeks, in the accursed heat. Now, at long last, it's almost over. The Ranger School nightmare relaxes at last. Did my thing, people think well of me. Why is it that everywhere I go in the army, there's this suspicion that I'm an intellectual, a physical or leadership liability? That being an intellectual is being a liability in war? I questioned a decision on training in private—I know better than to ask questions like this in meetings—and had to endure a half-hour lecture on why the institution of the army does things a certain way versus some other way. The tone left me no doubts that I was deeply in the wrong.

Something's changed between Giuliana and I—this month has been a small window into what life will be like in deployment, i.e. limited Internet and Skype capabilities—unlike the rest of the guys, who could mask their distance with cell phones, the fact that Giuliana's in England effectively meant that we just spent a month apart. And while after the first week, I didn't much notice, she sure did.

14 September 2009

Dear Brent,

It begins again. We returned from our Iraq-training rotation at Fort Polk, LA, only to learn that we'd probably be going to Afghanistan instead as part of the surge. Currently riding the "S-3: Air" slot, the S-3's chief helper with plans and briefing products. Working on staff and having a seat at the big table has been educational, if not particularly rewarding; luckily our S-3 is one of those capacious, ambitious, and driven workers, so the hard work he requires of us falls into a logical order. I had a slow start for the first couple weeks I was on board, but quickly proved my worth at JRTC. It comes down to being willing to put one's nose to the grindstone, but also to enforce standards with others. He's been a great boss for my time on staff, where all of the work one invests in a project is paid back in abstractions and intellectual satisfaction, and not participation.

You remember Torcello in Italy—Giuliana and I attended a wedding there this past weekend. It was a lovely time, although too short by a great deal, I had to make some serious concessions to take the leave, and am worried that I'm developing a reputation as a globe-trotter. It was necessary to the maintenance of my relationship with Giuliana. It was so good to return—to breathe in that good Northern Italian air, head down to a corner shop for *pain au chocolat* and a decent cappuccino—I miss the place, as I'm sure you do, and think about the trips we made to Asiago and into wine country often. My drinking seems to be wearing thin with Giuliana—I drank what I felt was a moderate amount (I was jovial and ambulatory—who cares how much I had, why should that be important?). What a charmed life we led—some of the best years of our lives—wouldn't trade them in for anything.

I don't know whether I'm ready to spend the rest of my life there. She wants me to learn Italian and wants to move closer to home eventually, get an apartment there to be close to her family. I'd like to do the same thing, but with *my* family and Connecticut. This is a danger of being together with someone who has similar priorities to you: unless that person lives in the same town, it can be awkward. As much as I love Northern Italy and would want Giuliana to be connected to her home, it would be terrible for me to have to live so far away from my friends and family. We'll work this out over the next few months, or resolve it after deployment.

I'm obsessed with this Iraq / Afghanistan planning thing, how up in the air our future is. This is exactly how it played out last time—the 173rd was supposed to go to Iraq, but the surge bumped us to Afghanistan instead. Now we're supposed to go to Iraq, but the surge in Afghanistan is pulling us in. Guess I'm really fated not to go to Iraq. Maybe that's where I'll go to die or something—like one of those awful "voyage of self-discovery" novels like *The Alchemist*—how would it look:

"Then I had a dream about a tree and a young boy. When I approached the tree, I noticed that it bore ripe pomegranates. The boy picked one and handed it to me. I asked him why he was being generous, and he said, 'Because I'm you as a child.' I knelt at his feet and wept. 'Why do you cry,' he asked, and I told him, 'Because I've come here to murder you,' and jabbed a knife into his throat. He screamed, a weak, reedy-voiced scream I would've delivered back when I was a punk kid, and his scream gladdened my heart."

I look forward to visiting you in Los Angeles this winter. Can't wait to see Frank again after all these years, and see how much scotch the human body can withstand without blacking out! Give all my regards and best wishes,

> Your humble servant & etc.,
> Adrian

Journal Entry: 21 October, 2009

Another unremarkable birthday—this one spent running through Live Fire Drills for Afghanistan on Fort Drum. Thirty-two years old, still muddling around in the cold. Ladling food out of a green cooler onto my paper plate for dinner, retiring to my sleeping bag on a rickety cot. Remembering to remember my "wet weather gear" to keep dry in the rain. Not sleeping. Treating my subordinates like children; being treated like a child by my superiors. Acting like a child, because that's what life is like in the army when we're playing pretend war for exercise.

The drift away from Giuliana is turning into a gulf. It's like waking up one morning and realizing that this person you care about is across the Atlantic Ocean, how unlikely that is in reality, like what were you thinking. After all these hours on Skype, visits at every opportunity, phone conversations in the middle of the night or early in the morning, it's hard to believe that it could end in nothing. Trying to ignore the problem and hope that it just goes away. Sometimes that happens in relationships—you weather the rocky parts and it gets better. Just need to have faith.

> *1 December 2009*

Dear Teddy,

Seeing you in New Haven and getting to watch Yale lose to Harvard by only a few points (I've seen worse scores—a respectable loss seems like the best thing one can hope for these days) was a great pleasure.

I apologize for going over the line with drinking a bit at The Game. I know I didn't do anything terribly inappropriate, but at the same time, things felt slightly out of control. Which, naturally, feels awful.

It's too bad Giuliana couldn't make it out then, but she came out for Thanksgiving. You met her when we went to Nashville earlier to see your daughter sing—I'm crazy about Giuliana, even if we've had some difficulties recently, I still think we can make it. Everything else being equal, it depends on building a solid foundation that can support us over the next deployment. I'm headed to Trieste to visit her and her family over the holidays—a lot will depend on how that ends up, and then what we can cobble together this spring. I'm not sure when I leave for Afghanistan, it could be as early as January, or it could be sometime late February or early March. These things are all up in the air, and it places a great deal of stress on the relationship. As she feels that she has to compromise to accommodate my mid-tour leave, and adjust to my schedule, other things that a normal couple would talk about or find ways to compromise on become contentious. You might imagine that I've become very opposed to the idea of any kind of compromise—dangerous shoals ahead. I still hope she and I can navigate our way through.

Meanwhile, the uncertainty that surrounds our deployment consumes everything else. Not knowing where you'll be in a month or a year, or when you'll be there, places a great deal of stress on everyone. It's worst for the people with families—and serves as a constant low-level distraction that gets worse as time goes on—older sergeants and some of the soldiers have been coming down with "injuries" and doing what they can to avoid deployment—guys who already have three or four deployments under their belts—the official reaction to this is that they're malingerers (an offense punishable under the Uniformed Military Code of Justice), but one has to feel for them anyway. Everyone else has to go, why should they be any different—save that they've been before—but that's what they signed up for—there's no way around it. Some of the sergeants on staff have begun making animal noises—clucking like chickens, meowing like cats then pretending to look for the stray cat in the office—does it matter whether they're doing this deliberately or not? Isn't the act of doing something irrational a sign of madness? If I were to take my pants off in the middle of a Stop and Shop grocery superstore, wouldn't I be crazy?

The excitement I feel at going back to Afghanistan far outweighs the disappointment I feel that I will never go to Iraq. There are many pros to a return to Afghanistan: I've been there before and know what the fight looks like, I have some idea of how the people are, of the capabilities of our interpreters, how to get things done. I know the agencies and the roles various individuals play in a society. There's a good chance I can get something done as a "battle-space owner." Amusing aside, we aren't allowed to have an "AO" or "area of operations" or call ourselves "battle-space owners" because our Afghan partners own the space—some kind of crazy Orwellian thought-control naming convention nonsense. I refuse to endorse it privately, but will maintain the public fiction as it is my duty to do so.

In other news, I was told nearly a month ago that I'd take command of Alpha Company, 1-87 Infantry in November—but this was based on the assumption that we were going to Iraq. Going to Afghanistan means that the handover will happen sometime next summer instead. Naturally I'm eager to get down to the business of leading soldiers in combat, and would have appreciated the opportunity to train my company according to the standards I know they'll need to meet in order to fight effectively in Afghanistan—I do worry that their current training may not be focused enough on rucking, carrying heavy weight dismounted—but these decisions are outside my hands. Trying to stay focused on the positives, trying to remember to "control the things you can, and release the things you can't [control]." This way I'll be taking command in combat—June / July should be the peak of fighting season, the meat of it, and I won't be missing much (unless I'm really unlucky) with April / May.

The year should go by pretty fast, if my last deployment was any indicator. It really dragged while I was there, but when I came back, life had moved on very quickly. The only way I've figured out to catch up with things is to drink my way back to the place everyone else occupies, switch myself off.

Look forward to seeing you before my departure—or, failing that, upon my return. One last hurrah!

Love,
Adrian

Journal Entry: 1 January 2010

The first day of the New Year. Wish I'd spent it in the Alps with Giuliana and her family. I could've stayed, should've stayed. Wandering through the streets with her, passing the tall, blond Austrian-Empire descendants murmuring Italian in the night, walking into bars heavy with fresh cuts of beef, aged ham, and liquors of every hue—everywhere a sense of close proximity, fellowship, friendship, belonging. Very limited drinking, and not once to excess, even by her modest standards. I've never seen such a beautiful *people* before—the city is full of decay, ancient and modern decay, everything crumbling, gazing out over the head of the gray, wintry Adriatic Sea—but the people—a city of fashion models!

15 January 2010

Dear Giuliana,

Thank you for inviting me to Trieste. Those few days represented one of the most relaxing and rejuvenating vacations of my life, and our best yet. It was so good to be there with you—not just to spend time with your family, whom you know I love, but also to wander the streets with you, see the sights. So many great places I never knew existed. The Carso, the docks, those incredible frescos in the church, the Roman ruins, Miramar—I just had no idea the place was so magical. I admit that for the first time, seeing those places in person the thought occurred to me that I could live there, that getting an apartment, learning Italian and navigating the streets, picking up coffee on the corner—those were things that were not just possible, but could be fun with you. It was one of the best trips of my life, and—I just wanted to thank you for it.

My unit got its marching orders, so I can finally tell you how this is all going to work out. One battalion (not us) is going to Kabul to train Afghan army recruits. Another battalion (the cavalry—technically they're called a "squadron," but that's just silly army stuff) is headed South to Kandahar to partner with the Afghans and the Canadians and fight the Taliban. We're headed North to a place called Kunduz to fight alongside the Germans and Afghan Police against the Taliban—the Taliban are trying to open a "new front" against the government, in a place the government used to assume was safe. We'll be the vanguard of the surge.

There's no question: I'll be taking an infantry company into combat. I'll be working alongside the Germans, so—I have no idea what that means, hopefully nothing like in the movies. I'm taking off in *April* so I'd like to see as much of you as I can before I go; we won't get a special time for leave because we're so close to Christmas break—and I'll be back sometime between March and April of 2011. If you can wait for me, I think we have a real shot at making this work. I've never said that before—I wouldn't have said it (didn't say it) the last time I deployed, in fact it was quite the opposite, I told a woman that I didn't think it was a good idea to stay together over a deployment—but I was wrong. If what you and I have is good, and real, then we'll find a way to keep it alive—many fail, but many succeed, and goddamnit it's worth it. What a story for the kids and the grandkids, right? Grandma and Grandpa met in England, fell in love, Grandma stuck with Grandpa while he was in the army, while he went to Afghanistan—that's possible, that happened in WWI and WWII, why couldn't it work for us?

It's going to be hard. I'm not going to have easy access to Skype over there, at least not in a way that's convenient for either of us—we'll have to make it work with letters and emails (which I know you hate) and occasional phone calls. It's worth looking the difficulty in the face because if we're naive about it, then the separation might get to be too much. Trust me on this one: when you don't see a punch coming, and it lands on your jaw, it's a lot worse than if you have a chance to roll with it. I want you to envision the solitude, what it's like to be pledged to someone you can't see and won't for a very long time.

And it's not all on your end. The hard part for you will happen during the deployment. The challenge for me will be coming home to learn that *even if you stick with me* you will have changed and adapted to that solitude—you'll have taken up yoga, or salsa, and matured in ways that will seem odd and unseemly to me. It will take us time to adapt—you to the old me (I'll be in a time capsule—or a time machine—I step in when I leave for Afghanistan, and step out when I return, like I was gone for an evening—but a year's gone by), and me to the new you. We will have our fill of challenges, I cannot even predict the full measure of them, all I know is that if we're serious about this—and I am—then we will be able to work our way back across the gulf that must spring up between us.

What must it have been like for an officer in the Austrian cavalry in the 19th century, headed weeks away by rail and horseback to Russia or some part of Germany to fight for the Empire? Wasn't that the same? They managed to find their way home, and—come what may—I promise I'll find my way back to you when this is all over. What happens next will be up to us. At least we'll have tried, that's worth something.

> See you soon (on Skype),
> Love,
> Adrian

21 February 2010

Dear Jessica,

Writing this letter is a bit of indulgent selfishness—I'm well ensconced in a happy relationship for the first time since we parted ways, and you've been in a solid relationship since things did not work out between us. I will never forget the moment you asked me if I would stay with you—I knew you had other options—and I could not face the uncertainties of war, the prospect of coming back changed (or not at all). Leaving you out of that discussion was, foolish; in any case, that's how I played it.

I'm deploying again soon—it's a little hazy, but could be any time from two weeks to more than a month from now. It's soon, is the point. People have already started leaving, and naturally that's put me back in the frame of mind I was in when I left for my first deployment, so long ago—another lifetime. Winter's already beginning to fade into spring—this was not a terrible winter, and over too quickly. Winter in upstate New York is a sight, the way the whole land is blanketed by snow, and then all at once it's melted and green starts to appear beneath it. The smell of regrowth—I have this fear that I'll leave on the first day of April, it'll be warm, and I'll have to tear myself away, back to that dusty, blasted, war-torn land. Would've been easier leaving from a blizzard. It always is.

My thinking isn't as clear as it could be, and I apologize for that—it took a major effort of will to overcome my feeling that, everything having worked out for the best for each of us, better to just leave things alone. But I'm an emotional person, as you know—an emotional wreck! Especially when it comes to moments like these. So—indulge me this whim—the desire to ensure that things are well between us, or at least not angry or bitter. It weighs heavily on my soul; it feels like a matter I don't want on the balance ledger if I'm called to account for my many failings and misdeeds.

I wrote my girlfriend, Giuliana, a letter recently; I was considering breaking things off with her, and late last year I really tried to break things off in the way that I did with you before the deployment—she wouldn't let me! Flew out to see me, was really sweet and understanding—we had an incredible time in Trieste over the holidays. I figure, now that I know what the risks are, why not just man up and give it a try? She's a wonderful girl with a steady and sunny disposition that balances out my natural tendency to take a cynical and pessimistic view of life.

So—it should be irrelevant by now but isn't—I need to know, before I leave, that you have a decent opinion of me, that you don't think me too awful. Whenever you have a chance, please let me know. Who knows, maybe we can even rediscover the friendship that I depended on for so long before things all went to hell. I can definitely use more friends as I embark on the last and most serious quest I'll see in my role as an army infantry officer.

> Fondly,
> Adrian

Journal Entry: 12 March 2010

The lifts have begun. I've had my bags packed since February—never fully unpacked into my apartment in the first place, there's so much impermanence, why perpetuate the fiction that this place is home for me. Why dust the shades, or clean the tub, or do anything unless there's a compelling reason for it? Barely have the energy to write—my job is the most thankless, procedural, essentially redundant job at my level—but still *necessary* enough to require energy. So at least I can look forward to being in Afghanistan, and having enough time in the day and night to get things done—being at work twenty-four hours a day. Already feeling less thirsty for booze—like my body's preparing for the inevitable purge. One wants badly to drink heavily in Afghanistan, and also not to drink at all. Cravings—sex, companionship, solitude, booze—they're contradictory, and end up canceling each other out. Save the craving for food, and for battle. Those are constant.

Can't quite picture what it'll be like for Giuliana.

20 March 2010

Dear Jim,

Figured I'd take the opportunity to send you one more letter. Everyone else is leaving, we're halfway through the deployment process, and I'm set to go in a couple weeks. There's a *New York Times* crew embedding with us, following the battalion around—maybe for as little as two months, or as much as six—difficult to say. It doesn't seem like they know themselves—I don't understand how that world works, how they secure funding, if they have to pay for meals and housing through the military, who insures them, any of it. Still—my first deployment, our sister battalion was covered by Sebastian Junger and Tim Hetherington in *War* and *Restrepo*—and here we are, being followed by the *New York Times*—these are the types of events that make one feel as though one is part of something bigger.

I was thinking about that after meeting the lead reporter, James Dao—a fellow Yalie (Pierson! I won't hold it against him), the photographer, Damon Winter (a Pulitzer-Prize winner!), and the producer, Catrin Einhorn; their interest in writing this story, which seems like it's going to be a story about people going to and coming back from war, is to explore the meaning of war for society, rather than another misbegotten, futile attempt to maintain objective distance while writing about a firefight from a ditch while bullets are screaming overhead. I remember talking with the guys from 2nd BN 503rd—the *War / Restrepo* crew—and it really seemed like to them, being part of a narrative or story gave their experience meaning. They went through some awful things, but those things were recorded and memorialized—that process gave the terror of war some significance outside itself, elevated it to the status of story or myth. I think it was useful for the soldiers.

A story that is well written and well produced is important for people to see—so they know what's going on—but everyone knows that's one of the things that makes journalism useful to society. I also believe, though, that it will be useful for the participants—help them to resist PTSD, to understand what happened as part of a framework.

So, I'm obviously making my company (I'm supposed to take command June / July timeframe now—our Alpha Company—I can't wait) completely open to them, and will let them know that if they want to ride out on a patrol, they can. You know the traditional skepticism-bordering-on-hostility to which most media are subjected; they will encounter none of that from me. Again, my feeling is that having the media to record events will only lead to those events taking on a meaning outside of the war—and you know how meaningless things can seem in war sometimes—and assuage any casualties or deaths we might encounter while on the offense. The people who get to participate in whatever stories come out of this project will, for the rest of their lives, be able to say that their experience in Kunduz Province had the imprimatur of the *New York Times*—it was worthy of coverage. That's actually true of many units out there, as you and I both know. Nevertheless, most units don't have such an opportunity. What's the worst thing that can happen? We're not going to be committing *war crimes*, for God's sake!

The importance of stories and storytelling is a great argument in favor of appointing unit historians to write the unit history upon return to home station—too much of a task for one man, but with significant resources (say, a lieutenant per company to do the writing for their section, a head editor, and a publisher to find a printer and raise the necessary money) easily accomplished in one or two months. All of the units in World War II did this at the brigade or regimental level—irrespective of service, so far as I can tell—if we don't do it now, it'll become exponentially more difficult.

Thinking about writing and recording stories, and what having the media around will be like over there has given me a lot of perspective on the importance of narrative, and made me think long and hard about what I want to do when I leave the army. I think—if I'd come here and had a command right away, and then been able to train and transition my guys, then had a chance at a second command—if things had worked out perfectly, I might've stayed. I'm not. So what next? Politics is really attractive—I don't know how Giuliana would handle that, as it would depend on my being in America—same with law school. Going back to school doesn't particularly appeal to me but I do have the GI Bill. Probably going to try to figure out how to get a Master's Degree or its equivalent.

It's good to have things to look forward to when I return. That's going to be what carries me through this experience. I know that from the last time around. The media will mean that there's a certain amount of interest in what's going on here from home, but more importantly, it will also mean that I can post up and have some really great conversations with these guys, which is certain to keep my mind off the tedium when things get slow and will help the hot summer months pass by. Some of the most engaging and memorable times I had were sitting down with the journalists who passed through Bermel during my last deployment—Tom Coghlan, Jason Howe, John D. McHugh.

> Hope all's well,
> Love to the wife,
> Adrian

P.S. I'm on speaking terms with Jessica again. Picked up the friendship like it hadn't been dead these past three years!

14

Journal Entry: 13 April 2010

Arrived at Camp Marmal for what I hope is no more than a two-day stay. It's very clean and well organized, none of the chaos and hustle-bustle of BAF; whatever their ability to patrol, these Northern Europeans are well organized. To the south, Mazir-e-Sharif stretches end unseen into the distance. To the east and west there's nothing but desert. And the North has that visual horizon particular to Afghanistan, without which I would be lost: the mountain range. Seems fairly small and low as these things go here, but we're not at elevation the same way we were in 2007–08.

The terrain is brown, with just a hint of green from the recent seasonal bloom. A Norwegian patrol was coming down from a pass in the hills when I arrived, tiny vehicles kicking up a cloud of dust that grew larger as they approached. Walking to dinner later I passed their muster area—the Norwegian soldiers were cleaning their vehicles, laughing and enjoying the end of their dangerous duty. When I passed their vehicle depot I took another look at the pass, the road winding up to and into the hills—what had they discovered there?

15 April 2010

Dear Mom and Dad,

I'm back. God, like I never left the place. What a trip—the combination of a coup in Kyrgyzstan and a volcanic eruption left us with interrupted and ad-hoc travel plans; we flew in through Kuwait instead of going through Germany en route to Kyrgyzstan, and then touched down in Manas after their political situation was resolved. It put me off schedule by about a week, all told, but at least most of that time was spent in a hotel room. I linked up with some of the guys from my future company—two of the platoons, and their first sergeant, and we were able to finagle our way on board a plane that was slated to take some marines south to Kandahar. A marine battalion commander was screaming at a dispatcher to "fix the problem" while we loaded his buses, and then we were driving and he and the rest of the marines faded into the background—the flight was ours. "Fortune favors the bold" and all that. I could understand his being irritated at having to stay in Kuwait, and that he was already behind schedule, but so were we! It's not every day that "captain" trumps "colonel," but my rival for the flight was so hung up on his "rights" and the regulations, that it was easy to outmaneuver and outfox him. I feel bad for his guys—if that's all it took to outfox a marine BC, they're going to have a tough deployment in RC-South with the Taliban. The stakes are higher than missing out on timelines.

The next stop after Kuwait was Mazir-e-Sharif. We landed at Camp Marmal, which is a sprawling and clean compound run by the Germans and containing Swedish, Finnish, Estonian and Norwegian components (now, U.S. as well); in one direction you can see mountains (as everywhere in the country, it seems), and in the other the city stretches out as far as the eye can see. For comparison I placed it beside Bagram Air Force Base (BAF) in my memory, and the U.S. hub, while bigger, suffered greatly in every other respect; Marmal is less trashy, nicer, and more efficiently run. Great Russian aircraft load and unload obscure equipment on Marmal's tarmac at all hours—it buzzes with restrained activity in a way that you don't feel at BAF, where everything is chaotic and frantic, disaster held at bay by the slimmest of margins—often a salute.

They also have bars there, for the NATO troops who can drink. Having great steins of beer available in a place isn't healthy for morale—not that I have a great desire to drink here, but it does bring up unusual questions such as: "what would war be like if you could drink?" And then I think about how every other army in human history has had access to ale and mead and whiskey—why shouldn't we have the same? Like I said, unhealthy.

They stashed us in the corner of Camp Marmal, away from everything (apparently there was a problem with some earlier U.S. Army infantry eating in the German dining facility and not following rules, or not showering, or hassling women, or any of the possible ways that U.S. Army infantry can get into trouble) and that scotched it for the rest of us. We ran through the mandatory training exercises—rollover drills, IED drills, zeroing our weapons, and then we were off to FOB Kunduz, where we are now, via C-130 Hercules (that old workhorse).

The C-130 is the plane I've spent the most time in, between Airborne / Ranger and RSLC schools and the 173rd—I think they had them operating during the Vietnam War—if we go to war again ten years from now, we'll probably still be using C-130s. They have this essential quality about them, like no matter how far technology advances, there will always be a place for them in the plan. It felt appropriate that a C-130 delivered me to FOB Kunduz. No plane is more friendly to me than an old cargo-net-holding, cramped, red-light, loud-drone Hercules.

Arriving at Kunduz I immediately noticed a huge "military graveyard" of accumulated Soviet and Northern Alliance / militia equipment, including helicopters, artillery, anti-aircraft weaponry, and tanks of all types and sizes. It's right next to our little FOB—how the two came to exist next to each other is beyond me. Apparently the Afghans consider it a memorial to the years of civil war between 1989 and 1996; to us it's a rather disturbing reminder of failed past attempts to bring bureaucracy and first-world institutions to the country. Many of the tanks and artillery pieces still have Soviet red stars painted on them; I took pictures and will show them the next time I have an opportunity. Our battalion artillery officer and I walked outside to scope it out while he was giving me the tour—he and two fellow staff officers reserved me a room and we'll live alone in relative comfort (considering that the place has inadequate air conditioning in the summer), safe from insects and the elements.

The Taliban are here—nobody knew for sure before we arrived, because the German reporting mechanisms aren't synchronized with U.S. reporting conventions—but some units have already seen shooting and IEDs in the roads. I won't be leaving the FOB much at all so I'm perfectly safe. We're on a plateau, far away from the huge mountains that separate Kunduz from its southern and eastern neighbors and well beyond effective rocket or RPG range. Our situation is nothing like past forts I've seen, which were built under or near high ground the enemy could use to attack us with their entire arsenal. We're safe in this place!

Speaking of which, Greg Ambrosia sends his regards—he's headed south with his company (Black Sheep) to "Baghlan" Province, so I won't see much of him as the deployment progresses, but will be able to track what's going on. Sounds like a fun job—he'll be fairly autonomous, with German allies, Afghan allies, and a few bad guys to corral up in the mountains. Well within his ability to accomplish. If they finish the fight in Baghlan before it's finished in Kunduz, they may come up to help us and I'll be able to see more of him. You never met the C Co commander, John Principe—he's the other guy I'd travel around with, to Montreal, Kingston, Syracuse and so forth—he's still on the base. There's a solid corps of officers here and I feel that it's going to be a good deployment from that perspective (really crucial, the support network).

Send cookies and other goodies when you can. The people who've been here already have already begun receiving packages and it doesn't quite seem fair—they're being generous with those of us who have recently arrived and aren't sorted out yet with mail, but it's better to give than to receive. I won't expect anything before May or June—but send *something*.

Love,
Adrian

Journal Entry: 23 April 2010

It didn't take long to get back into the swing of things. Got my own room—a small plywood box next to Scott, our FECC and across the hall from Matt, my partner-in-crime in the S-3 shop—it's a bit of a luxury on an FOB this small. A closet, a door, a thin piece of wood for a wall, the ability to shut the rest of the world out. That's priceless in a place like this, and for most of my deployed life, I've had that luxury. Hope it keeps up.

The infrastructure here is absurdly primitive. The generators went out a couple days ago and have been on sporadically since; means the AC doesn't work during the day, and the heat doesn't work at night.

These buildings are made of tin and concrete, and are good for keeping out wind and rain and that's it. Had to fly generator mechanics in from somewhere—hope they get fixed soon. Already missed two chances to talk with Giuliana on the phone, briefly—the generators scotched that, we were on backup power—does not bode well for this year…

★

2 May 2010

Dear Giuliana,

I'm writing you from sunny Afghanistan! I landed mid-April and missed spring by a matter of inches—apparently the week before I landed the entire land was green (apart from the massive mountains surrounding us in the distance, which even now are snow-capped). There were still a few red-blossoming flowers visible—one of the CAT-2 interpreters (there are three levels of interpreter, CAT-2 are very rare at my level, each colonel gets one for his battalion, CAT-3 is the best and least frequent) seems to be a bit of an artist and has been taking pictures of any and all "nature" he can find. No use complaining that I missed the arrival of spring; it's gone, and in its place, everything is that familiar old shade of brown and adobe, with the haze of dust that gets into and onto everything.

The accommodations are worse than anything I saw during my first deployment. We've been placed on an old "company-sized" FOB, or a fort built to accommodate about 150 soldiers; Navy "Seabees" (engineers) have been working around the clock to expand the space and make it livable for the 600 soldiers that will eventually be staying here. For the time being though, it consists of cramped quarters, a *terrible* gym swarming with flies and vermin, an embarrassingly inadequate rec room, disgusting shower and toilet facilities, not enough air conditioning units, never enough white milk, and an overwhelmed garbage and laundry infrastructure.

These seem like mean things to complain about, and I won't spend an inordinate amount of time whinging about them. At least there's a shower to be had once every other day or so, and water to wash my face and shave. Things can—and will—get a lot worse. I've seen what things can be like, and that was three years ago; the excuse we heard then for making us live like animals was "there aren't any assets, they're all in Iraq." Now the excuse is "there aren't any assets, they're all in RC-South." Come *on*! I'd love to be in a place where you can get on the horn and just get whatever you ask for, just once. Of course, the people on the receiving end of all this institutional largesse will be the very ones who complain loudest about how hard they had it when we're all back from this misguided episode.

The Germans! God—it's so odd to be working with them—on the good side, there's an entire extra company's worth of combat power here, and they'll be surging another *battalion* of soldiers here to help with the surge over the summer. Their FOB is immaculate—well organized and clean, you can imagine. This is something about their culture that is particularly well suited to the military (the source of a thousand jokes and stereotypes)—it prizes institutional systems, hard work, and efficiency above everything. On their base, which is across the plateau from our own fort, just a half-mile distant, you can almost believe that we have a shot at pulling this off, of clearing the Taliban out. I've met some really motivated officers and sergeants, and have a good feeling about my time as a staff officer.

This "staff" or administrative existence will get old very quickly, but I don't have a precise role on the staff now that my replacement has arrived. I was supposed to take command in November, so there's been another "me" here—you met him at the Winter Ball, Matt Adkins. Between the two of us, the workload is very manageable. He's more thorough and methodical than I am (his Air Force upbringing no doubt), and I'm more confident bullshitting my way through a half-baked last-minute briefing that I had just enough time to throw together because someone needed an assessment "yesterday." Again, we're a great team. There are some other fantastic people in the office (which is one room) that make it a pleasant work environment—our Intel officer, the FECC (lives across the hall from me), and our always-eager chemical officer; you met my boss, he keeps a lid on things, makes sure they don't get too far out of hand and that we make our deadlines. Rarely has to yell. This makes working pleasant for us and for him. He gets an unprecedented four senior captains (by our training, anyway), which gives him enormous flexibility as a planner—and we have enough intellectual ass to kind of fuck off a bit in the gaps and still out-produce our rival shops.

The trick I learned last deployment that kept me sane and on a more-or-less even keel was to get off the base once every week or two

(two at the most)—even if it was just a routine patrol. In this case that would be across the plateau to the German fort, or possibly to downtown Kunduz, to the Provincial Headquarters. These won't be dangerous patrols, but it's important to keep my brain engaged in the routine office work that is demanded of it; if I can't get new inputs, new air, new spatial relationships and images, I get depressed. My energy and motivation atrophy, and creative potentials fail and narrow, wither on the vine, so to speak. I start sleeping more. It got really bad last deployment as I was trapped on FOB Orgun-E, I was on the edge of despair—only friends kept me afloat. Ennui, not being able to get off the fort and help out according to my talents. Of course, that's not the way it's supposed to work. I'm grateful that I've had access to such a perfect mixture of patrols, friendships, and good leadership.

Write when you can and let me know how Oxford in the spring has been treating you; and send me some of those good English cookies if you get a chance. Miss you, and think of you often!

> Love,
> Adrian

Journal Entry: 10 May 2010

Had my first run-in with an unscrupulous terp of the deployment (certainly not my last). It's tough. This guy went out on no notice with a staff officer and spent the night with a bunch of Afghans—pretty hairy stuff, even if the Afghans were generals—he kind of put his neck on the line. In return he asked me to bring him to the S4 for a CERP project proposal. Basically the proposal was to deliver a generator with sufficient fuel to power his village. He wanted me to get him into the power business, set him up as a big man in his village. I'm sure if he'd gone back to his village with nothing, without even having tried, he'd have been a pariah. There's so much good to do here, it's impossible to know where to start.

I remember being a lieutenant fresh in theater, with no idea of how things worked—I actually imagined that the previous unit had mistreated its interpreters, and the Afghans. The truth here is that everyone has an angle, everyone's trying to work you for some advantage. Knowing that helps sort through where to put your efforts. I'm sure some of the lieutenants here are going through the same process now, assuming that their basic human impulses are enough to separate people who want to cheat them from their "friends." It's a hell of an institution we have going here—no such thing as friends, just allies of expediency.

The terp didn't get his generator. There's no money for it, for anything. Guess he won't be coming out on any more night missions.

25 May 2010

Dear Brent,

Our German allies have a platoon of *panzergrenadiere* in light "Marder"-class tanks that are equivalent to our Bradleys. Their APCs and tanks have the German "Iron Cross" on the sides. The soldiers still march, and—apparently—sing. I was on their FOB recently and watched as a convoy moved out—soldiers manning crew-served weapons, heads sticking out of hatches—and that "Iron Cross"—it was strange, to say the least.

How's that for a "hello from Afghanistan"?

I'll say this for the Germans: they know how to make a convoy roll. There've already been a few firefights and "events" in our area that confirm that the enemy is here in force; it's been the "feeling out" stage, with both sides circling warily, knives in front, looking for the best opportunity to strike. The majority of the fighters up here are more like gangsters, relatively few of the ideologically motivated "true believers," very small Al Qaeda footprint. Even though this is a rural area, it's shocking that GIRoA, the "Islamic Government of Afghanistan," could lose control over a place like Kunduz. It has a sizable ethnic Pashtun population, which is cause for worry; but on the whole the Northern Alliance is so well loved and mythologized I just don't know how the Taliban could've established not just a foothold but also a *stronghold* up here. It's really bad—here and in Baghlan, they have in fact opened a new front in Afghanistan; there are many areas, entire *districts* where we cannot patrol with less than a company (at which point we will have sufficient combat power to resist when they ambush us).

I've been keeping an eye on my future area of operations. There was a TIC up north when we first got here, it was an IED and some Small Arms Fire; I had this mild panic that all focus and attention would swing north and the fighting would be over before I had a chance to lead. Instead, the focus has fixed firmly on two districts to our west—no point in mentioning their names—we have a platoon at the district headquarters, and the Germans keep two platoons for a total of a company's worth of combat power (including, normally, some panzers). The Taliban are well ensconced, it's a twenty-five minute drive from our FOB—*almost* rocket distance—and quite obviously a place that requires attention before the outlying areas. The current A Co commander is a great guy, and I hope he gets a chance to get his beak wet—I don't think these things are "zero sum," that if he gets into fights with the Taliban that I will suffer—I just don't want him to do *all* the heavy lifting.

I've been pretty disappointed at how little we have up here in the way of assets. It's 2010, and somehow we're worse off than I remember in '07–'08; everyone in ISAF must assume that the Germans are taking care of us (they aren't—not that they *won't*, just that their ROEs with CAS are so restrictive that getting air support from them is like getting air support from a couple Air Force F-22s: worthless). There isn't enough lift, there aren't enough engineers, there isn't enough infrastructure, and we don't have any wood. I talked with guys in the Career Course who were at places in Iraq during the surge where the floodgates were on, and you could get an FOB built in a matter of days—whatever you needed, *BAM*, it was there getting flown in by a couple CH-47s. I've never seen that. Quite the opposite. I guess I never will, because even when I take over up north in A Co's area, I'll be the final kinetic shaping operation. Won't have much pull from that position.

I'll keep in touch and let you know how things are coming along. Think it's going to end up being a good deployment, with significant and worthwhile tactical challenges. The upshot of having few assets is that nobody is invested in our success or failure—therefore nobody's breathing down our necks for results, we're flying under the radar. That means plenty of latitude to experiment with weird tactics, and actually get shit done (instead of placating a constant rotation of generals and Congressmen and Personalities who demand what they call "measurable progress"). You know—I've bitched about the marines and their lack of discipline and general tendency to be spotlight rangers when and wherever possible—but you have to hand it to them. Even in a situation like COIN and Afghanistan, a totally unwinnable war, they are so afraid of losing relevance that they insist on getting in on the action (there weren't any MEBs keeping the border safe back in '07–'08 when nobody cared about Afghanistan, and I don't think in '05–'06 either), and then when they arrive, the war in Afghanistan is all about RC-South and their trials, how tough it is for them—*while they're busy failing on the world stage, we can actually get work done up north.* Hats off to them—like the petty thief in Fielding who can't help but pick the priest's pocket before his execution, it's more important to them to be the center of attention than actually accomplishing anything.

Sorry, there's no point in indulging those bitter feelings. I'm angry we don't have any assets up here. I know you're more of a "one-team-one-fight" advocate, and I have nothing but praise to sing for the marine officers I worked with in the Career Course—a great group of guys. When you have a level of perspective and professional respect, it's easy to give credit where credit's due; and everyone deserves credit. It's unprofessional to think anything else. I'll keep my griping on close-hold, it's between you, me, and the other friends I have who've seen things play out differently up close. I'm happy and proud to be here, in this position. To have a chance to make a difference, no matter how small that chance is—that's all a soldier can ask for. You take your best shot.

Humbly,
Adrian

★

Journal Entry: 7 June 2010

Summer in Afghanistan is a combination of dry heat and humidity. The driest and hottest you'll ever get. Deserts of discomfort—no green to be seen anywhere—that familiar phenomenon of broken A/C units and refrigerators, no cold drinks to be had anywhere at any cost save at the German FOB—strict rules prohibiting visits to the German FOB—no escaping the heat. No Internet. No phone calls. Flies and dust and the prison of sweat. Got a gift of twenty-four beers from the Germans, a true case. It would've been rude and I think odd to refuse—so I took it—keep it in my room. Haven't touched a single one, and likely won't for the deployment. A reminder that I can, and that I won't.

Standing out on the Hesco wall watching patrols leave the wire for contact in the morning and afternoon, seeing the vehicles drive off into the maps and PowerPoint slides I helped review, the plans of my friends, my friends themselves—yearning to lead my own patrols—make the difference I know I can—Lord, let me leave this staff work behind!

★

4 July 2010

Dear Jim,

I understand you're going to Vanderbilt for law, the same one as Russ Burke!? What are the odds… it sounds as though things are unfolding precisely according to your plan, and I'm sure that you'll encounter nothing but success along the way. Of course part of my motivation for saying so is that I believe it's in my and every American's interest for you to encounter success—personal and professional—but especially anything that can advance your political ambitions. I hope you still have political ambitions.

Staff life over here hasn't been bad at all, but it's been difficult playing the waiting game, watching fellow captains lead their companies into battle. It feels so strange and contrary to the nature of the thing to actually acknowledge it: I want to lead soldiers in battle. I want to take the fight to the enemy and not quit before he does. There's something egotistical about that idea, and I'm not sure exactly why having that desire inside me (which anyone in this position would—it's perfectly natural) gives rise to feelings of guilt, or a desire to conceal it (the desire) from all but the friends I know would understand—but there it is, at the base of everything, regardless of the high-minded reasons for which I joined the army, when I ditch the intellectualism and humanism, I just want to fasten the chinstrap on my Centurion's Helmet, raise my sword, and lead my standard-bearer into the thick of the fight. That's where I am now. And there's plenty of fighting to be done.

My change of command is in eleven days: July 15th. July 16th will be the first day I wake up, throw back a bottle of purified water before opening my dried eyes, shuffle over to the bathroom connex to shave, and walk into my command post. The prospect of that moment becoming reality has been the thing that kept me in the army—and it's almost here. I can finally live up to the example set for me by the best leaders I've had, and work to avoid the pitfalls and errors of the worst leaders I had. So long as people don't say that I'm a Toxic Leader when I'm done—so long as they say "he led his men honorably and to the best of his ability," then I'll be happy. I know most of these guys want to get into the fight, A Co's been largely sidelined while D Co and C Co have been fighting it out with the Taliban in the middle of Kunduz Province and two months of hearing war stories from the other companies is, I'm sure, driving them crazy. Well, it won't be long now—my predecessor has been hobbled by circumstance and bad luck (he's a great guy, we've gone drinking together several times—the handover won't be an issue, no dick-measuring contests or anything like that), but I should be able to get out and start walking over the lines the Taliban have drawn in the sand.

I have sympathy for my predecessor—Jeff Kornbluth—he's been in command for over two years, he just got bumped to major (hasn't pinned yet), and God knows he's had his time to lead and carry the guidon—but it must be a hell of a thing to leave command, to leave one's company. I can tell he and the 1SG get along really well, which is going to be a small challenge to overcome; Jeff and I are both fundamentally good people, but we have different leadership styles. I got to see the personality problems that caused firsthand last deployment when the old commander, whom everyone loved, was replaced by Captain Dixwell (of General Dixwell fame). Captain Dixwell was different, and that really chafed some people. He wasn't a Toxic Leader, he wasn't a bad person, he was quite skillful tactically, and genuinely cared about the welfare of his soldiers—in short, we were lucky to have him as a commander—yet some people had serious issues with his personality merely because he wasn't the old commander. I'm certain the same thing will happen with me.

I'll sign off on a brighter and more typically optimistic note: the EOD team coordinated a really impressive fireworks display this year using captured demolition and several bags of gasoline the mechanics had labeled as contaminated for some reason or another. Huge fireballs, blasts of pure American patriotism, visible for miles around (by virtue of our being on a plateau that rises above the surrounding area and in plain view of the Taliban's stronghold to the west)—I'm sure the Taliban told the villagers that work for them and pay them taxes that it was some sort of clever Taliban attack—at the same time, they must have looked at the wasteful, wanton display of excess—classic American maneuver—and been shaken, somewhere deep inside themselves, watching the fire reach skyward—what kind of an enemy blows things up for no other reason than that it pleases them to watch things burn? That's us. That's America. Even if we're not in a firefight or not at war, we will make massive explosions once a year 'cause we just love to watch shit burn and blow up.

> For the Republic!
> Adrian

13 July 2010

Dear Mike,

Just a few short days away from my Change of Command ceremony, now. I'm going to be a company commander! While I'm sure that fills you with existential fear—terror, perhaps?—it's the highlight of my military career; maybe even my life. After spending nineteen months as an executive officer, and having seen just about all an XO can see in terms of commanders and responsibilities, I feel that I have a fair idea of what goes into this job. As much as anyone can claim to be ready for it, I'm ready for it—the inventories are done, meeting the key individuals within the company is done, it's just battle circulation now, meeting my Afghan partners.

It's strange to be back here. I'm settled in by now, of course, Afghanistan has replaced what is "normal," and my quotidian grind consists of the usual things you remember from deployment—but doing it all for the second time has given me many opportunities to re-examine experiences from my first deployment, and a chance to see things happening around me more clearly—patterns, probabilities, commonalities.

Part of the experience has been acknowledging that from the moment I decided to stay in for another tour, to take another trip to Afghanistan, my mind accepted that I would be coming back some day (to war if not to Afghanistan). That prevented me from moving on and fully processing the things that happened to me overseas during the first trip. I've been stuck—I envy you your decision to get out, much in the same way you probably envy me my decision to stay in—of course neither of us could've made different choices.

That's all to say that my brain was eager to start drawing connections again, to learn more of the dark wisdom that was to be gleaned from this landscape. The day I first set foot back on Afghan soil it was like I'd never left. All the training and irritations and hassles that led up to the moment—things are not going well between Giuliana and I, we drift further apart with every month which is a result of my decision to stay in, to satisfy my need to command a company—it's all been worth it, I wouldn't have it any other way. This is the fundamental fact, which I don't think anyone can acknowledge in person, neither friends, nor colleagues: we're here because our egos drove us to be here (with some rare notable exceptions). We're here not because we volunteered to do a difficult job or any of the other nostrums that various well-meaning establishments feed the public, or we like to talk about over dinner at the DFAC, each man has his own deeply personal and essentially narcissistic reasons for doing this.

Caveat. People with families.

So—you remember Denis Johnson's *Tree of Smoke*? The more I think about that book the more I feel like it's the narrative equivalent of a black hole, the place we've never emerged from since Vietnam. Certain elements of the struggle have changed—technology's advanced on our side, so while the Taliban are basically the modern-day one-to-one stand-ins for the Vietcong and NVA, we now have drones and thermals and individual night-sights and laser-guided precision bombs, and one professional infantryman in body armor is worth five of your average drafted infantrymen, huddled together for shelter in the jungle (at least based on how Oliver Stone portrays it in *Platoon*. I don't know, I wasn't there). I'm sure the Rangers and SF units of today aren't substantially different from their predecessors—that was the lesson of Ranger School I've seen confirmed many times over, that at a certain level people start taking training really seriously because the stakes are just too high to fuck around with political correctness.

Tree of Smoke—I mentioned this for a reason—not just the static, chilling effect of bureaucracy, but that strange enmity described between C.I.A. agents and Special Forces elements and regular soldiers and infantrymen and marines—it's true. You saw it. You know what I'm talking about. Those "one-team-one-fight" speeches exist for a reason. And I've never read it expressed better than in the scene where the protagonist lobs a grenade into the SF compound with the intent of killing them. By the end, the enemy in Vietnam has become America—it's not the NVA or the Vietcong, it's our own tactics and strategies—it's our ability to kill without an ability to achieve victory—it's glamorizing the process and putting acts of valor on a pedestal, rather than using them as a jumping-off point to criminal inquiry.

It's pretty similar today. The isolated compounds "for secrecy." The division of assets and resources, the hierarchy of utility. Who's at the pinnacle of the military right now? SEALs, Delta, SF, Rangers, the various "Task Forces" I can't name and acronyms I'm not supposed to know about. Why? Counter-terror? We've invested literally tens of millions of dollars into researching, equipping, training, and maintaining a professional cadre of assassins "to keep us safe." Then, we allowed some brilliant but unscrupulous face in a suit—what was his name, and why did he do this to America?—to spread the fiction that *without* these assassins, we wouldn't be safe, that the only way to deal with the bad terrorist men was to keep murdering them. Not until they go away, because they'll never "go away," that can't happen, it's not the way the system's set up to run. There's no point in even imagining an end state for all of this because there isn't one—not through violence, anyway. Shouldn't the *real* "tip of the spear" be the SF B-teams that are out doing village stability ops, or the Civil Affairs guys carrying money for development projects? Isn't that—not just the tip, hell, the whole *shaft* motherfucker, the whole twelve inches—why we're here, doing this? The reason we're fighting in Pakistan and Afghanistan is that these were the places the British abandoned, never developed—Afghanistan was a skirmish zone, Pakistan was a militarized zone, and the rest of "Hindu" India received roads and the benefit of British education, bureaucracy, and other signs of modern infrastructure. Otherwise I'm sure India would be as much of a problem for us as China. Who knows, maybe India would've gone "Red" in the 50's instead of eventually settling down as a (corrupt, admittedly) Parliamentary Democracy.

Since our mission here is not (contrary to what everyone on the "high side" and kinetic side of things says) simply to keep killing Taliban leadership and fighters, but also to provide educational opportunities and build roads and acclimatize the Afghan people to working with each other to build consensus and develop plans for their country, to participate in the global economy, to take responsibility for their land and their welfare—why is that not how we *act*? Take it from me, we do a lot of talking about "doing the right thing," but actions speak louder than words. And who does everyone aspire to be? The guy with the baseball cap and beard, shooting OBL in the face. I've just told you that my ego would have me go to the sound of gunfire as well—that it thirsts for battle—I like to think that my intellect, my reason and its mandate to make this all have *meant* something in the long term is the thing that redeems me, and keeps me from being just another hooting, self-proclaimed knuckle-dragger. Another bully.

Speaking of which—you know that I've had some experience with Toxic Leadership—my current battalion commander, LTC Russell Lewis, actually believes wholeheartedly in the mission and is *not* a Toxic Leader. The other senior captains (one doesn't speak about these things with others) and I sometimes wonder what he's doing in command of an infantry battalion in the middle of a very kinetic area—if this was an error, or what—not because he's ineffective, but just because he's such a fundamentally decent person who understands COIN, goes out of his way to build relationships with everyone who's in a position to help him, and never holds ego or his position over anyone. He is a COIN master—because he legitimately believes that the Afghans have control over their destiny, and so far as we can tell, does nothing to benefit himself. No lobbying for VIP visits, no urgent attempts to make himself look good—just hard work to turn things around on the ground.

I know. You think I'm bullshitting. You're reading that and saying to yourself: "Adrian's writing this because there's a censor who's reading all the emails and doesn't want to piss off his future boss." No censors, and I'm not bullshitting you. This guy is the real deal. Doesn't raise his voice, doesn't waste time on bad slide presentations, doesn't make a big fuss over reputation or professional development. Purely outcome-oriented. Never been in combat before this—think he deployed as an S3 to Iraq, but he never talks about it—isn't gun-shy, always suits up and takes the same risks as everyone else—spends *hours* on the road meeting with partners (Germans, Afghan army, Afghan police, government officials) and—again—building partnerships—doesn't come back to base and bad-mouth the Afghans or the Germans. The guy's unreal. Like no battalion commander I've ever worked for—didn't think guys like him existed in the infantry. Like, there was some kind of rule against that.

Sorry, don't mean to brag or boast—now you're thinking, "Fuck you Bonenberger, how dare you crow about your good fortune!" First of all, I've already been on the other side of the house, as you know. Second of all, the iron law of leaders states clearly that *when you have one great leader, the next leader must be twice as bad to make up for it.* God knows that must mean that when LTC Lewis leaves, 1-87 Infantry will be led by a real Napoleon or Hitler—worse, an Eichmann, someone without the fortitude to have real ideas himself, save for the bullying instinct that brings him pleasure. That'll be the next guy. For the time being, I'm in a goddamned paradise of a position, about to serve for a combat leader in COIN that—drum roll—I actually *respect.*

My love to Connecticut and all that's still good in this world. Don't bother sending another container of "mouthwash," I won't have time to drink it this time around.

Adrian

GLOSSARY · SECTION FIVE

FOB: Forward Operating Base. A fort that serves as a battalion or company-plus Headquarters and logistical node. Usually has airfield capabilities ranging from Helicopter Landing Zones to small C-130-capable airstrips. FOB Kunduz was built by the Russians and was near a C-130-capable airstrip, and was also built up to the point where it could accommodate its own helicopter landing zone. It is located on a plateau, so unlike many other FOBs is difficult to range with rockets; shares the plateau with the German FOB ("Provincial Reconstruction Team" or "PRT Kunduz") and several ANA FOBs.

Camp: A really big FOB. The two "Camps" I visited in Afghanistan were Camp Marmal (RC-North Headquarters) and Camp Spann (1st Brigade, 10th Mountain's Brigade Headquarters).

Kunduz: A city and province in Northern Afghanistan. One of the last cities to fall to the Taliban. Province is home to a large Pashtun population from resettlement policies in the 20th century intended to diminish Tajik and Uzbek influence in the area. Sometime around 2007 or 2008 the Taliban began quietly establishing a new presence in Kunduz, and by 2010 they had assumed the tactical offensive in the area—this, along with a similar situation in Baghlan Province (immediately to the south of Kunduz) threatened to cut a major supply route that stretched from Tajikistan to Kabul. 1-87 infantry was dispatched to secure this area and check or defeat the Taliban.

Parwan: A province in Afghanistan that is largely free from Taliban influence.

Mazir-e-Sharif: The capital city of RC-North, home of Camp Marmal, the Headquarters (HQ) of ISAF in RC-North, run by the Germans.

Imam Sahib: A district in northern Kunduz that is named for its capital city, Imam Sahib. A/1-87's primary area of responsibility. Census figures put the population of Imam Sahib District between 250,000 and 400,000. I always thought that was kind of funny—using such an official-sounding term to describe what could only be a guess.

"What are we looking at for Imam Sahib, there, census guy?"

"Between 250,000 and 400,000, sir, standard deviation, of approximately +/- 40%".

Or

"So how many people live in Imam Sahib, census guy?"

"Based on our rigorous methodology and data-collection efforts, we've been able to establish with *100% certainty* that there are at least, say, 10,000 people, and as many as [audible popping sound as number is dragged out of tight asshole] 500,000. It could literally be that high."

Or—you know, fill in the depressing institutional scenario where someone just wants to be done with a project.

250-400,000. Come on. Just say you don't know. Right?

RC-North: the Northern section of Afghanistan, which is broken up into five areas by ISAF for ease of administrative military control—RC-North (the north of the country, center of gravity is Mazir-e-Sharif), RC-West (the west of the country, center of gravity is Herat), RC-South (the south of the country, center of gravity is Kandahar), RC-East (the east of the country, center of gravity is Peshawar) and RC-Central (Kabul).

NDS: Afghanistan's National Directorate of Security: think CIA plus FBI. Dreaded by Afghan criminals. I saw them take prisoners away in Paktika Province, and interacted with them in Kunduz where they oversaw payment to various militia factions. The single most influential Afghan agency.

ANP: Afghan National Police. The "normal" Police. My main partners in Kunduz, led by Colonel Abdul Qayum Ibrahimi. We had our disagreements, but shared tragedy and hardship, combined with ultimate success, and forged a strong bond between our groups. I looked at them like my own soldiers, and felt the same responsibility to them.

ABP: Afghan Border Police. The Police force specifically allocated to border checkpoints—like customs police. Had a very positive experience with them.

ANA: Afghan National Army. A lot better than people give them credit for. Sure they can't do logistics to our level, or even the level of the Greeks, but they're not fighting us or the Greeks. Logistical argument for us to remain in Afghanistan and train them seems to be a cover for contractors to make more money. We should have left after we got bin Laden!

ANCOP: Afghan National Civil Order Police. These guys were much better trained than normal ANP, and better equipped—they were assigned to static positions and very eager to get out on offensive operations with us. I think they were conceived as a sort of SWAT force—that's how they seemed to feel about the situation, anyway. Led by a terrific colonel, Andarabi—I'm guessing he's dead by now, all the good leaders over there get the knife.

ISAF: International Security Assistance Force. The official name for, collectively, the foreign military forces in Afghanistan—Germans, English, American, French, Polish, Romanian, Italian... everyone except the Taliban, and the Afghans themselves (They're "GIRoA," or "Government Islamic Republic of Afghanistan").

Click (unit of measurement): A kilometer.

MCLIC: Mine Clearing Line Charge. A rocket fires from a trailer, towing a hundred-meter-long line of plastic explosive charges. Damned big boom, sounds like a peal of thunder. Could also be called "Thor's Vengeance" but when I suggested that, the engineers looked at me like I needed sleep, which may have been true.

60s: 60mm mortar. Every infantry company has two of these. They can be fired from the hip. I say again: they can be fired from the hip.

M-ATV: An MRAP-class vehicle; "Military All-Terrain Vehicle." The vehicles we used on my second deployment to Afghanistan, and that are still commonly used as the standard infantry vehicle.

MRAP: Mine Resistant Ambush Protected. The generation of vehicles that replaced the HMMWV (or Humvee or Hummer), that had (generally speaking) better armor and a v-shaped hull to help combat the effects of buried IEDs.

MRE: Meal Ready to Eat. Better than they were in WWII, but still a step down from Peter Luger Steak House in Brooklyn.

IED: Improvised Explosive Device. A rudimentary bomb that can be made up of military ordinance or "Home Made Explosives (HME)," very unstable and explosive material. Vary in size and effectiveness. Can be delivered by vehicle (VBIED) or suicide bomber (SVBIED).

MEDEVAC: Medical Evacuation—I don't know the tactical difference between MEDEVAC and CASEVAC, but people tend to use "MEDEVAC" to describe helicopter evacuations of casualties, and CASEVAC to describe any ground-based evacuation (by soldier, mule, or vehicle).

MSM: Meritorious Service Medal. Awarded for service in garrison, sometimes awarded as an inferior award during the course of a deployment, when someone doesn't like the job you've done or bears a grudge against you. Standard award for 1SGs at the end of their service with a unit, but for some reason *not* standard for company commanders, although the company commander is the one with his name on the property book. Which is odd!

BSM: Bronze Star Medal. Awarded for bravery in combat, or for service in combat. The highest award you can receive as a platoon leader or company commander as an "End of Tour" award, or an award for service over the course of a deployment.

Valor Award: Given for bravery in combat. Of course, not everyone who receives a valor award acted bravely in combat, and not everyone who acted bravely in combat receives a valor award. This should not surprise anyone who has worked within an organization or institution.

SF Tactical A-Team: SF is Special Forces. In SF, like other organizations, various groups have different roles. So a "FID" team concentrates on "Foreign Internal Defense," or training local people how to fight as a group, and presumably to defend their interests against violent foreigners who seek to do those people harm. We might have, say, SF FID teams in South Sudan, helping organize South Sudanese to resist their bellicose northern neighbors. A Tactical team is a group of elite soldiers who have been trained not only to train, but to conduct offensive operations. They are exquisitely resourced, and it's like having a small army at your disposal. On top of these various groups, you have two tiers of SF units—there are "B" teams, which are (for whatever reason) considered to be inferior—like the bench—and "A" teams, which are like starting varsity teams.

RTO: Radio Telephone Operator. Holdover acronym from when we had Radio Telephones in WWII. He's the smartest soldier in the platoon or company or battalion. My RTO in Kunduz, the "Company RTO," was a soldier named Casey Rohrich. He was outstanding.

Commander: An officer with "command authority" or the ability to issue commands. This has mostly administrative implications.

Change of Command Ceremony: A ceremony where one commander relinquishes command authority to his commander, and his commander gives that command authority to another.

XO: Executive Officer. Second in command of a company. In Kunduz, my XO Captain Colby Frey. He did a great job. I felt bad because I'd been in his shoes in Paktika—the XO does the shitty admin jobs the commander doesn't have time for, and generally speaking is one of the most deeply resented officers (if not the most deeply resented officer) in the company owing to assigning details and getting in the weeds with procedural bullshit that everyone hates.

Senior MCCC Qualified Captain: An infantry captain who has graduated from the six-month career course ("Maneuver Captain's Career Course" when I went through it—the name changes occasionally), and is therefore assumed to be capable of drawing up company and battalion-level operations orders. A junior captain may not have been to this course, and his credibility is therefore diminished when it comes to offering suggestions or developing plans.

FSO: Fire Support Officer. The artillery officer detached to each company, to draw up fire missions for airplanes, helicopters, or artillery / mortars.

PSG: Platoon Sergeant. Typically the oldest, crustiest sergeant in a platoon. Usually an "E-7" or "Sergeant First Class" (SFC).

1SG: First Sergeant. Typically the oldest, crustiest sergeant in a company. Usually an "E-8" or "Master Sergeant."

HHC: Headquarters and Headquarters Company. The "prestige" company, or place where the battalion's best company commander goes to break his back performing thankless administrative tasks for credit with higher.

OIC: Officer in Charge. The officer responsible for a given group of soldiers.

NCOIC: Non Commissioned Officer in Charge. The sergeant responsible for a given group of soldiers.

Chalks: Also Sticks. The manner in which people are organized for air movement, whether offensive or administrative in nature.

Air Assault: An offensive operation using helicopters to deliver soldiers into an area held by the enemy.

RIP: Relief in Place. The process by which one unit relieves another in theater. In World War II this might've taken fifteen minutes and consisted of handing over foxholes and bunkers—in GWOT it's a much longer and more complicated process that lasts about a month.

ROE: Rules of Engagement. The legal and tactical standards governing who you can shoot at, and what weapons you can use to shoot at them.

SECTION FIVE

15

29 July 2010

Dear Giuliana,

I received your package before I took command and loved it—the vitamins were an especially thoughtful touch. I apologize for not writing or calling more frequently. The last month has been a whirlwind of activity, preparing for command and then observing my responsibilities as commander have consumed every bit of free time. Right before I took command there was an incident at the far eastern edge of my biggest district, Imam Sahib. July 13th. The Taliban overran a police checkpoint, and things quickly spiraled out of control from there. For the next five days (with a small break to conduct the actual "Change of Command" ceremony) we were on the move, pushing deep into Taliban-held territory. It worked: we were able to help out our Afghan allies, and my tenure as "Gator-6" was off to the best possible start, a series of not-insignificant victories—but I wasn't even on base. I have another two missions planned for the next month, one coming up really soon, and this is the first time I've had a chance to sit down and compose my thoughts. For the most part it's been little bites of time— twenty minutes here, forty-five minutes there—I sit down, write a couple words and before you know it someone's knocking on my door or I have to run to a meeting or I've ruined the letter with drool because I passed out mid-sentence and now there's blue ink smeared on my forehead.

You were wondering: "Why do you always write with blue ink?" There are two primary reasons—good reasons—behind that being my color of choice (besides its being my favorite color). The first one is that I have one good pen, and the ink is blue. I have a space pen I received as a gift that I use for journal entries and less personal correspondence.

The second reason is that the army (and military) sees blue ink as unprofessional, and requires that all professional and military documents be written in black ink and revised with red ink. As a minor rebellion against this stricture, I've written personal letters in purple ink, orange ink, and even on one memorable occasion, yellow ink (as you imagine this was a terrible idea and has not been repeated). Blue really is the best, the softest color. Rules like "black ink only" usually come about in periods of peace, when generals have nothing better to do than derive ways to bedevil and badger their subordinates. I'm sure Patton didn't care what color ink his soldiers wrote with.

I'm glad to hear that you're going to Africa with a friend for vacation, and I'm happy that you're rowing crew, finding fun new activities. You remember what we talked about before I had to leave: how you would be growing and changing this year, and I would be staying the same? See? It's happening! For my part, I feel that I pushed a "pause" button on my life when I left Afghanistan the last time—my life has become unstuck, now, and is moving again—not moving forward, it's more like a washing machine or a dryer—but at least it's moving. The cycle is not yet complete. The buzzer hasn't rung.

You shouldn't feel pressure—I understand that you have to live your life and the situation I've put you in isn't fair—you shouldn't feel like you're on "pause"—but please understand that writing, emailing, calling—that's the only way we have to connect for now. If I never hear from you, it puts a strain on the relationship, and especially as I'm in situations that are very trying, emotionally—I can't reveal this in public but I am in a very strange and vulnerable place, almost bordering on melodramatic. When I don't hear from you in ten days or two weeks, especially in the wake of an event that you know is important to me— my taking command—I can't tell you how depressed I get. I depend on you for correspondence. So, please, don't leave me alone out here! Miss you lots…

Love,
Adrian

3 August 2010

Dear Mom and Dad,

It's true, I'm a commander! Thank you for all the support and the letters and the packages—by all means tell your friends about Alpha Company, 1-87 Infantry. For Christmas care packages, for letters of support, anything. I've had some incredible help from old friends who've sent everything from snacks / candy, to dip and porn (a Yale frat—go figure) to comic books and graphic novels (my old friend Blair Butler from the G4 network). When flipping through the latest package from Blair, one of the books had a yellow Post-it note attached that testified to its being specifically relevant to soldiers, and it was one of the first to disappear from the command post. I can't tell you how inspiring it is, to see everyone from different political affiliations and ideas line up behind soldiers in combat. Our social milieu understands that these soldiers are poorly educated, politically conservative, crude, and from a Progressive perspective undesirable dinner party guests— our social milieu also understands that there's a national commitment, a pact, which is that these soldiers be given every consideration when they're at war. Say what you will about the infantry soldier as a man, about his priorities and political views, when he is needed to carry a rifle into battle against a clever and motivated enemy, none of those considerations count for a thing. Race, creed, sexual preference, those are all irrelevant details at the crucial moment (I would say, that's prob-ably true of *gender* as well). I've never felt such love and respect for my fellow Americans, my fellow citizens. People who'd be screaming at each other, who disagree vehemently over the definition of human life, about the morality of homosexuality, and everything else on down the line—they probably don't realize that they all have packages sitting beside one another in my command post, and that the quality of grat-itude experienced by the soldiers, sergeants, and officers does not vary one bit between them. If only people were more like those packages in their lives as citizens, I suspect we'd get more done—there'd be a common sense of political purpose, of participation. Americans across the political and religious spectrum would have something positive to share for a change. This vision helps me keep going, anyway!

My area holds tactical and political challenges. We must build co-alitions and institutional mechanisms to help the Afghans work better together. A substantial Taliban presence threatens my northern district, Imam Sahib—the government can't deal with the situation, for the simple but lamentable reason that each Afghan department approaches the problem as their own, and refuses to cooperate with the others. There's the NDS (which runs the militias and is like our CIA or FBI), the Afghan National Police (ANP), and the Afghan Border Police (ABP)—each works separately from the others. Afghans are a proud people, and stubborn about ceding any perception of authority or power. In this respect, ISAF and America provide the Afghans with a crucial service, by allowing different Afghan organizations to participate as equal partners without having to risk failure—this is the role we play in the war on terror, as a sort of arbiter or peacemaker for the Afghan factions that would otherwise be hard-pressed to cooperate. The Taliban don't outnumber the Afghans, they're just a little bit better organized.

I'm excited about the next months, and can't wait to do something real and lasting for Afghanistan, as well as add another chapter to the colorful history of Alpha Company. So much positive energy courses through my body each day, I've barely slept since "taking the guidon" (this is what we call the ceremony for becoming a commander). Normally I'd be worried that this sensation indicated a manic episode, but the other commanders all describe the same process—a sudden rush of vitality, followed by a muted awe toward one's responsibilities. My life is now the life of my company, my responsibilities are no longer the responsibilities of a single man, but of one hundred twenty, fifty, or however many men happen to be on the mission. Just as either of you were energized to solve a problem facing the household (probably posed when me or Christina were kids and getting up to some kind of mischief or another), I feel constantly on alert, looking to work to improve some pending problem or crisis facing Alpha Company or its soldiers. In a very real sense, I am Alpha Company—a soldier misbehaves and it affects me, a soldier succeeds and I share in his success— not in an egotistical way, but much in the same way that you must've felt toward your children.

Writing it that way makes it seem really condescending and patronizing. I haven't described it correctly, because I do not feel "better" than anyone, or entitled—I feel a constant sense of unworthiness, and an hourly fear that I am failing to live up to my job, that I'm not working hard enough on everyone's behalf. My 1SG, I know, feels the same way—we're very different people, it's not the same relationship

I shared with SFC James Krause (you remember him from Italy). If I could've imported now-1SG Krause to Afghanistan to serve alongside me as 1SG I would've done it—that would've been ideal—but the army doesn't work that way. Instead I get to meet a new person, who's been rock solid; he cares about the soldiers and that's the most important thing. I'm sure he feels as I do about his position—also that he would be offended by my earlier characterization—so please don't share that with anyone (the children analogy), although it's perfectly appropriate. In fact, we're all children, in the army—all of us, myself included. So maybe a better analogy would be mom as the oldest child, having to take care of her younger siblings growing up.

So happy, guys—my life is full of the perfect purpose. It was for this reason that I gave my identity and will up to the military—to take command. Each day I wake up and my soul is in harmony with the universe, I am doing what I was put on this earth to do.

Love,
Your son,
Adrian

14 August 2010

Dear Brent,

It's getting serious up here. Fighting season has arrived, and I feel like it's back in Paktika—the enemy's showing up in big numbers, we're seeing formations of between forty and seventy Taliban fighters in the woodline, they're maneuvering on us, shooting at us with mortars and recoilless rifles, infiltrating, suicide bombing, IED'ing, demonstrating tactical proficiency. Of course to hear most people talk about Afghanistan in the media, you'd think the only units over here were marines.

I had my first organic mission recently, and it was pretty much a draw. Well—a failure in the sense that I achieved the first of three objectives and lost men—a success in the sense that we ate a suicide bomb that wiped out the mid-level leadership in our Afghan Police partners as well as injured a bunch of my soldiers within an *hour* of stepping off and beginning the mission, I shit you not, but I kept momentum headed forward while everyone was telling me to abort. Through this unusual instance of me activating my "Iron Will" ability (don't know what the recharge time is on that one) and the faith of my superior officers, I was able to hold things together long enough to salvage some positives from an awful situation. The mission's culminating moment involved over 400 militia, police, and army moving forward as one unit, with no animosity or in-fighting—we really could've turned the mission into a success if we'd been postured to follow it up, but the way the assets were being committed was too piecemeal; there wasn't any organization or long-term plan. This was my fault. We'd planned to be on the offense for three days, and I made no contingency plans for follow-on operations; we should've planned for more. I feel that my status as the second "Shaping Operation" means that if I say that a mission is going to demand too many assets or resources, it'll get canceled and I will be accused of having eyes bigger than my stomach. This is fine—I still could have white-boarded possible alternatives. In any event, nothing went according to plan and I was happy that we were able to take what we did out of it.

Naturally the soldiers fought heroically. There were so many individual counts of valor that I don't know where to begin. That's really struck me out here, how dedicated everyone is to the mission—you know infantrymen, they just want to get out and shoot the fuck out of some bad guys. I saw my soldiers run through open fields under fire to flank Taliban positions. I watched Afghans moving forward to help injured soldiers and policemen. People sacrificing, enduring unthinkable risks in order to bring safety and security to a rural area that's been dominated by what amounts to a gang of thugs since 2005—extortion, no educational opportunities for women, you know the deal. I watched with my own two eyes as everyone clamored to get into the fight and ultimately did their part to pull it off.

Then there were the usual moments of absurdity and hilarity that always seem to accompany death and war. One of the platoons hadn't been in combat yet, and their platoon leader called me on the radio to tell me that he was taking mortar fire (I could hear the explosions, naturally).

"Is it effective?" I asked.

"It's –" [a blast interrupted his call—he was yelling into the radio] "it's 500 meters out and getting closer."

"Okay, make sure your guys are in the prone," I said—they were on top of a hill with no cover. "Can you see who's shooting at you?"

"I'm not sure," he actually said. "There are a couple Afghans about a click to our northeast. It looks like they're over some kind of tube. They keep putting things in the tube, and puffs of smoke are coming out of the tube."

Me [rocking back and forth and silently screaming]: "Have your FSO spin up a call for fire mission with the mortars. It's approved. Take those assholes down. You have the '60s."

"Are you sure, sir?"

"On my authorization! Initials Alpha-Hotel-Bravo!"

I remember grinning wildly, like a chimpanzee, and shrugging my shoulders at the dashboard of my M-ATV command vehicle. I didn't want my driver or RTO to see my face. I don't know if you've ever had that reaction to a small or seemingly insignificant event—something akin to hysteria, it's like finding oneself on a precipice—having to will yourself to step back, to regain control. The cumulative effect of the suicide bombing, the stress of everything, feeling isolated, and to top it all off to have this surreal conversation about whether or not a mortar team was actually shelling one of my platoons—it all combined to cause a very momentary desire to question my sanity. Subjectivity is not a pleasant thing to experience during combat, not at all.

Another scene that has stayed with me I was actually able to capture on camera. It was the morning after we'd taken the suicide bomb. I had spent the night in the bed of my M-ATV on a makeshift bed of MRE boxes, water, and rucksacks, and as you may imagine was a collection of aches, pains, frozen joints, and bruises from the exertion of the previous day's combat and the typically unfriendly sleeping arrangements. I stood up to check on the gunner—my RTO—and see how he was getting along.

"Look over there, sir," he said, pointing down the road. I turned, and saw that the rear of our formation was being guarded by a single ANP officer, who was nodding off. No C-wire, no anti-vehicle spikes, no sandbags—nothing, just a man in a conspicuous blue uniform, sitting on a tree stump, chin resting gently against his chest. A day after a suicide bomber had hit us in the rear of our convoy, killing eight of his colleagues.

"How long has he been like that?"

"He was lying down when it was still dark out. I was watching through my night vision," my RTO said. "At dawn he looked around to see if anyone was watching, then started pulling security."

"So, what you're saying is that he was essentially the first and last line of defense between us and the Taliban this whole night."

"Don't worry sir," my RTO said. "We've been watching his sector."

What else was there to say. I watched the ANP soldier for a little while, as he swatted desultorily at morning insects before giving up all pretenses of discipline and settling down for a morning doze. What's the war like for him? How does he imagine it, what do the Taliban look like to his mind's eye? He's here, he's in the same place I am, subject to the same inspirations and disappointments as I am. I can't escape the knowledge that things that would alarm or bother me (not having security up at night) obviously don't affect him in the same way that they affect me. As you know there's a massive cultural disconnect between America and Afghanistan, as wide or wider than the geographical distance between our two countries.

After returning from the mission we endured the usual administrative hassle of writing out awards. You know that I was never a huge fan of my first battalion commander—he got me to Italy, but he also never supported my development as an infantryman, and while I was there it was very, very difficult for me to refrain from disliking him personally and openly because of the animosity he quite obviously bore against me. Credit where credit is due, though—my first boss was terrifically magnanimous about awarding people he felt had done a good job, he wasn't a "badge protector." You remember Jim Krause, my first platoon sergeant, who articulated this "benevolent" award policy best when he said the following:

"Sir, in every event, there's always a person who was responsible for making it work, who pulled it all together. That person deserves to be awarded. Usually it's the person you'd want to award anyway— the go-getter, the self-motivator. It's good to award them because it inspires other soldiers to work hard and lets them know that people are watching their achievements. Occasionally it's a guy who isn't that squared away—usually messes up, doesn't have his shit wired tight. It's still good to award them once in a while when they deserve it because it shows that awards aren't for favorites. The most important thing is not to give awards out for nothing but to award intrepidity and valor, or skill during training. You don't want to ruin the award's mystique, but you also don't want to be an award-protector."

I'm paraphrasing, but that just about summed up his philosophy on awards. He came to this conclusion by getting screwed during an earlier deployment—someone hadn't liked him and awarded him an MSM (a garrison service award) rather than a BSM for an end of tour award. Rather than take it the wrong way (I'm sure he did in the moment, Krause has a clear picture of right and wrong), he incorporated the *right* way into his leader DNA. If nothing else, he was responsible (along with my first BC) for helping me approach awards the right way.

This is something people back in the rear don't really get, awards, how personal and political these things are. I've seen and heard of people receiving awards for things they shouldn't have, which is unusual, and witnessed firsthand people not receiving awards at all when they probably should have, which is very common. I believe that it's our responsibility as commanders to go out of our way to recognize achievement. Withholding awards for valor or service on the battlefield because a soldier was "just doing his job" is the stupidest thing I've ever encountered in the military. For myself, I've never had a "V" device pinned on my chest—I know that I'm capable of heroism—but I wouldn't let that affect the way I assign awards for soldiers. I wouldn't punish my subordinates because I was punished in the past.

So the past month or so, the three major incidents I was a part of, I have submitted or insisted on subordinates submitting for seven valor awards. Two Bronze stars with "V" and five Army Commendation Medals with "V." I could've submitted more. I want to make sure that everyone who deserves an award receives one for valor, but am also *certain* that it will never be enough. I'll look back years from now and regret not submitting more people. I'm doing what I can, I just want to make sure that all the soldiers who deserve recognition for a heroic act understand that their gallantry was observed and rewarded.

I am precisely where I should be in the present. My life is in near-perfect harmony—I can hear the music of the spheres every morning when I wake up, and in those infrequent moments before I drift off to sleep. I feel like I'm making good plans, making good decisions, and generally living up to the expectations of my office. It feels great. This is what I've been aiming for, a sense of balance, of co-existing with the world. My job at this instant is precisely what it needs to be, no more, no less. I'm a good commander, man. Leading from the front, carrying the load that I expect others to carry. Life feels correct.

Much love,
Adrian

5 September 2010

Dear Jim,

For the first time in a long while, I really miss having a shoulder to cry on. I'm not sure anyone other than you would understand what I mean by that, the emotions at work here. I put together a great mission, had helicopters, SF support, engineer assets, two platoons, and my partners all refused to show up. The *NYT* guys were there to catch it all, my ineffectiveness as a commander, the complete letdown. I've never been filled with such anger or impotence in my life. It was galling, mortifying, infuriating, hateful. My lowest point yet as a leader.

It was one of those things where you can't tell your partner everything about a mission beforehand or you risk compromising it when he tells his cousins in the Taliban that you're coming. So I told him that we'd be returning to the North (which he'd told me he *wanted*), then asked for support a couple weeks before, a week before, and finally a couple days before, *received promises that he would provide soldiers*, laid all the groundwork, and then… the day of, nothing. No ABP, no ANP, nothing. The militia were willing to roll—their NDS handler said he'd be able to ante up "whatever I needed" in terms of militia support, 100, 150, 200, whatever—but they're *officially* not my partners. I can't be seen working exclusively with armed gangsters with no oversight or accountability mechanisms. If it had been up to me I would've taken the offered support and the 200-some-odd U.S. soldiers we had in the form of the joint elements and rolled north to really tear into some Taliban ass—but I got reeled in by higher.

The cause, supposedly, was the removal of the old provincial police chief, a general (an Uzbek), and the appointment of a new guy from Parwan Province, also a general (a Tajik). This either emboldened my partners to stand up and say "no," or something else was going on (not sure what). It's Ramadan, so that might have contributed, but it's very unusual for Afghans to say that they will participate in a mission and then *all* back out at the last minute. Usually one can play a faction off against another, promise more aid to one group, curry favor with the other, whatever the case may be—this time I got nothing. And I'll probably never see most of those assets for a long time. How many times have you gotten a full SF tactical A-Team with a company of Afghan commandos to show up for a mission? Ever seen that? Well—I can put that dream to bed. Fucking bullshit.

While everyone else returned to base—SF to their base, the Apaches to Mazir-e-Sharif; the engineers and my third platoon brought the *New York Times* reporters back to FOB Kunduz—I and my first platoon decided to explore a village just south of Imam Sahib which was supposed to have some minor Taliban presence. We ambled down through the fields, bounding, ten of us, no Afghan support (of course, nowhere to be found that day). The town looked deserted, the doors closed and barred, everyone having run away or hidden in their compounds upon seeing us. We reached the last compound in the village, and one of the soldiers said, "Sir, smells like weed here." He was right; it was pungent, thick. I looked around, tried to see if there were any free-growing plants. Another soldier shouted to look on the ground.

We were standing on a dirt trail—a wagon trail—that was *covered* for twenty feet by a half-inch layer of marijuana, just drying in the sun. The terp was banging on a door, asking a woman inside the compound, who said that her husband was out in the fields. We decided that it was a bad situation—especially with the sticky-icky and the soldiers—so we started back for the vehicles. Got in a bit of a scrape, shot it out with the Taliban for an hour, made the vehicles, then headed home.

The skirmish with the Taliban, while indecisive, still made for a good tune-up, a positive note on which to end the day. In general, nothing satisfies an infantryman better than a good fight—even though my mission had been a total loss, a humiliating wash, depressing as all fuck, at least one platoon got to head home with a sense of accomplishment and purpose. Maintaining that attitude—maintaining good morale—that's the thing out here, not getting discouraged.

Another "asset" that was recently assigned to our battalion was a behavioral health major. A shrink. The idea there is that people can do sensing sessions and individual meetings with her after battle. I've been pushing it because I know it's the right thing to do, but when I go in myself—to set a good example—I just end up telling her that I'm good, and basically just checking the block. I don't care if others perceive me as weak, but I can't abide the notion that I actually am weak, and require help.

A fucking SF tactical A-team with Afghan commandos! Goddamn!

All best,
Adrian

11 September 2010

Dear Mike,

I imagine it's autumn in Connecticut now. That means the leaves are changing, there's that twinge in the air that smells like school and shorter days. It's getting chilly at night. I remember the first time I really felt the shift—it was during my year off from Yale. I wasn't in school, I was dating a really cute redhead who was in her senior year, and driving back from her place with the windows down on September 3rd or 4th, near the first day of classes—2000? Yeah—turning onto what was then called the Quinnipiac or "Q" Bridge (now the Pearl Harbor Memorial Bridge), and a gust of 60-degree air off the Long Island Sound made me think of every failure I'd experienced in life up to that time. I was 21, and it felt like I was going on 30.

What an asshole, I didn't know shit about life back then. Should've found a way to trick that redhead into marrying me.

I'm so sick of this. It's not fun. Being a commander sucks. I don't know what I was thinking, staying in—I guess the feeling of inadequacy that I didn't do enough my last deployment, a sense that I could make a difference as a commander, I don't know. It's just like being a lieutenant—at each step of the progression you look up and imagine that the person one rung above you on the decision ladder must have it so much better, and then you find out that you're wrong, like a jackass. "When I have my blue cord, people will treat me with respect." "When I get out of Ranger School, things are going to change." "When I get to my unit, things will be different." "Now that I'm XO, it's a whole new ballgame." "I've deployed, I have my combat patch, I'm big-ballin'." "A Senior, MCCC-qualified captain will demand the existential respect he should rightly command." "Having proven myself in combat, others will rightly accept my counsel without hesitation." It never stops, man. Never.

I feel like we're fighting this damned thing with both hands tied behind our backs. It's stupid. I can't do shit, I'm wearing a straitjacket. Everything I've accomplished has happened as a result of chicanery or deliberate misinformation. The times I've checked in with higher have resulted in confusion or misdirection, it feels like a miracle that anything's been done. I'm fighting to get a great mission approved, and *maybe* it will walk—I shield all of this from my subordinates, of course—but shouldn't it just be "hey, I'm the one who's out here, just let me do my job and resource me with what I need?" That's what I want to say, but of course that wouldn't get me anywhere.

Nobody knows why we're out here. Why we stayed in Afghanistan, why we went into Iraq. The "correct" answer is that the neo-cons in Bush's administration had an idea that taking down Iraq would spread responsible forms of government, that democracy would take root and flower. Because that's not what they *said* the reason was, they opened the door to conspiracy theories. Everyone has their own idea about the *real* reason we're at war: WMDs, oil, natural resources, a desire to isolate Iran, daddy issues between elder Bush and Saddam Hussein, connections between neo-cons and the Saudi royal family, and so on and so forth. In a very real sense, this proliferation of valid and uncontested explanations makes GWOT the first post-modern war. Competing narratives exist without being dispelled outright, and the actual reasons behind our involvement become less important and possibly even fade away with history, to be replaced by the act of interpreting the war's significance. I've explained the true reasons behind our involvement to I don't know how many soldiers, sergeants, and my peers, how and why it played out the way it did. Nobody really cares.

I'm getting older, Mike. You've already sailed for the civilian world, to process your experiences—it feels like I'm just accumulating more, to no clear purpose. Autumn's coming, the days are getting shorter, the air's colder—and that means winter's almost here, when the land will be blanketed with snow. I can't imagine the spring any more—that's all in the past—the best I can hope for is one last harvest. Nine years ago today, all this madness started—we started down the road to perdition. And here I am now—at the place I wanted to be, in combat—and we can't drink. What a cruel joke.

All best,
Adrian

Journal Entry: 15 September 2010

Preparing for the second try at returning to the Hill. We won't be able to make it into an outpost—that can never happen, after my Afghan partners bailed on me, I'll never be able to sell the same plan twice. At least we can keep the Taliban from rocketing and mortaring the city on the day of the elections.

Getting left high and dry by my allies in front of the *New York Times* offered a clear picture of what's at stake with the media. Even though one bad thing happened that could make me look like an idiot, I refuse to back down from the idea that greater media access is an absolute good. The only people who should fear the glare of the spotlight are those who have something to hide. If the reporters want to burn me, they certainly have enough material at this point—but I don't think that's their aim, here. I think they want to tell a truer story, not just another popular-but-trite Vietnam us-v.-them redux. So long as they're committed to staying out here to report and cover our deployment, they've got seats on my patrols. Oddly enough, I want them to succeed too, I want them to get the story they're looking for, so people listen, so it makes a difference… This is the way things should work on a deployment, media should have all the access they want to write stories, and the military should learn not to fear failure, public or private.

Back to the Hill. Going to be a straightforward mission—simple, but not *easy*. We'll run into a lot of resistance. Then, when the machine guns are dug in on the corners, and 3rd Platoon is established behind sandbags and in the fighting positions, and the mortar's dug out in the center, I'll go back to the district headquarters with 1st and take my nervous seat by the radio. And the Afghans will vote on whether they want to keep Karzai or not.

20 September 2010

Dear Giuliana,

It's been nearly a month since I last heard from you. Normally they say "no news is good news" but in this case, no news is a slap in my face. If you don't want to be together, if you don't have the desire to continue on in a relationship with me, then just say so and end it. This is absurd. I'm trying very hard to keep a sympathetic view of things, to see things from your perspective—I'm sure this is all very difficult for you—I hope you're doing the same for me, trying to understand the pressures I'm under out here.

Things are not well. Strategically there has never been less support for Karzai; while some people have faith that the ANP, ANA, and ABP (the Afghan military units) are improving, almost nobody trusts the government. They held national elections a couple days ago and the Taliban made things difficult. I feel like nothing I do makes a significant dent either way.

This is what I meant when I said things would get tough. I'm not sure what to say to you, a lot of the things that go on over here I can't talk about—but anything from you would be better than nothing, would connect us. I'm making an effort to keep this going, even though things are obviously pretty bad—I need you to pull your side of things too. I'm going nuts out here, and I'm not getting any support.

Please don't be angry with me. I want this to work out between us, I want to be able to come home to you. Your absence is making me very sad.

I miss you,
Adrian

★

24 September, 2010

Dear Jim,

I'm sorry to sing you back-to-back songs of woe, here. Feel rather awful about it. Giuliana is basically shutting me out, and things have been going wrong, tactically. My guys and the Afghans are all carrying their weight, doing the best they can, but since we ate a suicide bomb, I feel like we've been cursed. Stumbling from one near-defeat to the next, managing to rescue some kind of equivocal draw out of each mess to continue my tenure as a commander—I wonder if everyone feels this way after a mission goes awry?

The latest episode—I told you about the suicide bomber already, what it was like to walk through a courtyard of bodies, watching people kick pieces of people off to the side—and the stench. The latest episode, I was out with the *New York Times* folks for the elections, and I was going to secure a hill outside Imam Sahib to prevent the Taliban from mortaring or rocketing the polling sites. Qurghan Tapa Hill. We went up there with minesweepers because villagers said it might be mined—and it was—with weird Iranian plastic mines that defeated the sweepers. Two of my guys hit mines and got hurt bad, and then we got into a minor firefight. *Times* reporters saw everything, the real stuff. They were there. I'm glad, glad they got it all on video, got the pictures—that might make it sensible, somehow, turn it into a narrative if they end up using it—God, it was awful. I thought the second soldier to hit a mine had died, I was right next to the photographer, Damon Winter, and that's what I said: "he's dead." I can't tell you what it felt like. You know, so I don't have to, which is why I'm writing you instead of anyone else (and certainly not Giuliana, whom I'm coming to hate, living her life in England like nothing's happening, resenting me for being absent and distant).

The rest of the day was a series of MEDEVAC rendezvous and planning sessions with the Afghans—the same ones who'd sold me out during the last mission (you remember, where I could've invaded Pakistan I had so much firepower). I kept a little more than a platoon's worth of soldiers to secure the hill with my mortars, and was forced myself to stay at the district center with a minimal force to act as a QRF. The whole time I'm thinking about my guys. That night at the Imam Sahib COP (just four walls and a rickety metal gate) was one of the most stressful of my life, and I actually lost it on one of my platoon leaders and my mortar leader for failing to follow certain protocols. Isn't that insane? I was dressing them down when I should've been the calm one, the voice of reason. Never let it be said that I failed to learn my human limits during my time in Afghanistan. Every commander I've worked for would've been embarrassed to watch me.

I've got one more big mission lined up before fighting season slows down, an incredible air assault, which I've named "Operation Seemorgh" after the Phoenix-creature of Afghan legend. I've been planning it and looking forward to it for a long time, so based on recent experience I can expect something to go horribly wrong. At this point I don't care, I'd air assault in myself with an M240B if I could. I'm sick of it all, I just want to keep bashing away at the Taliban until they quit. I refuse to stop now. I will break them with constant patrolling, with superior and indomitable will.

There was a German platoon with us for the elections. I'd love a platoon of Panzers up here, and as many German paratroopers as I can lay hands on—I want their firepower—I want the image of American, German, and Afghan soldiers fighting side-by-side against the Taliban—I want Americans to see the Iron Cross on a tank's turret in the background of a picture with some U.S. soldiers and Afghan militiamen in the foreground—I want people to understand what this means, this thing we're doing, out here, at the edge of the empire. An end to the lectures, the condescending paternalistic diatribes about morality or who's right and who's wrong—there is only violence and more violence. Violence for violence's sake, honor for honor's sake.

I don't need Giuliana, Jim, or the cheesy army mental health / therapist / social worker who will just tell me what I already know about myself, which is that I've seen difficult things and that it's not my fault, or some variation on that inane theme. I don't need anyone. Standing alone at the edge, I have only myself—I am filled with a bitter but intoxicating sense of power—we will keep fighting, and we will win. Regardless of the cost. Fighting is all we have left, now—everything else is an irksome and insignificant function of an increasingly irrelevant civilization.

> I Remain,
> In Friendship,
> Yr Humble Servant, etc., etc.
> Adrian

7 October 2010

Dear Mike,

What are we doing. This makes no sense. I cannot understand it. I feel my grasp on humanity slipping away, mission by mission. The army believes that the answer to this is behavioral health. We'd do better with some religious / moral equivalent—sadly, our own multifaith shepherd / expert does not provide me with anything like the type of certainty I'd need to get through this or buck up. I'd naively assumed that a relationship with Giuliana would insulate me from the horror and the madness, but it hasn't—on the contrary, her frequent and lengthy bouts of silence only feed into my sense of solitude and alienation.

I had a beautiful and great air assault mission planned, which would have netted us a key area that has long been dominated by the

Taliban, but at the last minute it was canceled. I became truculent and insubordinate in front of a superior officer, who dressed me down appropriately and sent me to my CP to cool my heels. I gathered my wits and made peace with the new state of affairs, and we were sent through German-held territory to a desert to act as a blocking position for a spur-of-the-moment battalion mission. Fanned balls there for a while, rolled around the desert off-roading, burning the fuel taxpayers pay for on ghost-chasing missions—and now I'm just waiting for the next reason not to do the air assault.

My Mefloquin dreams have been incredibly weird lately. I'm not sure I mentioned that but I sort of pulled a "slicky boy" with the pills, I insisted to the doctor that the one-a-day kind was insufficient, I don't remember exactly what the song-and-dance was, something about an allergy, maybe, but he gave me "old reliable," the Mefloquin. The good stuff. The only anti-malarial medication I know. They say it's hell for the liver and not good for the existential crises, but I'm just addicted to the super-weird dreams! It's like going on a vision quest twice a week! With my increased cynicism, though, and skyrocketing disdain for procedure and authority that's been tied directly to recent professional disappointments, the dreams have become exercises in futility—absurdist jaunts that pit me against such impossible scenarios as

1) Reporting myself for a congressional violation

2) Having a sexual affair with an older married female major on the German FOB (no such major exists that I'm aware of)

3) Being recalled to America to guard a coffin that turns out to be my own

4) PowerPoint slides late for a meeting

Who dreams like that? If I weren't so certain of reality, I'd be worried I was losing my mind. Too busy to go really cream-cracker, though, lose my head entirely. Patrolling keeps things on an even keel.

Well I thought you'd like to hear about my troubles, it seemed like the kind of thing that you'd enjoy or in which you'd take some mean, squalid pleasure. You can pass it along to Bob, I'm sure the two of you have a fishing trip planned or some other kind of nonsense that I won't be able to attend. Damn you both. You'll get none of my Mefloquin stash when I return home, that's your punishment.

Thanks for reading,
Adrian

Journal Entry: 26 November 2010

Thanksgiving in Afghanistan: hot Mermite chow in an abandoned Afghan Checkpoint. Campfire, not big enough to warm us through the cold and plateau wind. Sleeping bag thick with frost and cold. Clear sky, with bright stars. Bombed-out fighting positions from some previous war behind us in the hills. Burned Russian APC half-buried in one of them. No friends to share it with, no booze to dull the senses. Just the psychological equivalent of that burning feeling one gets in one's muscles from extreme fatigue—the mantle of leadership is a heavy, heavy burden, and I'm sick with fear that I'm messing it up.

I'm recycling missions I haven't gotten to do yet, recycling ambitions unfulfilled while the fighting happens to the South, by Kunduz City and in Baghlan Province. Picking at cold turkey, cold mashed potatoes and frozen gravy. Struggling to keep my officers and sergeants motivated. Struggling to convince higher that my areas are important enough to resource. Struggling to keep it together. *Fucking struggling.*

5 December 2010

Dear Mom and Dad,

By the time you get this letter it'll be appropriate to say: "Merry Christmas, and a Happy New Year!" The boxes of gifts for soldiers have begun arriving—thank you and your friends (I'm sending letters to everyone who sends me or my guys boxes—or at least as many as I can—I'm worried that some may fall through the cracks) for all the hard work you've done. It's incredible, heartwarming, inspiring. I feel particularly well loved, but—I already felt that way—seeing guys who don't have boxes of their own getting hooked up by somebody from America—it's really moving. An old friend of mine from Japan, Elizabeth, we taught English together, organized her Bikram Yoga colleagues at the studio where she works to sponsor one of my platoons (1st). I've started seeing the packages from Reverend Lin of the Connecticut Blue Star Mothers. My friend Blair from L.A. keeps showing up with packages (not literally of course). It's—it's really great.

I know this will *probably* reach you a little on the early side—there's a lot of patrolling happening over the next month so I probably won't be on base much. That's why I wanted to get this out now. We've been very busy supporting missions—great news here, the Afghans have really started showing up since the old Police chief went away and General Kheyl arrived. Kheyl was buddies with Massoud back in the day—he draws a lot of water up here, and the militias listen to him. Some of the bigger players for the Taliban have decided to switch over to the Afghan side, and with the help of a couple really big missions we did with the Germans over the last month, two entire districts have shifted from "bad guy territory" to "trafficable without having to worry about IEDs."

It's worth mentioning that the first mission the Germans led in their area—*possibly* the first joint U.S. / German battalion-level Offensive operation ever, and *almost certainly* the first for the Germans since World War II—was (somewhat curiously given their history) titled "Blitz." One of those situations where our relative anonymity is a boon… not sure how people would've reacted to that, otherwise. Hanging out with those guys is changing how I see Germans in general, and more specifically their grandfathers who were, I'm quite certain, by and large doing the same kind of thing that I am. It's interesting that the Germans I've worked with seem to hate the Nazis more than I do. Nowadays, the Germans do Counter-Insurgency better than we do—more effective projects, better outreach and follow-through. I feel like together, we're exorcising the ghosts of WWII. And thank God! Let me tell you—seeing a Panzer tank steaming up to help out is a lot better than the alternative.

Matt Adkins took over as C Co Commander and has been kept busy with road-building, mine-clearing, and outpost-building projects. He's been really excited to get off the base for the same reasons I was—we both had to wait a little bit longer than we thought and consequently felt a bit burned out with computer slides. Greg Ambrosia's been here with HHC, same FOB as A Co (he was to our South at the beginning of the deployment) so he keeps me fired up with stories, motivation, cigars, and a constant earful of the challenges he faces. It's mostly just us company commanders that have to be there for each other—it could be worse, of course, the two majors (who work their asses off to keep the battalion running) have only each other, and the battalion commander has nobody but his family, I suppose, or the German battalion commander. I feel bad—there were a rough couple months where I was incredibly bitter about the decisions the leadership was making, because it seemed inconvenient to me and my goals. As things have turned out, though, they've been right—especially the BC, LTC Lewis. Giving the lead to the Afghans was the smartest thing anyone could have done. Not many people would've had the guts to do it but it's been paying dividends lately—we have the strategic initiative. It's premature, but if things keep going well we may be able to clear out this province by deployment's end. I don't know if there's a precedent for that.

Not much else to report. The Afghans are doing most of this themselves. We're out there working, but it's probably the safest place I could be in the world, surrounded by 125 angry infantrymen. We're not taking chances, so this holiday season just imagine me opening up a box or two and sharing it with some friends—no egg-nog or "holiday cheer in a bottle" this year, but plenty of warmth and camaraderie.

Keep those home fires burning—I'll be back before you know it—not in time for Christmas, sadly, but close enough so you won't know the difference. And I won't be coming back here. Not ever.

Love,
Adrian

Journal Entry: 4 January 2011

The package Teddy sent for Christmas had a couple issues of *The New Yorker* sandwiched between cookies and a copy of *Rolling Stone*. Reading "The Talk of the Town" I can barely recognize New York—I see a city in wintertime, where the sun sets quickly between the grasping metal fingers we've driven deep into the earth, while people in fancy dressware toast each other with crystal glasses—at the same time that I miss it, miss being a part of that life, I also hate it, and wish for awful calamity to even the level of experience. My relationship with Giuliana is broken. This is what I wish on civilians: a doomed effort to stay warm at night. The feeling of hunger that comes from a food shortage. The moral complications one encounters through simple necessity.

Even here in the "calm" North, villages are still plagued with sickness, child mortality rates unheard-of, widespread illiteracy, and warfare. The social golden standard in Afghanistan is a living situation to which we wouldn't expose our most hardened criminals. That's assuming there isn't a militia or gang or Taliban group breathing down your neck. People have no idea.

Why is it that days after our greatest victory I still can't see into the future, can't envision myself back in the "real" world, walking around, interacting with people? It's easy for me to see myself doing things on patrol, or planning another mission, but I try to see myself in civilization and draw a blank. Reading about sports does nothing for me, the Red Sox had a bad season and I could care less—seeing the society pages, scanning the latest in politics I just feel numb, like it's all happening somewhere impossibly distant. It's like reading a magazine through a broken universal translator device. If only I could've spoken with my grandfathers, or other WWII vets—the Vietnam vets that I've met are so wrapped up in their own experience, the bitterness they feel that they were treated poorly and we've been treated "well" (or at least better) that there's not much sympathy or ability to communicate in a satisfying way. I don't want to be like them: hateful, resenting others, resenting myself for having come through relatively unscathed.

8 January 2011

Dear Sasha,

Happy Holidays—I've had enough emails at this point, I vastly prefer letters to electronic correspondence, especially given the unreliability of our Internet connection. I heard from my sister that you were worried about me when I was quiet for a month—just wanted to let you know that that touched the hell out of me. It's not like I'm hurting for friendship out here—I've really appreciated yours, though. I don't hear much from Giuliana anymore—short sporadic emails now and again—I'm going to fly out to England when I get home, see what's going on, but I don't have high hopes that we're going to hammer things out. It deserves a chance, if she still wants it. Honestly, I'm not sure I can forgive her for essentially abandoning me out here, in my hour of need. I'm just too angry at her. We'll see.

Anyway—I was on the FOB when the article in the *New York Times* came out, and took a bunch of hell for it from my colleagues and superiors, as you might imagine. I didn't read the whole thing, but I read some of the comments, and that's a mistake I'll never make again. People said some awful things. I mean, it was a horrible situation—but those things happen in war. It felt like some people actually wanted me to feel worse than I already did about the whole thing. Inhuman.

I think the whole series has been done very tastefully, and overall I'm grateful that the article appeared. The truth is, being featured in the *New York Times* actually helped my soldiers deal with the situation—gave it a narrative, you know? They're part of something special, because it was covered by the media (given a *lot* of attention by the media). I saw that happen with the guys I knew from the 173rd in *Restrepo* and *War*—having a story to make sense of an otherwise senseless, terrible situation makes it comprehensible, puts it into a box people can open, examine, close, and generally appreciate for its value. I never would've said that before—it's the first time since college that I've thought that maybe there's something to nonfiction after all. Fiction is better for "truth," but nonfiction is better for peoples' souls. Who'd have guessed *that*!?

Write if you have a chance—I understand that you must be busy with other things—but either way I hope to see you when I'm home for leave. I'll be stopping through California and would love to impose on your parents' hospitality again. I'll let you know when the dates are clearer. I miss the ranch, with the hint of Beach Boys playing in the background—especially out here at the edge of things!

Your friend,
Adrian

8 January 2011

Dear Brent,

January 1st, 2011 at 0930 I was drinking coffee with the C Co commander, a guy named Matt Adkins, when he turned to me, pulled out a couple cigars, and said: "Happy 'New York' New Year's." We were at a compound after five days in the sticks. The engineers had finally cleared a path to us along this long, long road—took 'em days to do it—almost a month, in all. Matt handed me the second cigar and we lit up. I'm not a cigar-smoking man, but—boy. That was one hell of a great feeling. Thinking about what everyone must be up to back home. The ball dropping at Times Square. We were out there for another five days with a ten-hour break for refit. That was the closest I came to being happy in nearly three months.

But—we did it, man. I can't believe it—we fucking won. The Taliban are actually on their heels out here. The ANP general in charge of the Police is a serious former Northern Alliance Mujahadeen mover—the militias are lining up behind him—it feels like the beginning of a new chapter for Afghanistan: "A New Hope in the North." This is what we should've done all along, empowered the Tajiks and Uzbeks, told the Pashtuns to get lost. If we weren't going to get serious about fixing their problems, rather than fiddle-fucking around with representative democracy, we should've cut sling on the South, and built roads and infrastructure in Kabul and North. Oh, well.

The last bastion of Taliban presence and influence is in my district. I've barely been there the last month, just a couple short visits. Last there on December 14th, which, not coincidentally, was the last time I had any real enjoyment leading a patrol.

Got caught out in the open, man. Almost died. December 14th. In the middle of a fucking field. You know—one of those tilled fields, where the hard chunks of dirt mess with your footing and you can't run, but you can't really look around, either, and you're worried about the animal and people shit they have in piles everywhere, little land mines, and then actual land mines—thirty meters from cover to my front, and ten meters from cover to my rear. Woodline seventy meters away. I was between two elements, and two camel humpers opened up on me. Had me dead to rights. Hit the ground, then broke contact to the cover to my rear while a group of soldiers to my front laid down suppressing fire as all hell broke loose across the woodline. Rallied, then ran forward. After that moment, the farm, the stink of shit everywhere, it was over for me. The mission I just got back from was pure hell from that perspective, I was sure I was going to bite it, that I wasn't coming back. A good amount of hard fighting, and Jesus, more to come. I'm so done, man.

The only things pushing me forward right now are a commitment to keep sane and bring my guys back alive, anger at Giuliana for abandoning me (I have to live so I can tell her to her face how shitty this made me feel, how goddamned furious this makes me), and the nagging suspicion that I may need to write this all down. Wouldn't have considered the last part save that I've seen it firsthand with the *New York Times* guys—really good people, good reporters —what a narrative can do for people's sense of self worth. Maybe there's a way through this, a way ahead. I want to find out: I'm not going to just charge into things blindly, without a care in the world.

Part of the reason I feel like I've been able to do things —not constant heroism mind you, most of my soldiers are more heroic than I am on a daily basis—but I've done some fairly reckless things that my younger, less mature self was very proud of—has been due to a sense that it wouldn't be that bad if I died. Worse—I sort of wanted to die heroically, make people proud of me before I have the chance to come home and fuck things up, see my name on the walls of The Rotunda from heaven, and of course deliver the ultimate fuck-you to Giuliana for not supporting me more. Isn't that awful? Like, the worst thing a leader can do. I'm too full of ego, man. I need to get into yoga, bad. I'm not being facetious, I really need to level my spiritual side out or I'm going to go nuts when we get back to Fort Drum.

Leave is April. I'm coming out to CA, then I'm headed to England to see Giuliana and hash things out. Doesn't feel like there's a way forward but who knows, maybe we'll see each other and be able to come together, mend the fences... At the same time that I'm angry with her, I also know that she's a hell of a woman and certainly more than a schmuck like me deserves. It's almost like all the emotions I'm refusing to let myself feel have been poured into this one situation—it's more than I can contain or reasonably process alone.

Much love,
Adrian

9 January 2011

Dear Jessica,

I've been on a letter-writing warpath the last twenty-four hours! I got back from patrol a couple days ago—big mission, one of the biggest I ever took part in—and I'm already planning the next one. So much has happened and I want to put it all down before it all fades from my memory. Before it loses its immediacy and its impact.

First: I came to the end of myself at the beginning of December. I'm not going to divulge the precise details, because it's so totally unpleasant for me, I can't even talk or think about it objectively. Imagine encountering a political conundrum that you knew instantly, emotionally, fundamentally that you could not solve, that it was beyond your abilities as a human to overcome. That conundrum, that moment, is reaching the end of yourself, is plumbing the depths of an identity. In my case, I encountered a situation that ended certain longstanding and cherished ideas I held of myself as a hero, as a great leader. They were false. Since reaching the end of myself I've continued to go through the motions, to put one foot in front of the other—I led a morning raid on two compounds recently that from start to finish was an exercise in terror, whole hours of my life spent at the end of the horror movie, when you know for a fact that something mind-bendingly gross and horrible is going to ooze or burst out of the walls and accost the protagonist as she or he runs for safety.

Second: your package, with those baked goods, delicious treats, and readings arrived right before Christmas and I took the contents out on a particularly trying mission, consuming and reading everything over the course of the ten days I was there. It was a great consolation to me during a trying time.

Third: European redux—the first half of the mission was a joint mission between my unit and a unit of German paratroopers. I know your passion lies more with the French and Italians (and London, of course)—but for some reason the international flavor of the mission felt to me like it would impress you the way it impressed me.

This is an interesting phenomenon—when I think "international," when I write it, I have no conception that Afghan participation on a mission constitutes internationality, although their culture is far more alien than any European culture, although they are far more different and alien than our German allies. I wonder if I do not consider them because I am so used to working with them—if this lack of consideration constitutes a good thing, the mark of a successful alliance—or if it indicates a fundamental flaw, a deep-seated racism. I wonder if the Afghans are invisible to my subconscious eye, if they are below consideration.

Fourth: I return to America in March. I've had a short email from Giuliana to commemorate the holidays. Nothing to mention the press coverage we received out here—not that I expect it or need it for validation, but you'd think that the woman pledged to me would at least register such a remarkable event. I'd think that. She should have, and she didn't. I got a short email from her about rowing instead.

I apologize, this isn't the sort of thing I should be discussing in a letter with anyone but Giuliana. When I'm feeling happy, which isn't often these days, I just look forward to getting back to her and patching things up; when I'm feeling insecure or unhappy (which is the norm these lonely, cold days at the end of the deployment), when I feel that way (always) I think dark, unjust, vengeful thoughts about her, and lament the way I've been treated. I plot exquisite revenges against her, colorful fantasies replete with humiliation and righteous punishment. This is what I've become—a monster. Everything's so raw out here, Jessica, it's raw to the bone. I watched an insufferable, insipid movie recently and wept—*Gladiator*—and laughed at another legitimately moving story, *The Pianist*. Something's unbalanced and amiss.

Fifth: at the end of the last mission, I was on a line of nine vehicles looking northwestward into the fields. Shepherds had brought their flocks out to graze on the yellowed, dead grass. Afghan army elements lay on our right and left flanks, and police units swept the town behind us. The Afghan soldiers clustered around fires—where did they get the wood in the dead of winter?—and talked into the night. I sat in my vehicle and sent occasional situation reports. The Taliban were all gone. We were at the edge of the world, the last patch of wild earth had been civilized and tamed. What else was there to anticipate? That's when I had the last packet of cookies you sent me, and read a book my godfather sent, and composed a letter. That was two days ago.

I'm enclosing a rug, which I got for you special this time around. The prices have gone up since the last time I was here, and the quality doesn't seem quite as good. It doesn't make sense, all the rugs I was buying my first deployment were made up here in the North—I've removed the middleman and still pay a higher price. I explained that to the interpreter but it didn't make a difference. I look forward to sitting on your couch and chatting about it all some day soon. One more mission, a bit of bureaucratic nonsense, and I'm back—Jessica, I will see you then!

Love,
Adrian

10 January 2011

Dear Teddy,

I can't remember a Christmas where I didn't receive something to think about from you in the mail, but this Christmastime's offering, like the one in 2007, was especially well taken! I had to steal time away from my responsibilities to thank you because these gestures carry a special weight here, and the box you sent was a real boon. Although it took a certain amount of willpower to do so, I distributed most of the contents to soldiers who didn't have as much largesse and support as I did—this distribution occurred on the front lines of our most recent combat mission, which cleared out the primary Taliban redoubt in the North of Afghanistan.

As a matter of fact, I still have one of the Christmas gifts you sent me last deployment, a high-quality "Petzel" headlamp, the top-of-the-line model. This is one of my prize pieces of kit, with the red-light slide and three different settings, it's been on every mission with me since it arrived in December of 2007, training missions back home and actual missions out here. You said that if it was extra I should give it to a soldier, but instead I gave the headlamp I had at the time (an inferior model) to one of the guys in the HQ section and kept the one you sent. Let me think—my pocket binoculars, the Petzel headlamp you sent, my H&K mags, my Gerber tool—are there any other pieces of equipment that feel distinctly "mine?" That are specially and precisely belongings, in the way that Remarque described in *All Quiet on The Western Front*, or O'Brien later reprised in *The Things They Carried*? I think that might be all. Then again, the things that I think make me are probably not the things other people notice—that's not the way it works—to the public, I'm probably the guy who always wears clear eyepro, or a ratty old pair of gloves, or something I can't even imagine. We're not even what we want to be, who we think we are—we are who and what others perceive us to be.

The other contents of the package that were particularly useful were the magazines and reading material. It's so strange to read *Esquire* and *GQ* and *The New Yorker* while sitting at the front-line trace for civilization in a savage land—staring across fields, waiting for the intelligence analysts and decision makers to order us forward or bring us back home—that's what I did, between fielding reports and reviewing battle plans.

Maybe I'll end up trying yoga after all. I always thought it was something that guys did to pick up chicks, but if it's good for the spirit, I'd be an idiot not to try it. Anything to stay out of therapy!

Thanks again for the lovely Christmas package, it was a real life-saver,

> Love,
> Adrian

★

Journal Entry: 20 January 2011

Finally happened—the interpreters started asking me for things. Did what I could to avoid it, even put someone else in charge of managing their requests—which is what Captain Dixwell did to me my first deployment, a crafty move, the right thing to do—but going on patrols, it was only a matter of time. People wanting recommendations, and Visas, and special consideration. I let a couple interpreters go earlier in the deployment, they'd wanted to work with or for Special Forces. Happy to let them, happy to cut them free if they wanted to do hard work. But this—it's not frustrating because I don't want to help them, but because I can't, because my scrap of paper isn't worth the ink that I'd use to sign at the bottom, testifying to their heroism. They think I can get them to America. I can't even get myself to America.

★

26 January 2011

Dear Brent,

Here's the last letter I'll send you from combat, written on the last mission I'll undertake in combat, at combat's end. We've finished, the Taliban are gone. My area, the last holdout of active Taliban in Kunduz Province, is totally secure. For the second time in a decade, we can honestly say "Mission Accomplished."

Well, more specifically, the Afghans have done it. My boss, LTC Lewis, had a wild-eyed scheme to put the Afghans in charge and pretty much just resource them to fight their way through the Taliban, and against all odds it seems to have worked! It was an amazing sight: *hundreds* of Afghans, maybe a couple thousand, even, army, Police, Militia, Border Police, ANCOP, all streaming east to grapple with the Taliban and beat them down. Gunfire to the north, to the south, and—always—a half-mile or so forward of my positions, to the east. Our guys didn't fire a single shot. We just sat in a long linear convoy on the one main road (RTE SERPENS—all of the routes here have astrological names, ask the Germans why) leading east, pulling security for the engineers as they blasted their way through a huge belt of IEDs. Got seven of them, total—big ones, one wrecked a culvert—and I got to watch them employ the MCLIC several times, a massive mine-clearing device, and one of the bigger explosions I've been around recently. The MCLIC should be called "The Volcano Cannon." We traveled four miles in three days, then on the fourth day we traveled seven miles, having breached the enemy mine belt. Almost caught up with the Taliban then—the battle raged just a few hundred meters in front of us, and a few bullets zipped our way, pinged off the vehicles—but the dismounted militia overtook us and got stuck in before we could open up. It's better that way, the Afghans should do all the fighting, but my guys were hoping for a bit more, something to take the edge off sitting in a vehicle or sleeping in some sketchy former-Taliban compound, the stress of campaigning. I wasn't too keen about throwing the dice again, especially this close to going home, but then, it's the last hurrah—why not chuck the last smoke grenade and empty a few more clips into stubborn, Luddite barbarians? In any event that's not how it worked out. And I'm not going to waste time beating myself up or obsessing over the possibility that if we'd been able to clear out the road's last couple mines, that we'd have been able to drive through the district to our east at will, getting into free-wheeling firefights… maneuver warfare at last—not worth the energy.

Did I ever tell you about the caves my first deployment? I don't remember what they were called—sounded like "Kwajikheyl"—we learned about them when we arrived, how the Taliban had been using them as a supply depot, and they acquired a sort of mythic quality. Each mission we ran in the vicinity, we'd consider going after the caves, clearing them out, seeing what was in them—never did. To the best of my knowledge the SF units never did, either—at least not while we were there. The caves were firmly in "bad guy" territory, and to mount a company-sized mission merely to satisfy our human curiosity—well, that's not the sort of thing higher liked, and either way I wasn't the commander. Or I probably would've found a way to inflate their importance. 'Cause, man, I wanted to see the inside of them caves!

This deployment's version of the K-caves was an island—about five by seven miles—said to be inhabited by poverty-stricken farmers eking out a squalid existence from the sand and enduring floods and disease, as well as bandit enclaves. It fell just inside Afghanistan, but nobody patrolled it—no Border Police, no Police, nobody. So close to Tajikistan you could spit (at least on the nine-year-old map everyone was using). I had this foolish scheme to acquire canoes or zodiacs and land a platoon over there, check the place out, but it never came to anything. We couldn't get the boats, and in any event we never got close enough to the shore where it would've been practical to conduct the landing. It would've been cool to conduct an amphibious mission—in Afghanistan. That would've been a story for the ages.

So that's it, man. That's all she wrote. I have to hand this over to the next guys—some unit from Germany, a "legacy" unit (whatever that means—is 10th Mountain a legacy unit, because of the patch? The 101st?), former tankers or mechs that have converted to light infantry. You remember that feeling—giving it all over to the next guy, knowing that everything you did will now be his, all of the risks you took have settled into their predestined binary black-or-white form—the time for potential, for excitement is over. Having to deal with the inevitable property misunderstandings, the stress of where you stand respective to everyone else—redeployment—looking your future in straight in the eye…

I'm not looking forward to coming home. There's so much up in the air—the situation between me and Giuliana, my future in (and out) of the military, where I'm going to land, every day of my life after the end of war—I'll look forward to picking your brain about things when I'm in California, especially w/r/t the National Guard. Besides our visit, I'll be heading down to San Diego to visit Dad's buddy on the ranch—maybe we can all catch a baseball game together or something. On that topic—let Frank know I'm looking forward to seeing him again, we fell out of touch gradually after we went our separate ways—in the old days I'd write him myself, but it doesn't seem appropriate somehow.

Everything feels like it's ending, like it's finished. The Taliban are gone from this place, and I don't suppose they'll come back while we're here, not like they did in 2007, anyway. We're going home to a place that's changed over the last eleven months. My relationship with Giuliana is so deeply flawed and damaged that I can't really see patching things up—this is my fault—and then, on top of everything else, I feel like I can't communicate with anyone who wasn't over there. I can say things—I know all the correct things to say to make people feel comfortable, but the truth is that—*a* truth—if you've never had to keep going forward into the thickening battle, if you've never hunted and been hunted in turn, if you've never felt so terrified that you couldn't move, if you've never snapped and charged headlong toward the enemy, not caring whether you died or not—you don't know what it's like to live the life of the warrior, to live on the razor's edge. To ride the lightening. Especially after you've seen the consequences of slipping off the edge—your own death or physical injury. What could I possibly have in common with anyone who hasn't lived that as their everyday reality? What can any non-veteran have to say to me, what can they hope to teach me about life? None of them have stripped it down to its bare, savage essential, none have had the *courage* and *cowardice* (for it must certainly be some mixture of the two) to leap, unbound, into the chaotic maelstrom that is the violence of war—man's joyful, destructive impulses unfettered and let loose on earth. I am cursed, now, Brent—cursed to walk the world surrounded by the shades of people I once knew, cursed to remain friends with you, and Jim, and the rest of us, the accursed few—cursed to be alone.

> Yours & etc.,
> Adrian

5 February 2011

Dear Jim,

Apologies for remaining somewhat silent for a while. The unit that's slated to replace us is on its way, and we're wrapping up the last small mop-up missions before redeployment. Between final patrols and prepping for the property handover, it's been one massive hassle with none of the release of a big operation to keep things together. I've been having a miserable time adjusting to the new reality—pretty much made up my mind that the army's done once I get back home and reintegrate my soldiers—I'll be a normal, boring, bureaucratic functionary again. Letting go of Afghanistan, of this mystical space you remember from Iraq has been unusually tough.

A fair bit's happened since the last time I wrote you. We had a joint mission with the Germans that started with an air movement followed by a six-mile hike and a few days of fighting—then a big mission to clear the Taliban out of my area that involved hundreds of Afghans and no fighting on my part. It's all wrapped up; I visited a village where I never would've been welcome even a month ago, I'd have had to fight my way in and out, but now I can walk there with ten soldiers, a minimal bodyguard plus some Afghan National Police. It's called "Sey Kobruk," or, in English, "Three Bridges" (the town does, in fact, have three bridges). I took the walk the other day, just to confirm the reports that all Taliban had fled, then enjoyed a delicious dinner of "chicken *palau*" with the soldiers and Afghan Police—twenty bucks to feed twelve soldiers like kings—the sun shining overhead, everything peaceful, a brook running in the background—wasn't this the Afghanistan we were supposed to find in 2002, a place of tranquility lying beneath the scarred surface of war? I know that Kunduz is an aberration, that the police are much better here than in other parts of the country, that the population doesn't support the Taliban as much because they're Tajiks and Uzbecks—there's no "key" or master lesson to be learned here. I should feel grateful I was able to see this moment and live it, rather than looking for ways to undermine or doubt it.

I finally froze up in combat, froze up out of fear. I haven't written you since that episode—December 14th, 2010, the last day I got any active enjoyment out of the process of patrolling. It was awful, I was in an open field, no cover, with two ragheads blazing away at me from 75m away in a woodline. I could see the muzzle flashes and the bullets were zipping and buzzing around, showering me with dirt. Biologically we're conditioned to hear danger in low, throaty growls or hisses—there's something pathetic about the comical noises that bullets make, spinning and tumbling overhead—it should be more serious, death should sound important. Only thing to do was hit the ground and make a lower profile, which I did, then get to the closest piece of cover ASAP. The rest of my guys were in front of me, with the exception of my bodyguard who was doing everything he could to mimic my actions. Good guy, this was his first action. Think he feels like he got a bit more than he bargained for.

If it hadn't been for him, I might not have had the courage and willpower to pull myself off the ground. The soldiers of mine that were in cover to my front had opened up on the woodline, but rather than running forward I ran back—to the closest piece of covered and concealed terrain. Then I had to run forward through the field about a minute later. I didn't want to—God knows I didn't want to have to, if there was any way around it I would've found it—as my guys were shooting—up, down, 3-5 second rushes—I was hauling ass. Since that day, I've never enjoyed a patrol, been terrified of every one. I've still led every patrol I thought stood a chance of taking contact, every one of them, but my heart has been in my stomach each time.

And now it's over, it's all done. I know you think about going back, that you may be headed over here this summer—maybe that'll be me in a few years, though I can't really picture it now—if there were any more offensive patrols to be had, I'd do them, begrudgingly, out of a sense of obligation, but the fact that there aren't, that all of the doors have been opened, the rooms explored, fills me with a sense of nostalgia for the past. So fucked up, man! So twisted!

Enjoy law school, and I'll look forward to catching up in person when I return. Estimated arrival mid-March. If I'm not able to swing through Nashville (which will require heavy scotch and brandy drinking), you can expect to hear from me on the phone, per usual. Thanks for all the support out here, I'm going radio silent until "RIP complete." Last time I'll have to say that!

Much love,
Adrian

12 February 2011

Dear Mom and Dad,

We've started RIP'ing, the new unit's here and it's just a matter of time now before we're gone. Just doing little missions here and there— it's all over save the cleaning up and handover. The Taliban have all fled, no enemy stand against us, not even the IED guys. This place is safer than the worst areas in Detroit. I know I told you guys that before, and then you had to read a piece in the *New York Times* about how it was very dangerous here, so maybe you don't feel you can trust what I'm writing you now—please, please be assured, *this* time I'm telling the truth. Nothing to see here, totally benign, actually almost boring. I'm just itching to get home, where really interesting and important things are happening; especially as they're talking about moving me out of my room soon, and I don't like that idea one bit, my comfortable quarters, gone, given to the officer who's due to replace me.

So—it's tough to say what the weather will be like mid-March—I've heard it was a rough winter, which means that there could still be snow and the prospect of more snow. On the other hand, I've had extraordinary luck with weather my entire life, so from that perspective we could encounter nice weather. Or, at least, not have to deal with snow.

Which brings me to my next point: I'm thinking about Lake Placid for that weekend. I'm not going to be able to drive, but I'd like you guys to be there to welcome me back, and then we can head up together for a couple nights. Greg Ambrosia (who you remember from Jeff's place on Rabbit Island) will be there with his folks so we might be able to get dinner with them if my crude and unrefined conversation begins to grate at you, or fatigue your polite ears. There's a bunch of really nice places, but the Mirror Lake Inn is the one I like best. It's off-season so we may be able to get good rates; Geof and Mary Ann took me out to dinner there once and I was very impressed with the dining room at Mirror Lake, and the general atmosphere. Not too pretentious, a lot of wood; perfect antidote for someone who's been thirsting after civilization. And scotch.

I spoke with Giuliana on the phone when I was on a bigger base recently (long story, I was there for about a day). She won't be joining us at Placid, has a crew race that's very important to her, but we will be spending a couple weeks together in England in April. We'll both look forward to having a chance to maybe get back to normal. I haven't belabored you much with our issues, but the relationship is on life support at this point. I guess I should feel grateful it's still there at all. Well— we'll try. I remember that things were good, once upon a time—that's how it seems in my memory, anyway—maybe my memory's deceptive. No—I look in my journal and remember, perfectly, the night that I met her, I remember everything about the beginning of that wonderful adventure. God, we've gone so far from there. And I don't feel much about it, beyond a sense of anger and hurt that she stopped writing or supporting me—which is a selfish way to look at things.

Before I head out to England, I'll be out in California for a week or so. I figure I can drive down on weekends and catch up with you—my leave will consist of a series of increasingly drunken encounters with old friends followed by a salubrious sojourn with Giuliana, planned by Giuliana, in Rome; it promises to be a real celebration of life. Might even be able to see Adam Tsou at his new bar in Paris, *Candelaria*; he says it's a "craft cocktail bar / tacqueria." It doesn't make sense to me either, but knowing Adam as I do, if that's what he set out to do, he's found some absurd secret formula that's going to be wildly success-ful. Most importantly, I haven't seen him since he welcomed me home from my last deployment, and want very much to repay him with a visit.

We're shutting down shop here, winding things up—*honestly!*—and I won't have many more chances to sit down and write letters, so this is going to have to be my last to you guys. Thanks so much to everyone, my love to all the wonderful supporters of Alpha Company, and tell them that we're coming home soon. I hope to sit down with everyone for dinner and catch up properly.

Love,
Adrian

Journal Entry: 15 February 2011

Had a talk with the brigade commander today on the FOB. I wish I'd had him as a battalion commander earlier, before my opinions about the military hardened. He's an incredible leader—offered me HHC and a post at West Point if I stayed in. He understands that I'm on the fence—I mean, I'm not on the fence, I'm done, I'm off the fence, but he thinks that after I'm home for a little while I might change my mind. The trouble is, my hands shake before patrols. I dry heave. I doubt every decision I make, and have to physically restrain myself from ask-ing advice from privates, sergeants, lieutenants, anyone who will lift a piece of this responsibility off my back. I've lost my self-confidence. I got people hurt and killed with my choices. Getting up in front of the soldiers and talking to them requires almost superhuman effort. Death is constantly on my mind. What if something significant broke out—

war with Russia, or China, or Brazil? What would I do then—freeze? Order my soldiers to attack without me? Request a job on staff? Chickenshit—no. If you're not willing to carry a rifle and rucksack toward the enemy, you shouldn't wear the uniform. It's a good time for me to hang mine up, before I dishonor it with terror-vomit before a patrol.

Oh, I'm sorry—or I could go to Behavioral Health and have a head-shrinker tell me that I need help, then steal my time indulging my fictions. No one can know what I've done—not even telling the story will help people understand the truth.

17 February 2011

Dear Giuliana,

To begin with, I want to apologize for not trying harder to stay in touch. I understand why you pulled away, and I see now that I've been pulling away too, for a long time. It's difficult for you to read about me over here without feeling out of control—a pet peeve of yours (I remember!)—and believe me when I tell you that I've been numbed and less talkative than usual because I just don't know how to share a lot of the things I've seen with you, don't know how to talk about it. The shame I feel at having let my guys down. The fear I feel that I will betray my growing cowardice again in combat and get somebody hurt. And above and beyond everything else, the terror that these have been the best days of my life, that they've passed me by while I was too busy yelling into a radio or keeping my head down.

I tried, Giuliana, I really did: tried to notice the sunsets, to listen to the birds singing, and appreciate those bucolic moments of pastoral peace that would occasionally make themselves known and overwhelm everything around them, bringing me nearly to tears. Have you ever seen *The Ring Cycle*? I've listened to it a couple times out here, would really like to see it when I get home—this whole period of time feels like the opening scenes of Gotterdammerung—Siegfried by the river, the Rhinemaidens lamenting the loss of their Rheingold—a moment, frozen in time, where one has an opportunity to do things one way or another—and Siegfried spurns them, keeps the ring, no longer able to hear and understand the birdsong—the music kills me every time. I've had to burn everything beautiful around me, sometimes willfully, to keep a grasp on sanity. Willful, creative destruction, funeral pyre after funeral pyre to keep my sense of emotional equilibrium. I'm not sure I'm even capable of feeling anymore.

Rome—the whole trip sounds lovely, and you're a real sweetheart for putting it together. It's too bad you can't meet us out at Placid but I understand. The psychologists say that one of the biggest relationship pitfalls, the number one relationship killer is actually the soldier / sergeant / officer returning home from war, and expecting everything to be the same—I don't want to interrupt your new routine.

Correction—pardon—I want very *badly* to interrupt your routine and go back to the way things were, but I recognize that it's impossible. I should warn you—I'm feeling a lot of negative emotions about this, now—I want not to, I want things to be good, but it's just—well, we can talk about it in person. We need to. I'm afraid I can't simply let this matter lie. You know me, I need to flog a situation half to death before I'm satisfied with it. God, if only I could work that out! I'll try, Giuliana—I'll try before I come out there—I don't want to doom us with my selfish pride before I've even arrived. Where does this anger come from, why does it feel utterly irresistible!

It's over here, Giuliana—Afghanistan is sending me out, as though I never set foot here to begin with, utterly unchanged. It doesn't matter that the Taliban have gone, they were here and gone before, and they may return someday. It doesn't matter. This landscape is so harsh and unforgiving—on the one hand, the people I see in the fields trying to drag a living from the dust seem like heroes or madmen—on the other hand, they move slowly and without obvious desperation—it's only after a great deal of time spent around them that you realize that this transcends the fatalist predisposition of their culture. Then you realize that these people are the embodiment of despair: life without hope of improvement, waiting for an early and horrible death from disease, accident, or murder.

Can't wait to leave this place and these thoughts behind.

Love,
Adrian

1 March 2011

Dear Mike,

I can almost breathe again. Most of the battalion has already left, it's me and a few of my guys (we were the last ones in, and therefore have the honor of being the last to leave), plus the big XO and his logistics team. I'm headed out in a couple days to take care of the property book at Camp Spann, the brigade HQ—a couple straphangers, as always, one of them being a vehicle we had to sign for but was never delivered to us. Where did this vehicle go? Kuwait? Kabul? It's probably in some motor pool on one of the three major FOBs up in the North—such a thing is so enormous I can't get heartburn about it, besides which we've raised it as an issue in the past. I'm not going to get stuck with a bill for 1.2 million dollars because I don't have a "fat-boy" MRAP on hand and never did.

Have you figured out an angle on this whole mess, yet? Why it happened, what our part in it was, the significance of it all? I'm still trying. It got to be a real drain of psychical resources, maintaining the fiction that any of this will have made a lasting difference. I think I did a good job of keeping up appearances, toeing the line. That was my job, after all, to believe in the mission, to keep it going even when common sense and experience was giving me other information. Sometimes that worked. I like to think my soldiers, sergeants, and officers didn't think I was delusional because I kept looking for rationalizations, for examples and interpretations that buttressed our official mission here—maybe some of them did—what else do you do, in a situation like that. Complain about how everything's fucked up, and tell everyone who will listen that: "I thought this whole mission was a terrible idea, but I just did it anyway because I'm obligated to." That's bullshit of the highest order.

I know what you thought about Iraq, you know what I think about Afghanistan. The mental gymnastics aren't beyond our skill—although, in fairness, we're probably capable of Olympian-quality mental-gymnast routines (I suspect that this is one of the primary reasons that vets make such good politicians and corporate executives). Being able to fool ourselves some of the time, especially in public and around subordinates, still doesn't actually answer anything for us. Perception *isn't* the same as reality. A statement: "We're in Afghanistan to prevent the Taliban from oppressing women and children" doesn't fully en-

322 · Afghan Post

close the realities, any more than any other equally-valid statement.

I've talked with a few very well-read and well-educated officers who, when I ask them why we're here, say: "It's simple: Al Qaeda attacked us and we struck back." Having already understood that, I have to dig a little bit deeper and ask why we're *still* here. I try to skirt Iraq as much as possible for obvious reasons. "We wanted to make sure the Taliban and Al Qaeda never came back to power. We made some mistakes, but we've come a long way since 2003. And the drone strikes / night raids have been successful, we've almost completely dismantled Al Qaeda, and we're basically doing population control on the low-to-mid-level Taliban leadership." *Then* I ask about Iraq. "It was part of a broader neo-conservative strategy to bring peace through democracy to the Middle East through regime change."

That's the truth, Mike, that's how we got to be here. That, historically, is the reason you spent over a year in Iraq, and why I've been to Afghanistan twice. I've discussed this with others. As it's the truth, it should be compelling and shine its way through to my heart, to the hearts of others—and yet, nobody really believes it. It's like a shadow truth. The other truths out there are vastly more compelling, and are dancing circles around the actual truth. There are proliferations of truths, algae blooms: we've already discussed them. Oil, resources, global maneuvering, containing Iran or Russia or China or some combination thereof, racism, anti-Islamic Crusade, the list is pretty long. In my experience, no single narrative is substantially more valid, *emotionally* or even intellectually, than any others. We're living out the first post-modern war. Not even Vietnam was fully postmodern—not deliberately so—it took Vietnam to get us to this point, deliberate and conscious self-deception.

It makes it very difficult to set quantifiable goals, and therefore difficult to measure whether one actually experienced any real success or not. That makes this experience disturbing, unsettling. Here in the North, we were successful in terms of empowering the Afghans—I guess that was what we were doing, or supposed to be doing, on our level—we beat the Taliban until they could beat the Taliban, largely on their own. All the bad guys were killed or fled. So… why do I still feel like the whole thing was hollow? Maybe I don't believe that the neo-conservative agenda really was successful. Maybe I don't really think that the ongoing campaign to use drones and targeted assassinations can do anything but exacerbate, long term, the problems we have with the third world now that information and travel have brought it to our doorstep. I guess when it comes down to it, I must be a political radical and a progressive, rather than the reactionary I often imagine myself to be.

Here's another conundrum for you, as highlighted in a dream that I had recently. I was sitting at a café with my girlfriend (it was not Giuliana—I couldn't see who it was) in 1940 Paris, in the spring. I was an older man, and understood myself to have fought in World War I. I was wearing khakis and a tweed jacket. A parade of military soldiers was marching by, on their way to fight the Germans. After marching by for a little while, I realized that my old unit was marching up—when they did, I recognized some of the faces in the ranks—nobody was leading them, there was no commander—the entire parade stopped and began "marking time." I realized that they were waiting for me. My girlfriend said: "Don't go." I finished my café, stood up, and took up my place at the head of the unit. The first sergeant gave me a helmet, which I donned, and a pistol, which I put in my jacket pocket, and the parade began moving again. That was the end of the dream. I woke up and did not feel very rested. Was the dream a meditation on my future, the idea that once you make certain choices they're always a part of your life? Was it a death-wish? Something to do with Giuliana perhaps? Nothing—like the war—struck me as immediately true, as a good explanation.

The good news for us is that there's going to be plenty to write about. I haven't seen anything come out yet that tackles the really sticky questions about this war, the fundamental issues. I'm sure there are other people out there besides ourselves who are trying to make sense of it—it's likely that, as you've said before, the really good literature and art (movies, paintings, sculptures) to come out of the experience will be five to ten years delayed—the pace of things is picking up, though, so it's also possible that we've already begun to see the first examples. I haven't watched "The Hurt Locker" so I don't know if it's any good, but if it has a scene where a guy picks up a Beret Sniper Rifle and shoots down terrorists, I suspect that it is deeply flawed. The search goes on.

Look forward to raising a glass with you when I get back home— no more of my Dad's funky, spoiled white wine from 1979 that he unaccountably never drank (that was, without question, one of the worst hangovers in my life). Also—congratulations and of course I'll be at your wedding—look forward to hammering out the details when I get home. So long as Bob's not there. He's a drunk, and I don't trust him.

All best,
Much love,
Adrian

Journal Entry: 15 March 2011

Lying in my bedroom at a cush resort in Lake Placid. Parents in the other room. The whole drive up here I was thinking about how surreal this was, trying to process how I was supposed to be feeling. Listening to my parents babble joy at my return, try to figure out how to talk with them, how to interact without lying every third word. This isn't my life any more, but I have to act as though I enjoy it. What is the point to my being here? What would everyone think or say if they knew the truth about me? The violent fantasies I have when the smallest thing sets me off, the utter fatigue with everything and everyone the rest of the time—the lust and the thirst for booze—how could they understand? Who's seen what I've seen? They'd be horrified!

Talked with Giuliana on the phone for ten minutes, told her I was home. Sort of thought she'd be overjoyed, or something, but her reaction was just… surprised, maybe even annoyed. Wanted to throw the phone across the room, but pretended not to care, affected a tone of support and compliance, when what I really wanted to do was yell "fuck you" into the earpiece and have her choke on it. The future's headed at me like a brick wall rushing up toward a speeding car, but there's no steering wheel, no way to avoid it. We've dug in our heels.

Six years ago today I joined the army.

28 March 2011

Dear Sasha,

That's wonderful news, I'm so happy to hear that you might be in San Diego too! I'm trying to remain calm about the upcoming vacation and keep expectations in line, but the reality is that I'm very much looking forward to it. As you know, I'll be flying from California back to Connecticut, with a brief stop-over to wash clothes, and then it's off to England. Which I'm not really looking forward to—things have yet to improve between Giuliana and me—but I have to go out there and give it a try. California, on the other hand, will be a lovely judgment-free zone, where I can post up by the pool with a good book and a glass of scotch around your wonderful family, and soak in the *Southern California* sun. The fact that our vacations will overlap—is more than I can hope for, I don't want to be disappointed, so I won't— but I'll be very happy to see you if you are there! We can do lots of stuff together, we can go to a Padres game! It'll be awesome! (I'm assuming that you'd even want to go to a Padres game.)

It'll be especially nice as one of my soldiers killed himself two days ago. I was driving home from Fort Drum for the weekend, and my first sergeant contacted me out of the blue. He'd just left the unit to go home. I'd been thinking about texting or calling him, but was so wrapped up in my own weird adjustments that—well, I'll be flying out to his funeral in a couple days.

So on that note, the long answer to the question of whether I'm happy to have left Afghanistan would require pages and pages of ob- noxious, self-pitying crap. The short answer, therefore, is: "I'm really happy to have left Afghanistan and returned home." I've basically de- cided to leave the army at this point, but my leadership has convinced me to give it until after leave to give my "final answer" and submit my packet... I'll wait, out of respect for the superior officers who gave me so many opportunities and were good human beings in situations where that was not necessary. I need to leave the army and start heal- ing, which I can't properly do *until* I've left.

I do know that there are small happinesses I'm capable of feeling, that there are moments in life that I treasure, psychological space that I'm capable of inhabiting, even if it's only an occasional habitation. The ranch in San Diego is one of those places, which is why I assign such a high value to staying there a few days. It will always remain a place of joy and safety. A place where I can get some real, anxiety dream / nightmare-free sleep.

My dad had told me that your dad got the company T-shirt, but I didn't realize he'd sent it along to you; that was a really nice gesture. Makes me happy to know that you've been wearing it to the gym! I don't think Alpha Company's ever had a better representative—I'm almost embarrassed to put mine on these days, I'm getting so weak from torpor and a general desire not to push myself and further injure my knee or back. Still jogging though—maybe we can take a couple turns around the reservoir when I'm in town.

Well, this all makes me very pleased. It doesn't seem like I look forward to much anymore. Looking back isn't much good, because I never dig deep enough to deal with the issues I stacked up over the years; that leaves only the present, which I'm used to approaching with trepidation, stress-powered like some ancient inefficient piston-and-coal-operated device. There aren't many times when I feel fully comfortable powering down. If it seems like I'm putting additional pressure on you to come out to San Diego, that's probably true—I understand you're very busy but it'd be great to see you.

> Affectionately,
> Adrian

25 April 2011

Dear Jim,

I just finished a whirlwind tour through Europe and the West Coast. Things cracked up bad between Giuliana and I—we spent the better part of two days crying, she decided she didn't want to be with me anymore, just to remain friends, and I, having felt neither abatement in the anger I held toward her for abandoning me during the deployment nor a desire to have any relations with her besides those which we had had before, decided that rather than spending two weeks pretending to be friends doing what she wanted to do, I'd strike off on my own. I planned to visit my friend Adam, who has a bar in Paris, and the German officers I served with in Afghanistan. The first day alone in London was pretty rough, but I came out the other side all right—so long as one sufficiently dislikes the person you're leaving (you'd know nothing about this), the departure is bearable. You just have to put the good things out of your mind and focus entirely on the awful injustices the other person has perpetrated against you. Which is what I did, with assistance from an old college friend who happened to be in London at the time, living with her boyfriend. Smoking cigarettes also helped.

This was my second time in Paris, and it has grown on me. The city sits on the ground in a way that New York, Chicago don't—you can look out over it and see how Paris has settled onto the banks of the Seine over the centuries and millennia. Even D.C. and Boston—even *London*—miss the mark. Rome too, which I love, doesn't quite have the same atmosphere as Paris. I'd love to go back some day, but I'm realistic—now that Giuliana's out of the picture, it doesn't seem likely I'll return to Europe any time soon, maybe not for years.

I really don't know what to do now. I've decided to leave the army, and I know what the long-term plan will be: apply to graduate school for 2013, write some short fiction, become a writer. Without a family, what's that mean, exactly? I hope I don't become that creepy forty-year-old who has children with someone in their twenties. Even if "Dad" would be an airborne ranger combat vet (has a certain ring to it), what's that really mean when "Dad" is watching "junior" graduate college from a wheelchair? Looks like that's my future—if I'm lucky enough to have children. I've made choices in life, I have to live with them. And the way ahead—well, I've sacrificed marriage and children for professional happiness—I've doubled down on that—now I must forge ahead and accomplish that mission at any cost.

Good luck this summer in RC-North. There's still fun to be had up there, especially in the areas where the Americans haven't been since 2001—any Norwegian / Swedish / Finnish AO should have a fair bit of Taliban activity—avoid Camp Marmal if you can help it. Cushy living conditions, but surrounded by a wire fence, and you can't avoid the feeling that most of the people there don't understand that they're living in a war zone. There was a brief episode after BAF was attacked last year where you had to walk around with your weapon on "Amber" status—magazine in, no round chambered—I was returning from leave and conscripted a female soldier to drive me around base as she didn't seem to be doing anything and it's a long, long walk to get anywhere, and I asked her about what she thought of the procedure.

"Oh, I don't have any rounds in my magazine," she said. "We weren't issued any, but even if we were, I wouldn't put them in my rifle. Too dangerous."

Perfect. If I'd actually agreed with the policy of letting soldiers go months in a combat zone without zeroing their weapon in-country or carrying ammo, I'd have tracked down her supervisor, but as things stood, I figured I'd probably just get into an argument with him over how to do his job and in those situations the best thing to do is just to let things play out. Last time I was on Camp Marmal and encountered a stupid policy—in this case a "first-come, first-serve" approach to assigning quarters clearly designed for smaller units—I was essentially told to shut my mouth by the major in charge of the whole affair.

RC-North is still run by the Germans, and while my experience with them at the company and platoon level (and to a certain extent the battalion level) was very positive, part of that positivity came about as a result of the lower levels pointing to the constraints to which they were routinely subjected by their highest-echelon leadership, which is headquartered at... Marmal. Overly procedural, and the worst kind of risk-averse: the kind where you don't patrol or shoot back, and as a result the enemy accumulates combat power unchecked until one day you realize that you're surrounded by Taliban (which is what happened between 2007 and 2010 in Kunduz and Baghlan Provinces). Be careful who you go out on mission with, every country's infantry and tankers are proud, capable soldiers, but weird ROEs can make even a benign-seeming patrol a potentially life-threatening exercise. Don't tell Frankie I said anything about this, if she asks RC-North is totally safe.

My best to the whole family.

> With love and affection,
> Adrian

Journal Entry: 7 May 2011

Spring in the North Country—the spring I missed last year, thanks to Afghanistan—has arrived. My first in two years. Not like in the South, where plants always seem to be growing and blossoming, where growth slows down in the winter—it's different, frantic growth here on the shores of the St. Lawrence, up where winters get cold and snow covers everything in that thick blanket I can see in my mind's eye. Vivid colors pushing up in every direction, yellows, reds, blues, purples, greens—total visual overstimulation, after the paucity of Afghanistan.

Life on garrison is just as I thought it would be. The old team, the old camaraderie from war has already nearly faded, our life over there the echo of a dream. People getting ready to head to their next units, their schools, or mustering out—Ambrosia's headed up to join Principe at brigade, Matt's getting out in September, and our Battalion S2 is headed to a different unit—these are the changes I hate. And this is the last time I'll stand for it, stand for losing all of my friends. Never again.

I can't sleep alone in a house. By myself. I'd rather sleep at a hotel, or in a room on post. Solitude terrifies me, sobriety terrifies me, I don't even know what I'm scared of. Maybe it's looking out into Sacket's Harbor and thinking about walking into the water and not coming up for air. Or jumping from a high place. Or a Roman Bath. I'm terrified of nightmares during sleep, I can't be alone when tired, I can't drink enough not to care and still be able to wake up in the morning. It wasn't this bad in Italy, only because I could drink more. That was why.

24 May 2011

Dear Sasha,

I really didn't expect things to happen that way, but I sure am happy they did. Seeing you again in Austin was the first time I'd felt really happy and positive in months, maybe a year. I want to tell everyone that we're an item—I've never felt so strongly about pursuing a relationship before—I can't believe I'm so lucky as to have landed with someone I get along with like this. Seeing you walk toward me as I walked down the stairs toward baggage—it was like a dream—your hair waving, you smiled—that was it, Sasha, you had me. The rest of the weekend was one long series of pleasant moments, until I had to fly back, and you had to drive back to Houston.

I cannot wait to see you again. This must be what the end of history feels like—finally meeting the person you're destined to spend the rest of your life with. An end to the uncertainty, to the doubts about motivations, to the awful suspicions and worries over abandonment and betrayal. A real dialogue with someone you can trust. The certainty that another person is out there caring about you, thinking of you, wishing you well and hoping to get another chance to see you soon, and talk sooner.

You should come up to our "welcome home" dance, called The Summit Ball: it'll be held in a nice venue, and I'd be honored to have you on my arm (quite aside from wanting to see you again under any circumstances). Everyone knows about you, now—my roommates, the guys who I worked with downrange, my bosses, everyone—and they're all happy for me, pleased I've met such a brilliant and beautiful woman. Especially after watching firsthand the long, painful descent and wreckage of my last relationship. You'd be welcome like family. Please come if you can, I'll fly you up. And then I'll be there to welcome you at the airport, and snatch you up into my arms again, hold you close.

Is this what it felt like for our grandfathers to get home from WWII? I don't even know if they were with my grandmothers then—I assume so because of the timing of the thing, but then, you never know. After all of this—my struggles, yours, your seeing what I went through in Afghanistan, your *caring* what I went through—I feel an incredible bond with you, stronger than any I've ever felt before.

Your mission in life is an honorable one, and my ambition—to write—would not derail you from that calling in any way. I gave the army every chance and opportunity—it was very, very kind to me— but I know that I can't stay there. Our boss will be leaving soon, and a new boss will be coming in—once LTC Lewis leaves, somebody will replace him. I've seen really, really bad battalion commanders before. And nobody can guarantee me that the man who walks through the door to replace LTC Lewis will be half the man LTC Lewis is. As life moves in cycles, my prediction is that the next commander of 1-87, Summit Battalion, will be a massive, useless, flaming prick. A Toxic Leader of the highest order, which as *you* know from experience, is a terrible spot to be stuck in. Lame duck combat-approved company commander getting out of the army? Doesn't care about speaking his mind? Yeah. I'm gonna get creamed.

It's so easy for me to slip back into the military, I apologize, it dominates everything. You're the first person who's made me want to get better, to improve myself, to move past this phase of my life and take the next step. I'm excited for *myself*, but I'm also so damned excited for us, that we have this opportunity. It's a breath of fresh air, the first time I've looked forward to the future in months, if not longer.

Thank you for being such a wonderful friend. I want to do everything I can to make this work, to come back to life, and to put war behind me. I want a family. I want a life with you. I want all good things to come to us. I want each trivial moment together, each challenge, because I know we're up to it. I look forward to every minute of our time together, and the anticipation of that time will keep me going through the challenges we face when we're apart. Which, if I have my way, won't be forever, and it won't be much longer.

Everything I saw over there—the illiteracy, the servitude of women, the child mortality rates, the murder, the price of life so cheap, the trash, the disease, the lack of clean drinking water, the absence of roads and infrastructure, the human misery taken for granted, the massive families actively perpetuating the same—you and I can balance that out, together, creating our own happy moments on earth. We've been lucky—as individuals, and now, collectively, as a couple—so damned lucky—it's not an entitlement, it's another responsibility. To each other, to ourselves, to the world. We've made it this far and have this glorious, golden gift—the love of a person that deserves your love—how can we miss? Isn't this worth everything, every compromise and sacrifice? I think so—I know so.

It's been twenty-four hours since the last time I saw you and it already feels like an eternity. I miss you terribly and await your next embrace. I wanted the world to stop in Austin, but it didn't.

Hugs, kisses, and love,
Your Adrian

Journal Entry: 9 June 2011

Sasha came out for the Summit Ball, met my unit, and drove my drunk ass home in high heels when I went too hard, as everyone did. A real celebration, much deserved by everyone there who fought so hard and sacrificed so much—the drinking, the laughter, it all had an edge to it, a thought contained just under the surface that we were all busily avoiding with every toast, every shot. I was glad she got to see that with me. She needs to know what she's getting into, as much as possible.

Keep thinking about Pulaski, seeing what it must've been like for him in slow-motion replay—holed up in cover—alone—the decision— his .45—one bullet left—headshot. Should've bought stock in whatever company makes Jim Beam before redeploying. Some nights, nothing helps, not even good thoughts like the love of a woman, or friendship, or professional future happiness.

There's an old church across the street from my bedroom window.

Every night I look outside and see it, empty; every morning I have to brave the silent darkness, run to my car, drive like mad to work. I feel like I'm stuck in a Stephen King novel, a nightmare—the house I'm renting is at least a hundred years old, has an attic and a basement and God knows what all, and I swear it's fucking haunted. I can't get to sleep without at least five drinks. Sometimes even then I wake up in the middle of the night and have the sense that someone or something is in the room, or behind a door. My mind feels tired, but I can't sleep, and the more I don't sleep, the more my mind bends under the strain of fatigue.

Called Behavioral Health. There's a six-week waiting period, unless it's an "emergency," in which case I can get institutionalized and forever branded a weakling and coward. No thank you—I'll find a way to gut through this. Go in earlier to work, get sleep there. This house.

Journal Entry: 4 July 2011

Met some of Sasha's friends out for dinner tonight. Greek place. They seemed impressed to meet me—not surprisingly, everyone is these days. I told some war stories, bartered a bit more of my experience for social credibility, thoroughly dominated the conversation from start to finish, and—maybe—they walked away with a slightly better appreciation for the world, and themselves, than they started out with when they woke up this morning. We went out for a drink with one of the couples after, and then came back to Sasha's apartment for drinks and the fireworks display.

We didn't fight, but she wasn't in a great mood—something had set her off. She was speaking with her mother on the phone, wishing her a Happy Fourth, and I'd poured myself a tall glass of the Balvanie twelve-year Doublewood scotch she bought for me, and I was on the balcony looking over the city, the dark downtown towers illuminated under the bursts of color, and thinking about Japan, and how I'd got it right there, wondering why I kept losing the women I cared for most. Was overwhelmed by a sense of fatigue at the comfort of the place, the warm evening, and while Sasha was talking with her mother I was looking down from the balcony.

The sense of urgency, of pull, was palpable. I could do it. My muscles yearned for the edge, to tense, to do it, just fucking do it—every bit of my body compelling me forward, pushing while the ground and gravity pulled up at me like a magnet. I leaned, put my elbows on the railing, tested my balance, and it occurred to me that if I jumped, it'd never get any better or worse than it was in that moment, that the fatigue and anguish and the inevitability of defeat would be over for good.

Sometimes life is so precious, so beautiful and sweet, like a night with Sasha that's going to give way to morning, you just can't help yourself. I went back inside instead.

ACKNOWLEDGMENTS

First and foremost, I'd like to thank the The Head & The Hand Press, without which this project would at the very least be much less polished and sensible than it is now, and at worst, an abject failure. It was love at first sight when I found your webpage in late December 2012, and here we are over a year later with a book, a real book, that represents so much care and attention. It's been a pleasure to work with you individually and collectively—Nic, Linda, Kerry, Claire, Mike, Lisa, Joe, Chloe, Jordan, and Jeannette. A thing like this doesn't just happen—it takes a special collection of people, and friendship, and a quorum of faith. You guys are amazing, and without you this book would look radically different. Nic, your home is a place of rest and respite, and my couch is always open for you any time and anywhere you need it. Linda, our emails about writing and editing introduced me to some important writing and David Foster Wallace (and we still need to play geeky board games). Kerry, your efforts on the behalf of *Afghan Post* made something out of what would have been, in my hands alone, nothing. Chloe, your enthusiasm and confidence in my ability were a welcome source of strength. Finally, Claire, thank you for bearing with my inability to organize effectively, especially towards the end.

I'd like to thank my parents, for having me and putting up with me. My sister for the same, and also for not squealing on me when I was sneaking booze out of the basement during high school—that was cool of you. My extended family for always providing me with support and hospitality and not squashing my dreams. All the people who appear in this book for playing along, and the ones who don't but could've because you made it happen too.

I'd like to thank my godfather for being a source of positive inspiration in the world. The military leaders who taught me to be a decent and scrupulous infantry officer, and to hunger for victory on the battlefield.

My PTSD therapist who guided me to Cognitive Processing Therapy, and without whom I could not have told an honest story about war.

Lastly, I wanted to thank the love of my life for everything.

Adrian Bonenberger is a combat veteran who writes essays on military topics. He lives in Harlem with two roommates and a pet drone. Adrian has published with *The New York Times* "At War" blog, Doonesbury's "The Sandbox" blog, runs several blogs of his own, and has appeared on HuffPost Live to discuss emergent issues within the veteran community. He currently attends the Columbia Graduate School of Journalism.